HOW TO DESIGN AND TEACH A HYBRID COURSE

HOW TO DESIGN AND TEACH A HYBRID COURSE

Achieving Student-Centered Learning Through Blended Classroom, Online, and Experiential Activities

JAY CAULFIELD

Foreword by Alan Aycock

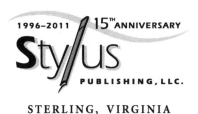

STERLING, VIRGINIA

Published by Stylus Publishing, LLC
22883 Quicksilver Drive
Sterling, Virginia 20166-2102

Library of Congress Cataloging-in-Publication-Data
Caulfield, Jay, 1949-
   How to design and teach a hybrid course : achieving
student-centered learning through blended classroom,
online and experiential activities / Jay Caulfield ; foreword
by Alan Aycock.
      p. cm.
   Includes bibliographical references and index.
   ISBN 978-1-57922-422-6 (cloth : alk. paper)
   ISBN 978-1-57922-423-3 (pbk. : alk. paper)
   ISBN 978-1-57922-603-9 (library networkable e-edition)
   ISBN 978-1-57922-604-6 (consumer e-edition)
   1. Student-centered learning.   2. Blended learning.
3. Lesson planning.   I. Title.
LB1027.23.C24   2011
371.3—dc22   2010052315

13-digit ISBN: 978-1-57922-422-6 (cloth)
13-digit ISBN: 978-1-57922-423-3 (paper)
13-digit ISBN: 978-1-57922-603-9 (library networkable
e-edition)
13-digit ISBN: 978-1-57922-604-6 (consumer e-edition)

Printed in the United States of America

All first editions printed on acid free paper that meets the
American National Standards Institute Z39-48 Standard.

Bulk Purchases

Quantity discounts are available for use in workshops
and for staff development.
Call 1-800-232-0223

First Edition, 2011

10 9 8

CONTENTS

SECTION THREE: INTERVIEW DATA

CONCLUSION

ACKNOWLEDGMENTS

I HAVE SO MANY COLLEAGUES, friends, and family to thank for making this book possible. I will forever be grateful to my friends and colleagues in the Learning Technology Center at the University of Wisconsin–Milwaukee, some who are now retired. Bob, you took a chance with me; I hope I never let you down. Alan, I have never met a finer teacher or a more trustworthy colleague and friend. Your intellectual capacity will always humble me.

A special thank-you goes to the remarkable hybrid teachers I interviewed for this book, who not only took time from their busy schedules but in many instances showed me around their universities and their communities. Mike, the dinner in Quebec City was unforgettable. I so enjoyed meeting and talking with each and every one of you, and I admire your passion and commitment to teaching and learning, and your love of students. I am equally thankful to the hybrid students I had the privilege of interviewing. Your candor and your perspectives were invaluable to this book in so many ways.

Another heartfelt thank-you goes to the numerous editors who read this manuscript, some of them in its entirety, thank you ever so much. Igor, your perspectives and your transcriptions were instrumental. Heather and Felisa, what would I have done without your encouragement and support along the way? Em, knowing how calendar challenged I am, you made sure I was in the right place at the right time; thank you. And your editing was so very on target and valuable to the book—and to me. My friend and colleague Leslee, you gave me hope that what I wrote might possibly be of value some day. Michael from the College of Com, you rock!! Eva and Jill, the examples from your years of expert teaching were perfect. Thank-you to Cheryl Coan for permission to use the assignment from her Communication Management in Public Service course, to Heather Salisbury for permission to use the assignment from her International Travel course, and to Jill Florence for permission to use excerpts from her film *Can We Become Homeless?*.

Another very special thank-you goes to John von Knorring, who encouraged me throughout my writing. Your constructive criticism was precise and given in such a gentle way that it motivated me to do the best work I could. I really look forward to meeting you some day soon.

I could not have completed this work without the encouragement of our dean, Robert Deahl. Thank you for supporting my passion for teaching and research. I am convinced that every academic administrator must thoroughly appreciate and engage in both of these activities to achieve excellence in academic leadership.

Finally, I am so grateful for the love and support of my family. To my daughter, Jamie, who proofs everything I write, thank you so much for reading what you must find so pedantic at times. To my son Steve, who supports me 24/7 when it comes to technology, thank you for putting up with my insistence that *now* is always the best time. To my son Jason, I so enjoy your wonderful sense of humor that always reminds me to take myself less seriously. To my talented husband, John, who loves me regardless of my passion for doing too much at once all the time, thank you for understanding my superwoman tendencies. And, finally, a special thank-you goes to my mom, who always believed I could do well in anything I put my mind to, who supported my love for learning for as long as I can remember, and who is truly my best friend. God bless you, Mom. I love you.

FOREWORD

I'VE KEPT ABREAST AS BEST I can of the burgeoning literature on hybrid (or blended) teaching, so I feel comfortable in saying that the book you now hold in your hands is well worth your time; I believe it to be basic to any instructor's appreciation of the full value of blended teaching and learning. To explain my assessment of Jay Caulfield's book, I need to tell you how it came to be written.

When Jay Caulfield joined the University of Wisconsin–Milwaukee Learning Technology Center, we were near the beginning of our efforts to create a program for faculty blended course redesign; by the time Jay left us to join Marquette University, our program was nationally known. So the time Jay and I worked together was one of considerable creativity for both of us. Also a heck of a lot of traveling: With others on the center's staff (Amy, Carla, and Bob) we crisscrossed the Midwest from Illinois to Minnesota and traveled throughout Wisconsin, offered conference sessions in Denver and Madison, and worked with numerous faculty and departments on our own campus.

In two senses, then, Jay and I shared an odyssey as the hybrid program emerged, and both of them are relevant to my remarks here. First of all, we had to figure out what our program should look like. We already knew that—as Jay mentions in Chapter 1—it needed to be based on theory, but at the same time it had to be intensely practical, representing our own experience of teaching blended courses at the University of Wisconsin–Milwaukee and elsewhere. Faculty needed to know the ideas, tips, and experience as clearly as we could convey them, so abstractions were not foremost in our program design, and Jay has followed this principle in this book.

We also learned as we went along what we needed to include in our course redesign program. For instance, we knew from the outset that we would need to emphasize online discussions and small group work as basic tools of forming an active learning community online and face-to-face, but this book includes chapters on understanding your students and helping to manage their expectations and their experience in a blended course. This emphasis on students' needs and perspectives became part of our awareness only after we had begun to offer our redesign program. In retrospect, it makes perfect sense, but we had not quite thought through the consequences of our assumptions about the nature of blended learning. So we undertook a pilgrimage in our own role as instructors, and like all such journeys, there were unanticipated discoveries and a sense of greater understanding, which incidentally is vividly reported in many of Jay's accounts of teachers' initial efforts at blended teaching.

An odyssey in a second sense emerged as Jay and I and others traveled around the country offering our program. We encountered faculty from different regions and disciplines and from a wide range of institutions. Their question generally was always the same: What technologies should we adopt that will allow us to succeed in offering blended courses? This question illustrates the somewhat naive notion that a magic tool would take you from a traditional face-to-face, passive mode of instruction to one that embraced all the latest advances. Yet you will notice that Jay's chapter on technology comes rather late in the book. As she reminds us, wise technological choices don't necessarily correspond to what is hottest in the marketplace; instead, pedagogy drives your technological decisions. What do you need to redesign your course for active learning? What will encourage your students to participate, collaborate, and engage with the course learning goals? It's still true, as national studies remind us, that a huge percentage of online work involves text-only tools.

Finally, as the title reminds us, this book is a guide, not a manual or a textbook or anything that pretends to have more authority than experience confers. There is no canon of blended or hybrid instruction, no single correct way to plan, design, teach, and assess this mode of learning, as Jay so correctly demonstrates. Going hybrid is itself a work of exploration and experiment: Try something and see if it works; if it doesn't, try something else instead. Patience and a sense of humor are thus the sine qua non of blended course redesign, but after all, teaching itself is meant to be open-ended in precisely this fashion. Hybrid teaching is, as I believe Paulo Freire would have said it, a pedagogy of liberation.

Alan Aycock
University of Wisconsin–Milwaukee

PREFACE

THIS BOOK IS WRITTEN for all who teach, and especially for those who have chosen to teach in a hybrid learning format. It is a practical handbook about outcomes-based practice applied to hybrid design to use when designing and teaching a hybrid course. Many faculty who have enrolled in a hybrid faculty development program claim that learning to teach in a hybrid format improved their overall teaching. I have had the privilege of observing some excellent hybrid teachers along my never-ending journey to become an expert teacher, and I have had the opportunity to teach over 80 hybrid courses in the past 11 years. It is my hope that what I write regarding hybrid teaching, which includes my observations of other successful hybrid teachers and some of my own hybrid experiences, will generate further reflection, dialogue, and research. I have discovered that for the students I teach, the hybrid design when well orchestrated creates a collaborative, student-centered teaching and learning experience.

A number of learning theories, principles, and concepts are the framework for my writing, including critical planning questions teachers might ask themselves when designing a hybrid course. These questions were first identified by the faculty in the Learning Technology Center at the University of Wisconsin–Milwaukee several years ago. The faculty there have been conducting workshops on hybrid teaching for almost a decade now, and they are considered experts in the field of hybrid course design. I was privileged to have worked in this environment for nearly 3 years. The passion and excellence of those I met there was evident throughout the duration of my stay. I have yet to find a more dedicated team of teachers who are willing to share what they know and who are eager to give faculty credit for their teaching successes while providing expert advice in a respectful and humble way to those who accept the challenge of designing and teaching a hybrid course. I will forever be grateful to my colleagues at the Learning Technology Center for teaching me how to improve my teaching, and how to receive and give reflective and constructive criticism on the teaching and learning experiences we shared. Furthermore, I welcome input from and dialogue with teachers who are interested in continuing the conversation about the practice of hybrid teaching.

What This Book Is Not About

This is not a book about institutional planning for the use of technology in teaching, nor is it a book about technology per se. It is not a book about how hybrid design may save a university or a corporation money or increase revenue by gaining access to additional student markets. This is not to say that all these topics aren't important or of interest, or that they may not be mentioned in the context of designing and teaching a hybrid course; in fact, one or more of these desired outcomes may occur as a result of developing degree programs taught in a hybrid format. They simply are not the purpose or the focus of this book.

SECTION ONE

INTRODUCTION

CHAPTER ONE

WHAT IS HYBRID?

Good teachers possess a capacity for connect-
edness. They are able to weave a complex
web of connections among themselves, their
subjects, and their students so that students
can learn to weave a world for themselves.

—Parker Palmer (1998, p. 11)

B EFORE ASKING WHY TEACHERS might consider choosing a
hybrid course design, a discussion of the definition and concept
of *hybrid* is warranted. Ross and Gage (2006) identify three major
types of blended learning in higher education, specifically

- ◆ technology-enhanced courses,
- ◆ hybrid courses or reduced face-time courses, and
- ◆ blended programs or degrees. (p. 156)

Technology-enhanced courses have a technology component, but the
classes meet according to the traditional schedule; that is, time in the
classroom is not reduced. In a technology-enhanced course, the instructor may place a course syllabus online, with URLs of websites to enhance
learning. In blended or degree programs a student may choose some mix
of online, hybrid, and traditional courses.

*Hybrid courses, the focus of this book, may be defined as courses that
have reduced "face time" that is replaced by time spent outside the traditional classroom.* Time spent outside of the classroom includes online

learning and, similar to some traditional courses, may include experiential learning that takes place in the community or in an organization without the presence of a teacher. For example, a hybrid course could include a community project in addition to the online component and the traditional classroom or face-to-face (F2F) component. A hybrid course should not necessarily be limited to in-class and online environments. The designer may incorporate any method of teaching and learning that has been demonstrated to be effective for the discipline and content being taught. Beyond the more concrete definition of hybrid, the concept of hybrid, what Shulman (2005) might refer to as the *signature pedagogy* of hybrid teaching, refers to the interwoven higher level cognitive processes involved in structured, outcomes-based, student-centered teaching and learning occurring in multiple environments.

Often, definitions of hybrid focus on the percentage of time spent learning in the classroom and the percentage of time spent learning outside the classroom. Although this statistic may be determined for each hybrid course and is likely to vary significantly among teachers and courses, it is not the salient feature that defines the essence of effective hybrid teaching. Hybrid courses place the primary responsibility of learning on the learner, thus making it the teacher's primary responsibility to create opportunities and foster environments that encourage student learning, rather than simply telling students what they need to know. Although a traditional course design may create an active learning environment, many do not. Instead many traditional classes continue to incorporate lengthy lectures with little or no opportunity for students to interact with one another or the teacher, creating a learning experience, in which learners become dependent upon the teacher to tell them what they need to know, placing the primary responsibility for learning on the teacher. This point is illustrated by a written comment from a student who was evaluating a statistics course. The comment reads as follows: "If I don't understand what statistical significance is, it is because the teacher didn't explain it well enough." In many instances, teachers need to help students move toward taking more responsibility for their learning.

A well-designed hybrid course is a joint and provocative exploration of the discipline by teacher and learner in which the roles of teacher and learner are fluid—sometimes the teacher takes the role of learner and sometimes the learner takes the role of teacher. It does not by any means lessen the responsibility of the teacher to intimately know the fundamental concepts, methodologies, and principles inherent in his or her discipline and to engage the students in learning. Knowledge of the discipline and how to effectively teach it is the foundation of creating any meaning-ful teaching and learning experience. Hybrid further enhances the ability of the teacher to create multiple effective and engaging environments, in class, online, in the community, or in an organization, and to select a blend of those environments where learning essential concepts, theories, and principles of the discipline are most likely to occur. A traditional F2F class, on the other hand, often limits teaching and learning to interactions in the classroom.

To further illustrate, when teaching a hybrid class in nursing, the first assignment may be a reading about heart abnormalities. After reading the text, students are asked to visit the Auscultation Assistant website (www.wilkes.med.ucla.edu) (Cable, 1997), an online simulation of ab-normal heart sounds. Students then meet online in small groups, and the teacher asks them to decide which heart abnormality is present when they hear a specific abnormal heart sound. Each small group hears a different heart sound. Everyone in the group needs to contribute to the online dis-cussion. The teacher may or may not guide the online discussion, which is a difference between a totally online course and hybrid course design. In a totally online course, the teacher must guide the discussion online where all interaction between the students and the teacher takes place. In a hybrid course, however, the teacher may decide to guide the discussion online or to observe the process of how students arrived at the solution to a problem and then discuss the process and the solution during the next F2F class, which may be the more effective venue. When students meet F2F, they listen to each group's heart sound and decide whether the group correctly identified the abnormality. If students are unable to solve the problem, the teacher asks critical questions that help them eventually identify the correct abnormality. In this example, by reviewing the students' online dialogue and listening to their in-class explanation of why they chose a certain abnormality, the teacher also becomes the learner, which means the teacher learns how the students process information when identifying the abnormality. By knowing process, the teacher is then able to ask critical questions to steer students toward the correct answer.

Using critical questions to assist students in learning is an example of what Vygotsky termed *scaffolding* (as cited in Lipscomb, Swanson, & West, 2004) and is an important component of a hybrid design. Jesus Christ, considered one of the most effective and engaging teachers of all times, taught most of his lessons while traveling from one place to another, often using parables to illustrate and make memorable points.

Today we might refer to such parables as case studies. He engaged his audience in his lessons, often asking them critical questions that helped them understand the moral of the stories he told. Socrates did most of his teaching by walking around Athens, employing philosophical questions to bring others into dialogue that encouraged the pursuit of wisdom. Gandhi interacted with the masses by communicating a peaceful yet compelling vision of freedom that was so powerful the Indian people were willing to die in pursuit of it. The point is that these exemplary teachers understood that learning would be most successful in environments that fostered inquiry and dialogue; in other words, learners had to become active participants with the lessons being learned. This is what is meant by creating student-centered learning environments. According to Lea, Stephenson, and Troy (2003), a student-centered learning approach includes reliance on active learning, an emphasis on student understanding, increased student responsibility for learning, increased student autonomy throughout the learning process, and a respectful interdependence between the teacher and the student. This is a very different approach from teacher-centered instruction, where the teacher tells the student what needs to be learned. A hybrid course design provides teachers with an opportunity to involve students in online interaction as well as in-class interaction. Opportunities to interact with electronic content, as in the case of simulations, and with peers outside the classroom prepare students to have meaningful F2F interaction inside the classroom.

Today hybrid has become known as a way of teaching that uses technology in lieu of some portion of time spent in the classroom, and for the most part that is true. However, it is important to point out from the start that technology is a tool to help create engaging, interactive, and effective student-centered learning environments regardless of whether it is used during class or outside the classroom. It is not the primary focal point of hybrid, and as soon as it is made so, it decreases the likelihood of designing a hybrid experience that is as effective and engaging as it could be. To further illustrate this point, think for a moment about a chef who is in the process of creating an exciting new dish. To do this well, he needs to first apply his knowledge of the inherent principles of culinary art to help him create the right combination of ingredients for his creation to be nutritious, attractive, and delicious. If his primary focus is on the pan he is going to cook the dish in before he selects the ingredients he is going to use, he limits his creation to dishes that must be cooked in a specific pan. The same is true about designing a hybrid course. If the focus is on technology instead of applying knowledge of the discipline to determine which principles students need to know and how to best teach those principles to them, the possibilities of creating the most effective and engaging hybrid course design are limited to the technology chosen.

In summary, the foundation of hybrid teaching is built upon creating student-centered learning environments whereby the teacher's primary role is encouraging students to become active knowledge seekers versus spoon-fed learners. The teacher may create an effective student-centered environment by identifying provocative student-centered learning activities designed in any number of environments inside and outside the classroom to involve the student in learning the principles of the discipline. The use of multiple interactive learning environments outside the classroom makes interaction inside the classroom more effective and productive.

CHAPTER TWO

THEORETICAL APPLICATIONS

There is nothing so practical as a good theory.

—Kurt Lewin (1951)

THIS CHAPTER AND THE NEXT FOCUS ON THEORY, with only secondary attention on practice. Additionally, Chapter 3 includes two detailed examples of experiential learning. In the remaining chapters, theory is invoked to validate practice, and this is intentional. Theory applied to practical experience is in itself an important andragogical principle. Reflective practice is one of the founding principles of Ignatian pedagogy, which is the foundation of Jesuit education. Jesuits, known for their high-quality teaching institutions, have been educating students for over 450 years (Lowney, 2003). Brookfield (1986) said the highest goal for education—individual and societal transformation—is only attained through "critical reflectivity" (p. 105). Critical reflection leads to improved practice, a goal of all conscientious educators.

This chapter also emphasizes learning and social science theory specific to adult learners versus educational theory or theory specific to children and adolescents. Rather than attempting an exhaustive review of theory, I selectively address theory relevant to creating an effective hybrid classroom. For readers interested in a comprehensive review of adult learning theory, numerous excellent texts exist on the subject, including but not limited to works by Dewey (1938), Knowles (1980, 1984, 1990), Mezirow (1991), Merriam and Clark (2006), and Brookfield (2006). Given the interrelatedness of motivational theory to student engagement and learning, this chapter includes a discussion of certain aspects of motivational theory and incorporates the findings of several studies about achievement motivation for distance learners. It also addresses distance education theories and practices, especially those related to adult learning theory and hybrid teaching and learning.

Before going further, however, let's set the context by beginning with a few brief definitions. I define theory as a testable set of related ideas or constructs used to explain a recurring phenomenon. Learning implies a change in behavior as a result of receiving and acting upon new information. As implied by the term, *learning theory* focuses on the learner versus the educator. For example, self-directed learning is based on the andragogical principles identified by Knowles (1990) and illustrated in Table 2.1; these principles focus on the learner. Teaching theory is closely related to learning theory and focuses on creating appropriate opportunities for learning. For example, if we know adult learners effectively learn

Table 2.1 Pedagogical Principles Compared to Andragogical Principles

Pedagogical Principles	Andragogical Principles
Learners learn what the teacher tells them they need to know.	Learners need to know why information is important to learn; educators need to make this evident.
Learning is the primary responsibility of the teacher.	Learning is the primary responsibility of the learner.
Transferring information is the most frequently used method of teaching, and learner experience is minimized.	Drawing on the individual's personal experience and relating that experience to information from the discipline is the most frequently used method of teaching.
Readiness to learn course content is determined by the teacher, and uniformly applies to the entire class.	Applying scaffolding techniques, such as group interaction, simulation, and case analysis, is frequently used to enhance each individual's readiness to learn.
Content to be learned is determined by the logic of the discipline.	Information is best learned when applied to real-life situations that are relevant to the learner.
External motivators (grades, monetary rewards) are considered primary motivators of learning.	Intrinsic motivators (self-esteem, need to achieve) are more important than extrinsic motivators.

by drawing upon life experiences, then our teaching practice and the assignments we create should encourage learners to draw upon such experiences. Whereas the term *andragogy* broadly refers to adult learning occurring in any learning environment, it should not be confused with the term *adult education,* which has a slightly different focus. According to Knowles (1980; Knowles, Holton, & Swanson, 2005), adult education has three subfields: an organized set of activities with stated goals, the *process* of adult learning, and adult learning linked to social practice. Adult learners are beyond adolescence; it is difficult to be age specific as individuals differ in achieving stages of growth and development. Pedagogy refers to the art and science of teaching children and adolescents, and andragogy refers to the art and science of adult learning, including pedagogical principles when applicable (Knowles et al.). Problem-based learning encourages groups to work collaboratively in solving identified problems. In project-based learning, the student chooses the project, and the teacher may develop the learning outcomes associated with the project. Discovery learning occurs without teacher interaction, although a learning outcome may be identified (Klahr & Nigam, 2004).

Adult Learning Theory and Practice

For centuries, teachers taught adults by primarily applying the same principles as with teaching children. It is only during the last half of the 20th century that we began to see a major shift among philosophers, educators, psychologists, and social scientists that reflected the understanding that adults learn differently than children.

Knowing when to apply pedagogical principles versus andragogical principles or when to combine both is part of the art of teaching. Assessing each student's experience, demonstrated knowledge of the principles of the discipline, intellectual capacity, stage of growth and development, learning style, personality, primary motivators, and a host of other variables is paramount to knowing how to successfully engage students in learning. It is important to note that hybrid teaching and learning cannot be primarily dependent upon pedagogical principles because much of the learning in a hybrid class takes place outside the classroom and is, for the most part, self-directed. Depending primarily on pedagogical principles is incongruent with self-directed learning.

An inherent conflict exists in classrooms today. Many adults have been taught according to pedagogical principles. Their willingness to make the transition to andragogical principles when appropriate is dependent upon the teacher's willingness, competence, and persistence in applying them. Some students will resist. Just as some workers want to be told what to do and when to do it, some students have similar preferences. Unfortunately that is not what today's workplace is demanding of its professionals. Second, research on student-centered learning (Schwartz, Mennin, & Webb, 2001) that applies andragogical principles indicates that students are more likely to understand and remember what they are studying. The literature often refers to this type of learning as *deep learning*, which leads to better long-term performance, improved motivation, more favorable supervisory evaluations, positive feelings toward learning, and increased use of resources for further self-directed learning. In summary, applying andragogical principles appropriately will better prepare adult students to become successful learners as well as successful working professionals.

When is it appropriate to apply andragogical principles to an adult learning environment? The answer depends on the teacher's accurate assessment of the learner. If the learner is willing to accept primary responsibility for learning and has adequate life experiences to draw upon, then it is likely that andragogical principles may be applied. Although pedagogical principles may be necessary and appropriate if the learner is not willing or capable of accepting primary responsibility for learning, the move toward andragogical principles should become the goal for teachers and adult learners.

To illustrate, I teach applied statistics. Based on adult students' unfamiliarity (lack of experience) with the statistical concepts and the application of those concepts to everyday life, in most instances I must combine pedagogical and andragogical principles to create the conditions for effective learning. On the other hand, when I teach leadership theory, I depend primarily on andragogical principles because most adult students have practiced leadership in some formal or informal way, and they will readily relate their life experiences to the theoretical concepts. The same students are frequently enrolled in my statistics and leadership theories classes. The difference lies in the situation. In one instance, students are likely to have life experiences to draw upon, in the other instance, they may not. That said, both these situations have exceptions, which makes assessment at the individual student level very important; otherwise, the students who are the exceptions are likely to have a poor learning experience. One of the more challenging classes to teach is when the readiness of the learners is spread across the continuum, requiring the teacher to continually assess where individual students are in the learning process to apply the most effective principles.

Constructivism

Jean Piaget, a developmental and cognitive psychologist, first proposed constructivist theory in the early 1900s. Its foundational premise is that we are born with the ability to associate experiences. As we grow we develop our motor and perceptual capabilities, which in turn allow us to further explore our environment and to construct increasingly sophisticated paradigms (Siegler, 1998). Lev Vygotsky, a Russian psychologist who conducted much of his research in the 1920s and 1930s, is considered a social constructivist (Siegler). Piaget and Vygotsky primarily worked with children. Vygotsky's theory attributes much of what we construct in the way of knowledge as being closely related to whom we socially interact with in our environment. Thus, it is through structured dialogue with others that we construct knowledge. According to Vygotsky (as cited in Wood & Wood, 1996), our ability to construct knowledge earlier than we may be able to do on our own is related to how well teachers guide us while we are in the zone of proximal development. This zone as defined by Vygotsky refers to the gap between what a child can achieve alone and what a child can achieve through problem solving under adult guidance or in collaboration with more capable peers. It is here that Piaget and Vygotsky differed in their thinking, as Piaget believed that children could not develop beyond the growth and development stage they were in.

Adult learning theorists, such as Brunner (1966), Knowles (1990), and others, incorporated constructivism as a primary principle when teaching adults. In identifying teaching principles for adults, Knowles (1990) stated,

> The teacher helps the students exploit their own experiences as resources for learning through the use of such techniques as discussion, role playing and case method; the teacher gears the presence of his own resources to the levels of experience of his particular students. . . . The teacher helps the students apply new learning to their experience, and thus to make the learnings more meaningful and integrated. (pp. 86–87)

Semple (2000, p. 25), a cognitive psychologist, summarizes principles of constructivist thought as follows: Knowledge is constructed from learner experience and is cognitive rather than external. Learning is a personal interpretation of the world based on beliefs and values; it is an active process dependent on experience and contexts relevant to the learner.

Several empirical studies indicate that constructivism practiced in the classroom increases learner performance and satisfaction (Barman & Barman, 1996; Kim & Fisher, 1999; Rhodes & Whitten, 1997; Tynjala, 1998). Constructivism is also a major component of self-directed, problem-based, and discovery learning. In addition to its influence on general education and the field of cognitive science, constructivist thought has greatly influenced distance education learning theory where structured dialogue is considered an essential component of an effective distance learning experience.

Inquiry as a Means of Teaching

Brunner (1961), a cognitive and a constructivist theorist, is known for his work in identifying *inquiry* as an effective teaching and learning practice. When practicing inquiry as a method of teaching, Brunner (1966) identified four criteria:

1. Experiences that most effectively implant in the individual a predisposition to learning;
2. Ways in which a body of knowledge can be structured so that it can be most readily grasped by the learner;
3. Most effective sequences in which to present the materials to be learned; and
4. Nature and pacing of rewards and punishments in the process of learning and teaching. (pp. 40–41)

The first three criteria are evident in Knowles's andragogical principles (see Table 2.1). The last criterion relates to behavioral theory, specifically schedules of reinforcement. Behaviorist B. F. Skinner (1965) proposed several schedules of reinforcement (rewards) that enhance learning. According to reinforcement theory, the schedule of rewards has a strong influence on whether individuals will continue a behavior, which from a behaviorist point of view becomes *learned behavior* through repetition. For instance, giving a reward each time for a behavior is less effective than giving a reward intermittently. From Brunner's work, a number of similar teaching and learning concepts have become popular, including self-directed, problem-based, and discovery learning (as cited in Knowles et al., 2005).

Learning Style

Learning style is generally described in the literature as a preferred method of processing information. To illustrate, if I am a kinesthetic learner, I prefer to learn through body movement, and I am generally adept at motor skills, using them as a way to communicate to others. The National Association of Secondary School Principals' Learning Style Task Force (DeBello, 1989) defines learning styles as follows: "Learning styles are the characteristic cognitive, affective, and psychological behaviors that serve as relatively stable indicators of how learners perceive, interact with, and respond to the learning environment" (p. 5).

According to Dunn (1990), a prominent learning style researcher, students can learn almost anything if educators recognize and are responsive to the students' learning style strengths. This thinking is also aligned with aptitude research, which indicates that students with specific aptitudes may learn more effectively when corresponding teaching methods are employed (Cronbach & Snow, 1981). Studies that have correlated learning styles with learning performance outcomes have had mixed findings, which according to Cronbach and Snow have been related to inadequate sample size. Several studies, however, indicate learners learn more effectively if content is taught in a way that reflects their preferred style of learning (Benedict & Coffield, 1989; Dunn & Dunn, 1992, 1993, 1998, 1999; Kern & Matta, 1988).

Generally researchers agree, however, that learning styles research is inconclusive. The Institute of Educational Policy (Phipps & Merisotis, 1999) specifically identifies learning styles as an area that needs further research: "The research does not take into consideration how the different learning styles of students relate to the use of particular technologies" (pp. 5–6). Regardless of inconclusive research, learning style inventories are quite popular, such as Dunn's (Dunn & Dunn, 1999) learning style inventory, VARK's (http://www.vark-learn.com/english/page.asp?p = questionnaire), and Kolb's (Kolb, 1984) learning style inventory. Most psychologists agree that different learning styles exist. From a research perspective, the challenge is that there are different forms of measurement being applied to the same concept.

Often in my teaching practice I have referred students to the VARK questionnaire as it is available online and free of charge. Most students find the terminology in the instrument and in the explanation of results very familiar and comprehendible. In general, students report they enjoyed completing the VARK questionnaire and reading the results because it helps them understand how they learn best, which in turn has an impact on the way they study.

Multiple Intelligence Theory

Cogitive psychologist Howard Gardner's (1993) theory of multiple intelligence originally described seven forms of intelligence; he later added two more (as cited in Pritchard, 2009). See Table 2.2. The premise is that individuals possess different degrees of each type of intelligence. Somewhat analogous to learning styles theory, multiple intelligence theory suggests that those learners who know which intelligences they excel in will better understand why they more readily process certain types of information (Stefanakis, 2002). For example, a learner who has a high degree of visual-spatial intelligence will readily understand new information offered in the form of graphs and pictures.

Teachers applying multiple intelligence theory realize the importance of relating new information to multiple forms of intelligence. For instance, a teacher may ask students to first reflect upon how they experienced a particular event such as September 11, 2001 (drawing upon intrapersonal intelligence) and then ask how they believe someone else in the group may have experienced it (drawing upon interpersonal intelligence).

Creating Democratic Classrooms

In any profession, culture influences practice. If the profession is misaligned with cultural values, it will eventually modify its practice to become aligned or it will become extinct. Sullivan (2005) had the following to say regarding professions: "Professionalism also means duties to the public. Chief among these duties is the demand that a professional work in such a way that the outcome of the work contributes to the public value for which the profession stands" (p. 23). Gardner, Csikszentmihalyi, and Damon (2001) said: "A professional realm is healthiest when

Table 2.2   Gardner's Multiple Intelligences Applied to Learning Tasks

Type of Intelligence	Description	Applied to Learning Tasks
Linguistic	Understands grammatical structure and word usage. Fluidity in using words to communicate.	Writing and speaking assignments. Word games.
Logical-Mathematical	Fluent in the understanding and use of mathematics and logic.	Simulations involving logic or strategy. Numerical problem solving.
Musical	Understands rhythm and enjoys reproducing musical sounds.	Learning to play musical instruments. Musical composition.
Spatial-Visual	Thinks spatially. Sees ideas in picture form.	Drawing images. Using graphics on a computer.
Kinesthetic	Learns through body movement and often communicates using gestures.	Learns a new physical skill such as dance or tennis.
Interpersonal	Works well with people. Is very perceptive of others' feelings and perspectives.	Leading a group in completing a task. Working with others to organize an event.
Intrapersonal	Heightened sense of self-awareness.	Writing reflective journals.
Naturalistic	Understands the value of nature and the environment.	Working on an environmental sustainability project.
Existential	Big picture thinking about the realities of life and death.	Studying historical events and philosophical perspectives.

the values of the culture are in line with those of the domain, when the expectations of stakeholders match those of the field, and when the domain and field are in sync" (p. 27).

How does this thinking apply to the teaching profession? First and foremost, as we live in a democracy, it would seem that our teaching should reflect democratic principles as eloquently summarized by Knowles et al., 2005):

A democratic philosophy is characterized by a concern for the development of persons, a deep conviction as to the worth of every individual, and faith that people will make the right decisions for themselves if given the necessary information and support. *It gives precedence to the growth of people over the accomplishment of things when these two values are in conflict* [emphasis added]. It emphasizes the release of human potential over the control of human behavior. In a truly democratic organization there is a spirit of mutual trust, an openness of communications, a general attitude of helpfulness and cooperation, and a willingness to accept responsibility, in contrast to paternalism, regimentation, restriction of information, suspicion, and enforced dependency on authority. (p. 109)

Maslow (1972) emphasized the importance of creating safe learning environments that are not only perceived as physically safe but as psychologically and socially safe as well. If adult learners are concerned with safety in any one of these dimensions, applying Maslow's motivational theory, motivation will decrease, negatively affecting learning potential. Establishing a democratic classroom environment is one way to likely ensure perception of a psychologically and socially safe environment.

Aligning Teaching Practice With Adult Learning Goals

In a study that explored the major reasons adults value continuing education, Houle (1961) found three, each of which is associated with a category of learners. The categories are not mutually exclusive and are likely to overlap. The first category of learners, goal oriented, use education to identify specific goals or needs, and they view education as one of the primary means of achieving those goals. This group may seek education in many different forms including formal or informal methods. *If the teacher constructs work that helps the goal-oriented learner see the relationship between the concepts and the goal, learning potential increases.*

The second category of learners, activity oriented, choose learning experiences based on the degree of interaction they entail and the likelihood of forming relationships. *If the teacher includes social interaction as a major component of class work, activity-oriented learners will probably learn more effectively.* The third and final category, learning-oriented learners, has characteristics aligned with those of lifelong learners who are interested in learning for its own sake. *The teacher who provides information regarding available learning resources will engage these learners as well as provide them with future opportunities for more learning.*

As already mentioned, one of the founding principles of andragogy is experiential learning, which, as its name implies, means that adults learn through experience with or without the presence of a teacher. Because learners need to feel safe in discussing their reflections on what they have learned, experiential learning will only flourish in a democratic environment where teacher and colleagues value hearing about each other's life experiences.

As student engagement has been identified as one of the better predictors of learning (Brint, Cantwell, & Hannerman, 2008; Carini, Kuh, & Klein, 2006; Ewell, 2002), teaching practices that assist adult learners in recognizing the value of what they are learning will increase their engagement and ultimately their learning potential. In a study involving graduate students and learning tasks (Caulfield, 2010), student perceived value and student perceived effort associated with a learning task were excellent predictors of student engagement. Findings from this study suggest that teachers need to help learners relate their life experiences to the learning task at hand, for it is through this association that learners recognize the value of the learning task and become more fully engaged in learning.

Teachers as Role Models

Bandura (1977), a prolific researcher at Stanford University, is well known for his work in a number of areas including social learning theory. Although a behaviorist, he recognized that individuals learn not only through doing but through observing others. His well-known research on aggressive behavior in children in the 1960s gave credence to his theory. Children were asked to observe an adult punching a Bobo doll. After observing this behavior, children became more aggressive, indicating that behavior may be learned from observing a role model.

Students often consider their teachers as role models, which gives teachers an opportunity to demonstrate skills important to learning, such as active listening, critical reflection, collaboration, and respect for every individual in the classroom. Role modeling these behaviors creates a democratic learning environment.

Brief Summary of Distance Learning Theory

All the foregoing applies to all modes of teaching and learning, including hybrid classes. Although a hybrid class is not a distance learning class per se, distance learning characteristics do apply to the online portion of the class. For some hybrid students, total time in a classroom (often referred to as *seat time*) may be only 20% of that spent in a traditional class.

Keegan's distance learning theory. Several distance learning theories are worth paying attention to, especially because they show some connection to adult learning theory. Keegan (1996) attributes the following characteristics to distance education:

◆ Quasi-permanent separation of a teacher and a learner throughout the length of the teaching process;

◆ Quasi-permanent separation of a learner from a learning group throughout the length of a learning process;

◆ Participation in a bureaucratized form of educational provision;

◆ Utilization of mechanical or electronic means of communication to carry the context of the course; and

◆ Provision of means for two-way communication so that the learner can benefit from or initiate dialogue. (p. 111)

Again, although a hybrid class is not distance learning, these characteristics do apply to the online portion of the class. Keegan emphasized that unless teachers work toward removing the distance between the teaching acts and the learning acts, it is likely that students will become disengaged, leading to attrition. Practices likely to reduce the distance include presenting learning materials in a readable style, anticipating student problems, carefully structuring course content, using graphics where appropriate, using multiple examples, conducting telephone conferences, having frequent online communication, and giving timely feedback on assignments. Most of these actions encourage regular and frequent dialogue between the teacher and students, an integral component in creating successful online learning environments.

Moore's transactional theory. Moore (Moore & Kearsley, 1996) published his transactional theory of distance education in 1986, although he presented his ideas on transactional theory as early as 1972. He intended his pedagogical theory to be broadly applicable to all forms of distance education. Moore recognized his debt to the work of Desmond Keegan and of humanistic psychologists, including Carl Rogers (http://web space.ship.edu/cgboer/rogers.html), Borje Holmberg (1995), and Abraham Maslow (1972). Moore believes that in any learning situation there is always a certain degree of transactional distance, which he considers a continuous variable. He draws from the conceptual framework Boyd and Apps (1980) developed when they defined the construct of transaction as interplay between individuals, the environment, and behavior patterns occurring in a specific situation. Moore defines transactional distance as pedagogical versus geographical in nature, in that transactional distance refers to the *cognitive* distance that occurs between teachers and learners as a result of differences in understandings and perceptions in any learning environment.

According to Moore (Moore & Kearsley, 1996), two methods can reduce transactional distance in education. The first is to increase dialogue between the teacher and student(s), and the second is to decrease the predetermined structure of the learning experience. Moore describes dialogue as the "interplay of words, actions and ideas and any other interactions between teacher and learner when one gives instruction and the other responds" (p. 201). He defines structure as elements of course design, such as learning objectives, case studies, videos, individual projects, and group work. An example of a highly structured element of course design is a video in which every word is predetermined. A third variable in Moore's (1993) theory is the autonomy of the learner, which he defines as "the extent to which in the teaching/learning relationship it is the learner rather than the teacher who determines the goals, the learning experiences, and the evaluation decisions of the learning program" (p. 31). Thus, Moore suggests that the degree of learner autonomy may, to some degree, influence the amount of transactional distance that may be tolerated to achieve learning goals, with autonomous learners tolerating more transactional distance. In the ideal learning state according to Moore (1993), the learner displays a high degree of autonomy. Thus, the degree of transactional distance needed for effective learning is dependent upon the relationship between structure, the intensity of the dialogue, and the autonomy of the learner, with more autonomous learners being able to tolerate more transactional distance. The variable relationships in transactional theory are displayed in Figure 2.1. For example, a highly structured assignment, such as viewing a video, has no dialogue associated with it, thereby increasing transactional distance. In this situation, the learner is placed in a highly autonomous situation in that learning is achieved by solely interacting with the video content versus interacting with the content, the teacher, and other students in the class. Conversely, if the teacher assigns a small group discussion assignment pertaining to the contents of the video, dialogue increases, transactional distance

Figure 2.1   Moore's Transactional Theory

Structure ↑ + Dialogue ↓ → Transactional Distance ↑ + Learner Autonomy ↑

OR:

Structure ↓ + Dialogue ↑ → Transactional Distance ↓ + Learner Autonomy ↓

decreases and the learner becomes less autonomous through the dialogue that occurs.

Moore (1990) also supports constructivism as an important method of learning. He believes that a learner constructs knowledge primarily through dialogue. It is a process whereby the learner internalizes what is being learned by finding a personal application for the new concepts while determining the worthiness of those concepts. Finally, Moore (Moore & Kearsley, 1996) believes that what makes any course an effective learning experience is a consequence of course design and delivery rather than whether students are learning in a physical classroom or by distance.

Literature on achievement motivation (Pintrich & Schunk, 1996) and andragogy (Knowles et al., 2005) indicates that learners who are highly motivated to achieve will set their own learning goals. Thus, aligned with Moore's theory, high achievers may be autonomous learners who tolerate transactional distance to a greater degree than those who are less autonomous and require less dialogue in a learning environment to achieve their learning outcomes.

Holmberg's theory of distance education. Borje Holmberg (1995) has worked in the field of distance education since 1955 and has received many awards, including honorary doctorates from Deakin University in Australia and the Open University in the United Kingdom. His theory of distance education centers around three concepts: Distance education requires higher-level learning; individual study requires a certain amount of maturity, self-discipline, and independence; and feelings of empathy and belonging promote students' motivation to learn. Holmberg presents his theory of distance education and teaching in a number of hypotheses, which he invites researchers to empirically test. His initial hypothesis, "Organized learning can occur without the presence of a teacher"

(p. 176), has been supported by findings from several research studies (Daley, 1993; Schmidt, Arndt, Gaston, & Miller, 1991). Holmberg's second hypothesis, "Intrinsic motivation is a crucial condition for learning," (p. 176) is not restricted to distance education and is aligned with Knowles's (1990) principles of andragogy. Shunk (1991), a prolific researcher in the area of motivation related to learning and performance, reports that intrinsic motivation has a reciprocal relationship with learning and performance. In other words, just as motivation positively affects learning and performance, learning and performance positively affect motivation. Holmberg's third and fourth hypotheses are related: "Learning is promoted by students' fitting subject matter into existing cognitive structures," and "Learning is encouraged by frequent, helpful communication with others" (p. 176). These hypotheses are aligned with constructivist and social interaction theories, which suggest that the behaviors of one individual influence those of another and vice versa (Turner, 1988).

Peters's industrial/postindustrial theory. Otto Peters, past vice-chancellor of the FernUniversität-Gesamthochschule (distance teaching university) in Hagen, Germany, is the author of several books on distance education and received the International Council for Open and Distance Education Prize of Excellence in 1999. The basic premise of the industrial component of Peters's (1993) theory is that distance education is a product of industrialization, and because of that, it has been heavily influenced by principles of industrialization, such as rationalization, division of labor, assignment of tasks to specialists, mechanization, and automation. Peters points out the following striking similarities:

1. The development of distance study courses is just as important as the preparatory work prior to the production process.
2. The effectiveness of the teaching-learning process is particularly dependent on very careful planning and adequate organization.
3. The function of the teacher is split up into several subfunctions and performed by specialists as, for instance, in the production process at an assembly line.
4. Distance education can only be economically viable if the number of students is great: mass education corresponds to mass production.
5. As is the case with the production process, distance education needs capital investments, a concentration of the available resources, and a qualified centralized administration. (p. 39)

Peters classifies F2F education as a form of preindustrial instruction similar to the work of a craftsman. The postindustrial component of Peters's theory is based on the premise that the principles of distance education need to be radically redefined to align with the postindustrial society we now live in. Peters draws attention to the three economic trends Wood and Zurcher (1988) identify as most important in the postindustrial era:

1. The proportion of labour employed by the tertiary or service sector will increase dramatically;
2. The "new" technology will emerge [referring to computerization];
3. The decision-making structure of the new economy, and eventually that in society at large, will change significantly [in that decision making will take place within groups of individuals versus taking place at hierarchical levels]. (p. 22)

Since Wood and Zurcher identified these trends in 1988, the service industry has had explosive growth over the past three decades, computerization and digitalization are dominant technologies, and the emphasis on delegating decision making to those closest to the process is prevalent in today's management literature.

Peters (1993) describes how these trends affect the design and use of distance education today. The growth of the service sector has dramatically increased the need for highly educated professionals, and lifelong learning is an important factor in the workplace. Because of the need for continuous learning, individuals will more and more turn to distance education, which gives them the freedom to learn where and when it is most advantageous to them, reducing time spent away from home, family, and other responsibilities.

Technology is permeating every aspect of our society, including education and more specifically, distance education. The evidence is in the significant expansion in web-based learning over the past two decades. Related to the change in decision-making structure, group interactions play an important part in the learning process, and thus need to be included in the design of distance education. Finally, adult learners play a more active role in deciding what, where, when, and how something is to be learned. Distance education may better give students those choices. All of this points to the importance of applying constructivism and andragogy when teaching adults.

Bates's theory and practice in the use of technology in distance education. Tony Bates has written nine books and numerous articles on distance education, focusing primarily on the use of technology. According to Bates (1993), at the end of the 1980s a vast majority of distance education was print based, without the use of any digital technology. Bates said the following are the major reasons technology is becoming more and more important in distance education:

♦ A much wider range of technologies is becoming more accessible to potential distance education students;
♦ The costs of technological delivery are dropping dramatically;
♦ Technology is becoming easier to use by teachers and learners;
♦ Technology is becoming more powerful pedagogically;
♦ Distance education institutions will find it increasingly difficult to resist the political and social pressures of the technological imperative. (p. 213)

In other words, to remain competitive in today's technological environment, distance learning institutions will need to remain current in the use of technology.

Bates named three generations of distance teaching institutions: correspondence schools; those using a wider variety of media including telephone and television; and those incorporating information and communication technologies. Bates pointed out that the successful third-generation distance education institutions apply technology in a way that benefits learners. Bates also asserted that the use of technology has provided learning experiences not otherwise available in F2F learning situations. He further stated that the cost of producing high-quality distance teaching materials will not drop, as production will continue to require "people who can combine good pedagogic practice with an understanding of the strengths and weaknesses of different media and technologies" (p. 232).

Bates (1993) proposed four hypotheses related to the use of technology in distance education:

1. The need for multiple forms of experience is required before learners internalize and fully comprehend concepts (Bates, p. 223). Applying this thinking, the best learning environments should

include multimedia, exposing students to multiple ways of learning. This thinking is aligned to learning styles and multiple intelligences theory as well as constructivist thought, which emphasizes the importance of constructing knowledge through experience. Bates invites empirical research to test this hypothesis.

2. Media are neutral regarding content, but specific regarding skills (Bates, p. 234). By this Bates means that some media will assist in the development of skills but others will not. As an example, he cites broadcasting as being less effective than print in helping students develop deep comprehension, while videos may help students apply knowledge to new situations. Surface comprehension may be achieved by using one medium, while deep comprehension may occur after being exposed to multiple forms of media. Results from at least two empirical studies support this hypothesis (Bates & Gallagher, 1987; Salomon, 1983).

3. Media can be matched to appropriate models of thinking (Bates, p. 226). Research by Salomon (1983) indicates that some media may be better than others at helping students grasp particular concepts. For example, television and computers may generate images that help cognitive processing through visualization or through symbolism. Visual learners may particularly benefit from this type of media use. Bandura (1977) has used television to model behavior that is internalized and may actually encourage similar behavior by the viewer. According to Bates, "This means that a good understanding of what is required to teach a particular subject needs to be combined with good knowledge of the pedagogic strengths and weaknesses of different media" (1993, p. 230).

4. Learners need to interact both with the learning material, and with tutors or instructors, and other students, in order to learn effectively (Bates, p. 229). This hypothesis is supported by the theories of Keegan, Moore, and Holmberg. Bates emphasizes the idea that computer-mediated education, which includes synchronous and asynchronous dialogue between students and between students and the teacher, will increase the effectiveness of learning. This aligns with constructivism and social interaction theory.

Anderson's equivalency of interaction theorem. Terry Anderson, an educational psychologist from Athabasca University, has been researching interaction in learning environments for over 20 years. In his earlier work with Garrison (Anderson & Garrison, 1998), he identified three modes of interaction between students and teachers in distance education. The modes for students were student–student, student–teacher, and student–content; the modes for teachers were teacher–teacher, teacher–content, and content–content. In his later work Anderson (2003) drew upon the student interaction modes in what he termed the equivalency of interaction theorem, stated as follows:

> Deep and meaningful formal learning is supported as long as one of the three forms of interaction (student-teacher; student-student; student-content) is at a high level. The other two may be offered at minimal levels, or even eliminated, without degrading the educational experience. High levels of more than one of these three modes will likely provide a more satisfying educational experience, though these experiences may not be as cost or time effective as less interactive learning sequences. (p. 4)

Anderson said he has learned from students over the years that they prefer different modes of student interaction. Not all students enjoy or need high levels of each mode of interaction to learn effectively. His findings support Moore's (1993) transactional theory, which states that more autonomous learners need less dialogue. These results could have important implications in how interaction is structured in any learning environment, including hybrid.

Over the years, I have found that graduate students enrolled in a hybrid class learn quite well when interacting with content in a structured way outside the classroom. Content interactions could comprise any number of assignments, including a short essay about a particular reading or community experience. Having completed a high level of content interaction by writing the essay, students are already invested and engaged in the topic when they come to class, and the in-class discussion is more meaningful and efficient than if they had only completed the reading or had the community experience without further critical reflection.

Variables Related to Groups Interacting With Technology

Frequently hybrid learners are asked to work in small virtual groups. To improve group performance through the effective use of technology, McGrath and Hollingshead (1994) researched the impact technology has on the behavior of work groups. They discovered through their extensive review of the literature on group theory, including groups' use of technology, that many variables are involved and can be categorized into four groups: input factors, organizing concepts, process variables, and outcome factors.

Input factors included such things as member attributes, group attributes, the nature of the task, the technology used, and the physical, social, and temporal context. The interaction of input factors influences organizing concepts which are determining how the group functions as a processing system, generating a consensus system, and determining a vehicle for motivating and regulating behavior. Process variables, influenced by the organizing concepts, focus on the following processes: participation of group members over time, how the group organizes and uses information, how the group generates consensus, and how the group behaves, which affects group cohesiveness over time. Finally, outcome factors dependent upon these processes are task performance effectiveness, customer satisfaction related to group outcomes, and member reactions regarding group process.

McGrath and Hollingshead's (1994) work implies that these variables need to be considered when organizing and assigning group work in a hybrid class. For example, when the teacher assigns students to a particular small group, it may be helpful for at least one member of the group to have good technology skills (input factor here is member attribute) so that the technology does not distract the group from its primary objective of completing the assignment. Having a concentrated focus on the task at hand will determine how the group functions as a processing system (organizing concept), which will in turn affect how the group processes information (process variable) as its members work together. All this influences the group's task performance (outcome factor).

Community of Inquiry

In their book on blended learning, Garrison and Vaughan (2008) discuss what they refer to as a *community of inquiry* (CoI), defined as "a cohesive and interactive community of learners whose purpose is to critically analyze, construct, and confirm worthwhile knowledge" (p. 9). The three elements of a CoI are social presence, cognitive presence, and teacher presence. Social presence refers to open communication and group cohesion with the ultimate goal of emotional bonding and camaraderie. To achieve this goal, the authors stress that the CoI must be a trusting and safe environment. These ideas are aligned with those of Knowles et al. (2005) when they speak of building democratic learning environments. Maslow (1972) writes extensively about the importance of creating safe learning environments so effective learning may occur.

Cognitive presence refers to making the connection between ideas and exploring those connections through dialogue and application. This thinking is aligned with constructivist thought. Teaching presence refers to the course design and the actual teaching, including facilitating focused discussions. Garrison and Vaughan (2008) use the CoI framework to assist readers in understanding hybrid learning environments, emphasizing that the hybrid methodology is well aligned to the CoI paradigm. The authors emphasize that a major goal of a CoI in a blended or hybrid learning environment is working toward achieving specific learning outcomes within and outside the F2F classroom. Furthermore, they suggest the CoI serve as a guide to research and practice for teaching and learning environments with online components.

Studies Pertaining to Achievement Motivation of Distance Learners

As we have already noted in discussing Holmberg's (1995) second hypothesis and Knowles's (1990) adult learning principles, intrinsic motivation aids learning. In general, researchers across disciplines support the theory that motivation has a positive influence on learning outcomes. Over the years, several studies have focused on identifying personality traits of distance learners as compared to those of traditional learners. Study findings suggest that successful distance learners are likely to have an internal locus of control, a high need for achievement, and prefer learning via active experimentation (Jonassen & Grabinger, 1988). These findings are not surprising in that individuals who have an internal locus of control believe they are the ones who determine their success and failure, which means they are likely to accept primary responsibility for their own learning. Those having a high need for achievement are more likely to work more autonomously in achieving goals, including those related to education. Thus, the increased transaction distance that Moore (1993) speaks of becomes more tolerable for autonomous learners. Finally, adult learning theory emphasizes the importance of experiential learning.

Certain personality factors helped predict success in distance education students, including self-sufficiency and introversion (Biner, Bink, Huffman, & Dean, 1995). Self-sufficiency implies taking initiative in accomplishing tasks, which is important for online students who complete work more independently. Introverts are more comfortable reflecting on ideas before communicating them to others; asynchronous communication provides time for reflection.

For distance learners, Coggins (1989) found an indirect relationship between the need for peer and faculty affiliation and course completion. In other words, distance learners who do not have a need for high affiliation with the teacher and with other students are more likely to complete an online class. For students who have a higher need for affiliation, the importance of creating social presence in the online and F2F components of a hybrid course cannot be overstated, as social presence fulfills that need to some extent. Gibson and Graff (1992) report similar findings in that successful distance learners needed less peer affiliation and had more self-confidence regarding their performance and competence in completing their degrees as compared to unsuccessful distance learners.

A few studies have focused on distance learners' primary goals concerning education. These studies indicate that the majority of distance learners have what Thompson (1998) terms *instrumental goals* versus *developmental goals*, meaning that instrumental goals are focused on advancement in the work setting while developmental goals are focused on learning for the sake of personal development. Those individuals who are most motivated by career goals are generally more successful online learners. In a study involving 2,300 FernUniversität distance learners (von Prummer, 1990), 84.4% of the students indicated their primary goal was to attain advanced professional qualifications (instrumental goal). Developmental goals, such as goals relating to general knowledge, did not rank in the top three goals of the study.

Also, von Prummer (1990) noted significant gender differences in that 84% of women as compared to 73.4% of men ranked "opening up new areas of knowledge" as a primary goal. Women ranked self-esteem as more important than men did (74.1% compared to 56.8%). Last, women reported more interest in intellectual stimulation than men did (74.1% vs. 56.8%). These gender differences may influence student performance on certain assignments. For example, women may be more interested in an assignment they may find intellectually stimulating regardless of whether it is closely related to career aspirations, while this generally may not be the case for men.

Shu-Lun Wong (1992) investigated differences in study behaviors of distance education students as compared to F2F students. The study was conducted at Memorial University of Newfoundland, and the sample consisted of 201 students, 89 distance learners, and 112 F2F students. Most participants were business students. After controlling for age and sex, distance learners reported being more influenced by intrinsic motivators than did F2F students. Furthermore, findings suggested that distance education students show more interest in course work. Finally, F2F students had higher scores in fear of failure, superficial learning, and achievement motivation. The researchers hypothesized that higher scores in these areas may be a result of the competitiveness of undergraduate study. Nonetheless, these differences in study behaviors may at least partially explain why distance learners are reported to learn more effectively than those enrolled in traditional classes (U.S. Department of Education, Office of Planning, Evaluation, and Policy Development, 2009).

Results of a study by Gibson (1996) indicate that academic self-concept may have an impact on the rate of attrition for distance learners. Gibson interviewed 16 distance learners several times during their initial year of enrollment in distance instruction. Information from these open-ended interviews indicated that academic self-concept, defined as "the student's perception of self as a learner," (p. 24) is dynamic rather than stagnant and is influenced by environmental and institutional factors. Gibson classified these factors as either *process* or *content* factors. Process factors included personal success, self-growth, skill deficiencies, the ability to juggle multiple priorities, and the number of courses taken over a short period of time. Content factors included mastering a variety of content areas, clear expectations from the faculty, and a fairly structured course design. Further findings suggest that academic self-concept plays an important role in persistence in distance education, and that appropriate interventions such as constructive and timely feedback on assignments and frequent dialogue may enhance academic self-concept, decreasing the likelihood of attrition.

Coming Full Circle: How Does Information in This Chapter Apply to Hybrid?

While we do need to pay attention to learning theory, theory specific to distance learners is for the most part quite dated, and theory specific to hybrid learning environments is almost nonexistent. Perhaps the key message is that we should skillfully apply existing learning theory to the different modes of course delivery made possible through advances in technology. Moreover, as researchers, we should identify opportunities that may further develop learning theory based on observations, experiences, and practices as we employ different models of course delivery. Some would argue that the distance learning theory that does exist is really a form of adult learning theory. Still others would argue that adult learning theory in and of itself does not completely meet the definition of theory. In any case, a sufficient body of research provides evidence that adults do learn differently than children. Moreover, findings from multiple studies suggest that appropriately applied pedagogical and andragogical theories assist teachers in creating engaging and effective adult learning environments, regardless of whether those environments are F2F or online.

CHAPTER THREE

EXPERIENTIAL LEARNING

> You cannot help but learn more as you take
> the world into your hands. Take it up rever-
> ently, for it is an old piece of clay, with millions
> of thumbprints on it.
>
> —John Updike (2008)

THIS CHAPTER BEGINS WITH several definitions of experiential learning and a relatively brief explanation of its complexities from a theoretical perspective. Readers interested in comprehensive theoretical reviews may refer to a number of works, including Boud and Walker, 1991; Dewey, 1938; Fenwick, 2001 and 2003a; Jarvis, Holford, and Griffin, 1999; Knowles, 1984; Kolb, 1984; Merriam, Caffarella, and Baumgartner, 2007; Mezirow, 1991; and Schön, 1987. Next, Fenwick's (2003a) five perspectives of experiential learning are discussed. As the role of the teacher and learner is a topic of discussion in the experiential literature and is relevant to hybrid teaching and learning, discussions on role identification for each perspective are included. The chapter concludes with two detailed descriptions of applied experiential learning activities within a hybrid course, each applying the five perspectives in Fenwick's framework. Examples highlight the role of the teacher and learner.

Definitions and Theoretical Background

One of the major premises of behaviorism in the field of psychology is that we learn through conditioning, which occurs when we interact with our environment (Hergenhahn & Olson, 2000). For behaviorists, observable interactive behavior demonstrates learning. At about the same time behavioral psychologists such as Watson (http://www.psych.utah.edu/gordon/Classes/Psy4905Docs/PsychHistory/Cards/Watson.html), Thorndike (http://www.muskingum.edu/~psych/psycweb/history/thorndike.htm), Skinner (http://webspace.ship.edu/cgboer/skinner.html), and others were researching behaviorism, well-known educational philosopher John Dewey (1938) published a book titled *Experience and Education* that clearly put forth the idea that learning takes place from experience in a social context. Dewey stated, "The principle that development of experience comes about through interaction means that education is essentially a social process" (p. 58). Dewey identified two dimensions of learning. First, he said learning occurs when the learner connects past experiences with novel experiences; he termed this cognitive ability *continuity*. Second, he wrote that for learning to occur the learner must be actively engaged in or interact with the novel experience; this ability he termed *interaction*. As an example, a learner may experience seeing a certain breed of dog for the first time, which is a new experience. However, having had dogs all his or her life, the learner is an avid dog lover with many past experiences relating to dogs (continuity). Based on those past experiences, the learner thinks the dog may be some type of retriever. Thus, the learner asks the owner of the dog several questions about the dog (interaction). He or she learns from the dog's owner that the dog is a Chesapeake Bay retriever, which is very similar to a Labrador when it comes to training. However, according to the owner, the Chesapeake is a bit more temperamental.

Note that both dimensions are important in this learning experience. It is more likely the learner felt comfortable in questioning the dog owner because the learner already knew about dogs (continuity existed). It is also more likely the learner will interact with his environment because of his interest in dogs (interaction occurs). According to Dewey (1938), because continuity existed and interaction occurred, the learner's paradigm concerning dogs transcended the previously existing paradigm. In simple words, the learner learned something new about dogs.

Although John Dewey brought the tenets of experiential learning to the forefront, he never coined an exact definition of the term. He did, however, define the role of the student and the educator. Simply stated, in experiential learning, the role of the learner is to construct knowledge grounded in social interaction, while the role of the teacher is to assess a learner's readiness and capabilities to learn and to provide the appropriate experience, specifically one in which the learner is engaged and capable of constructing new knowledge through observation, experience, and reflection (Roberts, 2003). The theory that learning may occur through direct observation in social contexts is supported by behavioral psychologist Albert Bandura (1977) and personality psychologist Walter Mischel (1973). Both researchers link one of the major tenets of experiential learning theory to behaviorism, specifically social cognitive learning theory.

Later work by experiential learning theorists has led to several definitions of experiential learning. Jarvis, Holford, and Griffin (1999) wrote, "Experiential learning may be defined as the process of creating and transforming experience into knowledge, skills, attitudes, values, emotions, beliefs and senses. It is the process through which individuals become themselves" (p. 46). Kolb (1984) said, "Learning is the process whereby knowledge is created through the transformation of experience" (p. 38). Kolb's experiential learning cycle is heavily referred to throughout the educational literature on experiential learning and learning styles, and is illustrated in Figure 3.1. Briefly, Kolb theorizes that learning begins with individuals' observing or being engaged with a novel experience. Next they reflect upon that experience, creating a paradigm or abstract conceptualization of their perceived experience. Finally, they test their paradigm using a similar future experience. Kolb also identifies four learning styles that correspond to these stages of learning.

The following is an example of how Kolb's learning cycle might be applied. The supervisor of a subordinate in a new job might be treating the subordinate with the utmost respect (concrete experience) while showing the person how to perform a job task. Later that evening, the subordinate reflects on the supervisor's respectful behavior (reflective observation) and comes to the conclusion that the supervisor must behave respectfully toward all individuals in general (abstract conceptualization). For the remainder of the week, the subordinate observes the supervisor interacting with a number of individuals, and the subordinate decides his or her paradigm is correct (active experimentation).

Knowles, whose work is summarized in Chapter 2, identified the importance of experience as one of the principle components of andragogy. Saddington defines experiential learning as "an independent learner, cognitively reflecting on concrete experience to construct new understandings, perhaps with the assistance of an educator, toward

Figure 3.1   Kolb's Experiential Learning Cycle

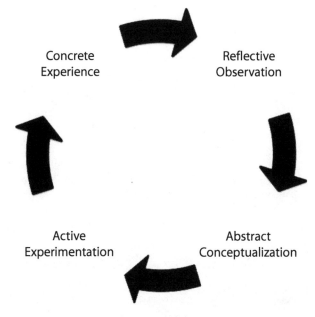

Concrete Experience

Reflective Observation

Active Experimentation

Abstract Conceptualization

some social goal of progress or improvement" (as cited in Fenwick, 2001, p. 7).

From this brief overview of the theoretical underpinnings of experiential learning theory, it becomes apparent that experiential learning is very much related to a number of other pedagogical and andragogical learning theories, including constructivism, active learning, and problem-based learning, all of which are discussed in Chapter 2. A number of theorists (Britzman, 1998; Hart, 1992; Michelson, 1996; Sawada, 1991) challenge how we learn from experience, including whether reflection is a cognitive process, whether learners are capable of removing themselves from an experience to reflect upon it, whether social and cultural context should be considered, and whether emotion and desire, which are not fully addressed, play an important role in experiential learning.

Although theorists do not completely agree on how we learn from experience, there does seem to be general agreement that learning from experience has been occurring for centuries.

Why Fenwick's Five Perspectives?

Fenwick's umbrella framework for experiential learning, which includes several key andragogical theoretical concepts discussed in Chapter 2, is well suited as a frame of reference when constructing experiential learning experiences. Experiential learning may be a substantial and vital part of any hybrid course design, as it places responsibility for learning predominantly with the learner; the primary roles of the educator are to create effective experiential teaching and learning activities and to serve as facilitator, coach, and evaluator throughout the process.

Tara Fenwick (2001) poses two questions about experiential learning: "What does it mean to learn from experience? And, what, if any, is an appropriate role for educators in this process?" (p. vii). She then suggests the following five perspectives. From an application standpoint, keeping these perspectives in mind may be valuable when creating the opportunity for experiential learning.

Constructivist perspective. As discussed in Chapter 2, this perspective purports that reflection on concrete experiences aids the learner in developing and testing new paradigms. Increasing knowledge regarding a novel and concrete experience may then be tested on similar future experiences. This is and has been the dominant experiential perspective in the adult learning literature, where the teacher's role is one of facilitating novel experiences, and the learner's role is reflecting on the novel experience. It is predominantly through reflection and validation that new paradigms transcend old ones and new knowledge is acquired. Constructivism leads to critical questions such as, "How do social context and power structures influence the shaping of existing and expanded paradigms? And how do the environment and social context have an impact on the testing of those paradigms?"

Major challenges in evaluating constructivist theory include being overly deterministic in attempting to understand learners' perceptions of their experiences and the relationships between experience and knowledge. Critics Davis and Sumara (1997) said,

> Constructivism is a theory of knowledge and experience that seeks to bridge perceived gaps between knower and world and among knowers. The belief in the isolated subject further supports the notion that the "individual" is *contained* in a context rather than regarding the individual as an integral part of a relational fabric. (p. 111)

Second, it is paramount for teachers to avoid interventions that detract from learning while encouraging those that enhance learning. As Fenwick (2001) commented, "The point is that educators' consideration of and intervention in others' experiential learning is neither neutral nor innocent" (p. 3).

Psychoanalytic perspective. The underlying theme of this perspective is working through conflict between the conscious and the unconscious. Major proponents of psychoanalytic theory include Bracher (1993), Britzman (1998), and Ellsworth (1997). One of the tenets of this perspective is giving adequate time to learners to work through conflicts, which may otherwise evoke resistance to learning. Thus, the role of teachers becomes one of helping learners work through these dilemmas by first learning to listen to and work through their own psychic dilemmas. The role of the learner is to take the time necessary to resolve inner conflict. Fenwick (2001) wrote, "To learn, people need to be deliberate experimenters in their own learning, willingly engaging in traumas of the self" (p. 33).

For example, managers who give employees adequate time for and assistance in working through inner conflict that arises as a result of impending change will likely experience less resistance in implementing that change. In another example, because of predetermined views of student athletes' lack of interest and ability in academics, a teacher may evaluate student athletes more harshly than other students. Until the teacher recognizes and works through his or her personal bias, this practice interferes with good teaching for those student athletes.

Regarding this perspective, Fenwick (2001) proposes a critical question, "Are all workings-through to be honored and encouraged?" (p. 34). In some instances, repression of conflict may be a survival technique that is needed to maintain emotional stability. There are students who have voiced concerns about teachers who attempted to probe into their internal conflicts, causing them discomfort in the classroom. Teachers need to achieve a balance between encouraging learning through resolving inner conflict and making students feel uncomfortable by invading their privacy, especially in the presence of other students.

Critics of the psychoanalytic perspective such as Lave (1988) question whether it is too internally focused, with little regard for the cultural and social dynamics that learners experience on a daily basis. Mezirow (1996) makes the point that as rational beings, we cannot focus on psychic dilemmas indefinitely, but instead work through those dilemmas, forming paradigms that serve as future frames of reference to be tested and potentially validated.

Situative perspective. This perspective emphasizes that the learner learns by the act of doing and learning is situation specific (Lave & Wenger, 1991). Knowledge emerges from interactions with community (culture, values, relationships) at the time those interactions occur. According to Lave (as cited in Fenwick, 2001), this implies that knowledge is in a constant state of flux, dependent not only on community but on circumstances (purpose of activity, challenges) and on tools (technology, images, objects, language) present at the time. Here the educator's role is to help identify and facilitate authentic community experiences, helping students to discern meaning from their participation and coaching them to eventually be capable of performing the activity on their own. The learner's role is one of active community participation and discernment of value provided to the community. Critical questions that arise from this perspective are, "Is the learning environment successful in accomplishing its learning goals? How do the various participants, tools and objects interact together? What meanings are constructed?" (Wilson & Myers, 2000, Chapter 3, para. 2, 300).

Critics of the situative perspective include Anderson, Reder, and Simon (1996) who argued that several empirical studies demonstrate that learning transfers across contexts, and that such transferability is dependent upon variables such as the nature of instruction and the way the material is studied. Second, they argued that not all learning is benefited by complex social environments and that in fact some learning is best accomplished independently. An accountant who needs to learn the tax code is an example. Salomon and Perkins (1998) argued that organizational learning may lead to superficial changes in behavior without changing underlying belief systems. In reference to business settings, this concern is evident, as they wrote, "This low road rather than high road character of organizational learning should not come as a surprise. After all, first and foremost, organizations are performance systems, not learning systems" (p. 15). Finally, according to Ellsworth (as cited in Fenwick, 2001), the situative perspective does not address the flux in positions that individuals may experience as related to relationships, power, knowledge base, and progress with the community activity itself. Nor does it address community resistance, which may block effective learning experiences.

Critical cultural perspective. This perspective focuses on how power and inequity existing among various cultures and social groups may hinder social transformation through experiential learning. As long as boundaries exist between groups and cultures, experiential learning for individuals attempting to blur those boundaries may be somewhat limited by other individuals or groups who benefit from keeping them intact. Critical cultural educator McLaren (1995) said:

> It should come as little surprise that public opinion among those groups most advantaged by wealth and power is more supportive of the public school system and current reform efforts than it is on the basis of those disempowered by race, socioeconomic status or gender. For those very populations that will be increasing in numbers in the coming decades—particularly African-American and Latino youth, conditions in this country's school systems have worsened appreciably. Groups actively lobbying for minority positions on issues dealing with race, social and welfare concerns are now being labeled within the conservative agenda by spokespersons . . . as "ethnocentric" or "separatist." (p. 11)

Fenwick (2003a) wrote, "When adults participate in systems and exchanges where power is unequally distributed, where the focus is on technical rational control and where they are unaware of their own human potential, they shrivel" (p. 31). Thus a goal of critical cultural perspective becomes one of blurring the boundaries that interfere with the transformation of individuals within cultures and social groups through experiential learning, thereby better enabling working together "to fight dehumanizing conditions and create a more democratic, equitable, sustainable reality" (Fenwick, 2003a, p. 33). Globalization could potentially work as an asset in achieving this goal by blurring cultural boundaries.

Critical adult educator Foley (1999) believes that individuals acquire knowledge through social action experience, which builds self-confidence and greater understanding of power structures. Through this form of experiential learning, learners become aware that they can make a difference if they are willing to engage in social action.

The role of the teacher in critical cultural perspective is to assist learners in becoming more aware of how misuse of power and the presence of oppression lead to inequities. Further, teachers need to help learners successfully engage in social action that works toward achieving equity and freedom. The role of learners is to transform themselves into social change agents. Critical questions include:

> What social and cultural capital is valued most in a particular community, and which group is reflected in it? . . . What is considered legitimate knowledge among a particular group or a whole society? Which

kinds and whose knowledge count most—in higher education, in different workplaces, in community and family life? (Fenwick, 2003a, pp.
32–33)

Critics of the critical cultural perspective, such as Foucault (1988),
believe that reducing human behavior to something that is dominated by
coercive and intractable power is too simplistic a view. Other critics such
as Sumara and Davis (1997) believe the views of oppression, power dominance, and resistance to minority movements espoused as destructive and
irreversible forces by some critical cultural theorists are self-limiting and
perpetuate negativity.

Enactivist ecological perspective. Fenwick (2003a) said, "Ecological theorists explore how cognition and environment become *simultaneously
enacted* through experiential learning" (p. 34). This perspective is
grounded in systems thinking. Learners and contexts become integrated
and inseparable systems; the modification of these systems through intentional interaction between them results in change, leading to a higher
level of unity that may be achieved through interdependence. An example
is the dialogue between learners and between learners and teachers in the
context of a classroom, which is viewed as a system. The dialogue cannot
be predetermined; yet as a result of its occurrence, learners and teachers,
whose roles become intermingled throughout the course of the dialogue,
are changed through experiencing the dialogue in the context where it
occurred. The collective experience itself is larger than any one individual's thoughts, emotions, and perceptions. Participants in this system then
take the collective knowledge that emerged from the dialogue and share
it with others in different systems (family, community). Fenwick (2003a)
said, "Knowledge cannot be contained in any one element or dimension
of a system, for knowledge is constantly emerging and spilling into other
systems" (p. 11). Learning then becomes a "continuous invention and
exploration, produced though relations among consciousness, identity,
action and interaction, objects, and structural dynamics of complex systems" (p. 10). From an enactivist ecological perspective, Sumara and
Davis pose the following critical questions. "How does one trace the various entangled involvements in a particular activity in a complex system,
while attending assiduously to one's own involvement as participant?
How can trajectories of movement of particulate actors in relation to the
system's objects be understood and recorded in a meaningful way?" (as
cited in Fenwick, 2001, p. 49).

From this perspective, the role of the teacher becomes one of integrating what goes on in the classroom with what goes on outside the classroom, aiding learners in seeking better understanding of the world by helping them to make sense of unpredictable and often messy and complex interactions. Learning is an ongoing collective process; it does not take place in a vacuum. Integration may be enhanced by dispelling the notion that a classroom is within the confines of four walls. Instead, the classroom becomes the world we live in with all its beauty and ugliness. As Davis and Sumara (1997) wrote:

> Rejecting the cultural arrogance underlying the belief that the formal educational setting is the principal location for study of cultural knowledge, we are suggesting that other sites be seen as places of teaching and learning: shopping malls, restaurants, food banks, retirement homes, churches, festivals, hockey games, etc. In our desire to separate the schooled experience from life outside the classroom, such locations have not been regarded as an integral part of who we are. Instead, inside the classroom they are named "the real world," and nodding reference is made to this distanced realm through contrived word problems and fragmented discussions of social issues. Thus, at the same time, that school and not-school are dichotomized, educators often delegitimize their own project by naming it as *not* [emphasis added] part of the real world. (p. 123)

From the enactivist ecological perspective, the role of learners is to actively and consciously participate in the fluid systems they live in, for by so doing new knowledge emerges. They need to recognize that existing thought patterns may no longer apply to present and future systems, learning to be comfortable with ambiguity while being eager to explore new and emerging patterns that transcend previous thought.

Fenwick (2001) identifies some criticisms that are likely to arise from the enactivist ecological perspective. Constructivists are likely to postulate that not everything an individual thinks about is made communal, and that the knowledge some individuals have should be shared. The role of ethics in this perspective is unclear. From an ethical viewpoint, which conduct is ethically correct, and do ethics change as the systems change? From a critical cultural perspective, how does experiential learning void of considerations such as social structure, power, and dominance actually occur? These questions do not in any way invalidate the enactivist ecological perspective; however, they encourage reflection on complex issues that have neither simple nor definite answers.

In summary, Fenwick's (2001) framework for experiential learning includes five perspectives: the literature dominant constructivist perspective, the psychoanalytic perspective, the situative perspective, the critical cultural perspective, and the enactivist/ecological perspective. A theoretical, and in many instances an empirical, body of literature exists for each perspective that may serve as a guide when creating experiential learning activities in a hybrid course. The summary of the perspectives provided in Table 3.1 is not meant to imply that any one of them functions in exclusion to the others; instead it is likely that tenets from each are relevant to experiential learning as a whole. For some experiential learning activities, certain perspectives may be more insightful than others.

Examples of Experiential Learning Applied to Hybrid Course Design

The two examples of experiential learning in this section focus primarily on activities outside the classroom versus those online or in the F2F classroom, which are discussed in the remainder of the book.

Mediation

The first example of experiential learning is taken from mediation classes taught by Eva Soeka, director of a graduate program in dispute resolution, and several teachers from the program. The program's students are predominantly experienced professionals working full-time (median age mid-40s), including attorneys, human resource professionals, and government employees.

Honeyman and Yawanarajah (2003) define mediation as

> A process in which a third-party neutral assists in resolving a dispute between two or more other parties. It is a non-adversarial approach to conflict resolution. The role of the mediator is to facilitate communication between the parties, assist them in focusing on the real issues of the dispute, and generate options that meet the interests or needs of all relevant parties in an effort to resolve the conflict. (para 1)

Discussions with Soeka centered on how previous learners who had never practiced mediation became proficient at it by the time they graduated from the dispute resolution program. In fact, she told me that only a few students could not master the technique (personal communication,

Table 3.1 Fenwick's Experiential Framework: Five Perspectives Summarized From Chapter Narrative

Perspective	Major Theme	Critical Questions	Major Theorists	Criticisms	Role of Teacher	Role of Learner
Constructivist	Reflective observation of novel experience leads to new paradigms that are then tested in similar future experiences.	How does environment and social context influence emerging knowledge? And how do they affect testing emerging knowledge?	Piaget & Vygotsky	Overly deterministic. Isolates the subject from social context and environment.	Create or expose learners to novel experiences. Refrain from interjecting bias into learners' reflective observation.	Reflective observation of novel experiences. Test new paradigms on similar future experiences.
Psychoanalytic	Experiential learning occurs without resistance when learners are given adequate time for internal conflict resolution.	Should the resolution of internal conflict in all cases be encouraged and honored?	Britzman, Ellsworth, & Bracher	Too internally focused with little regard for the influence of social and cultural dynamics.	Work through own internal conflict and help learners do the same by giving them adequate time and encouragement.	Take the time to work through internal conflicts that interfere with learning.

Table 3.1 (Continued)

Perspective	Major Theme	Critical Questions	Major Theorists	Criticisms	Role of Teacher	Role of Learner
Situative	Learning occurs by the act of doing and is situation specific.	Is the learning environment successful in accomplishing its learning goals? How do various participants, tools, and objects interact together? What meanings are constructed?	Lave & Wenger	Empirical studies indicate that learning transfers across contexts dependent on certain variables. Not all learning is benefited by complex social environments. Organizational learning may lead to superficial changes in behavior.	Identify and facilitate authentic community experiences. Help learners to discern meaning from community experience. Coach learners toward independently becoming active community members.	Active community participation and discernment of meaning and value to community.
Critical cultural	Learning may be enhanced or hindered dependent upon understanding the distribution of power and the dominance of certain social structures.	What social and cultural capital is valued most in a particular community and which group is reflected in it? What is legitimate knowledge among groups and society? Whose knowledge counts most?	Foley & McLaren	Reducing human behavior to that dominated by coercive and intractable power is too simplistic a view. Views of oppression, power dominance, and resistance to minority thinking are self-limiting and perpetuate negativity.	Heighten awareness in learners that misuse of power and the presence of oppression leads to inequities. Encourage learners to engage in social action that works toward achieving equity and freedom.	Transform into agents of social change.

Enactivist ecological	Founded in systems thinking, experiential learning occurs by cognition and environment becoming simultaneously enacted.	How does one trace the various entangled involvements in a particular activity in a complex system, while attending assiduously to one's own involvement as participant? How can trajectories of movement of particular actors in relation to the system's objects be understood and recorded in a meaningful way?	Sumara & Davis	Not everything that an individual thinks about is made communal. Knowledge that some individuals have should be shared. No clear moral and ethical role exists. Social structure and power dominance are not considered.	Integrating what goes on in the classroom to what goes on outside the classroom. Aiding students in seeking better understanding of the world they live in by helping them to make sense of unpredictable and complex interactions.	Actively and consciously participate in the fluid systems they live in, recognizing that existing patterns may no longer apply to present and future systems.

October 12, 2010). She attributes the overall success of the students to the experiential method of teaching that the program is founded upon.

After being assigned theoretical and practical contemporary readings on mediation and after discussing those readings during class, learners practice mediation in the classroom while their colleagues and the teacher provide extensive feedback on their work. In a subsequent class, the students learn advanced theory and continue with more advanced practice in mediation, again receiving extensive feedback on their work. Finally, near the close of the program, students conduct several mediations in a courtroom in the presence of a teacher whose primary role during the mediation is to coach them if needed. Before entering the courtroom, students thoroughly prepare for the mediation situation. Soeka said that by having a solid understanding of theory, during the mediation students learn to adjust their approach as the situation warrants (personal communication, October 12, 2010). The actual mediation, which may take as long as three hours, often involves very emotional situations for parties involved in the dispute. Students would not likely experience this type of learning solely through classroom simulation.

Example 3.1 is a reflective journal written by a mediation student following each of three mediations in which she served as the primary mediator. Note that for each of the three mediations, a different teacher was present as coach, enabling the student to receive feedback from three expert mediators who have a slightly different focus based on their educational backgrounds and research interests. To maintain confidentiality, names of the students are not given.

Example 3.1: Student Journal

Mediation No. 1: Landlord/tenant dispute
Chris Harris Taylor, coach

Being my first mediation, I probably over-prepared, to a point where I had a several-page opening to read in order to set the stage for this mediation. The issue for this mediation was that the tenant was unwilling to pay rent because he felt the condition of the property wasn't in the shape expected as a tenant.

I went through the opening in great detail—too much detail. My opening covered all of the key points, but the opening statement was probably 8 to 10 minutes long—too long for the nature of the disagreement. After going through some level of fact-finding, my biggest area of opportunity was that I wasn't sensitive enough to the parties' emotions. I worked to understand the facts, although not in such great depth that I was focused on the problem rather than the solution (good). I didn't adequately identify with the emotional frustration (particularly the defendant's), which likely prolonged the issue itself. And, this was vital because the defendant had some psychological issues, which warranted being a bit more on the understanding side.

I did have to caucus and that went really well—I was able to do a reality check with both of the parties (separately in their caucus), and was able to bring that back to move forward to resolution. Overall, the case settled, and to the satisfaction of both parties. Neither of them walked out of the room receiving less (or paying more) than they wanted, based on their comments to each other.

My strong points: I had a good command of the process; I was thorough in the opening; I set expectations well for the parties to know how to respect the process; I commended them for being there; I caucused well; I was able to redirect frustration to the problem.

My weak points: I was too thorough in the opening; I didn't identify enough with emotions; I went into the facts a little more than I should have on a few of the precise points, as I was trying to understand the real number involved in the dispute.

Next time: shorter opening, more understanding of emotion.

Mediation No. 2: Landlord/tenant dispute
Eva Soeka, coach

Second mediation—vastly different, both good and bad. In this mediation, I shortened up the opening remarks quite a bit; however, it was still too long. This mediation was a bigger challenge as the defendant did not understand anything about the legal issues of her dispute. She left her lease and pursued a different rental property thinking that her departure ended the lease; however she had a renewable provision in her contract.

What made this mediation more difficult was that it seemed the defendant didn't truly care about the outcome. Her best alternative to a negotiated agreement (BATNA) wasn't very strong. She said several times throughout the mediation that she would walk out of the room and go home. The issue that I tried to help her understand was that she was putting her grandmother at risk because the lease had her grandmother as a co-signer. My involvement was more to get the defendant to stay in the room long enough to talk about what a possible resolution might look like. At one point, during caucus, she called her grandmother on speaker phone and had a conversation saying that she didn't want to pay anything and thought this whole process was ridiculous.

The caucuses went fine this time around—the defendant was in more need of some reframing whereas the plaintiff was very practical about what he wanted out of the mediation. At the end of the mediation, they successfully settled, with the defendant paying the plaintiff over the next several months.

My strong points: better opening statement (more concise and hitting the key points), some level of emotional understanding (but still not enough), good use of caucusing helped keep the defendant focused on the resolution possibility.

My weak points: still a bit long on the opening, still needed more emotional understanding, too much fact-finding.

Next time: more concise opening, even more emotional connection/understanding.

Mediation No. 3: Landlord/tenant dispute
Moira Kelly, coach

Third mediation—well, to start off and to be candid, I had a hard stop to be conscious of due to rescheduling this mediation at the request of the Small Claims Court. Because of this hard stop (a meeting downtown at 11 AM), I felt a bit rushed, which, in hindsight, may have actually helped.

The opening was pretty solid—more concise, hitting the key points. Getting each party's perspective of what happened was solid, and the entire mediation only took 25 minutes. The parties really wanted to resolve this—in fact, I had a repeat participant in the plaintiff of this mediation (same as the defendant in my first mediation) which I thought might have been a result of him having been through a successful process on another occasion and him wanting to attempt that again.

We did not caucus in this mediation, and at the end of the time, the mediation resolved with only $100 changing hands from defendant to plaintiff, on the spot.

My strong points—efficient and effective opening, good focus on the facts and ultimate driving issue, sympathy for how the parties felt through the process.

My weak points—I did not appropriately seat the plaintiff and defendant as they each had an accompanying guest, and I did not put the plaintiff and defendant closest to me; I probably rushed the mediation too much despite getting resolution, due to my own schedule; I did not acknowledge to the defendant that I had mediated a case for the plaintiff before (something I wasn't sure about introducing).

Overall summary: I was very impressed in how the process of using this practicum really does enhance one's skills in only a few mediations. I was nervous during the first one. By the third, I was on a mission to resolve an issue. I thought the process made a lot more sense by the end of the second mediation and relayed to the teacher that I thought going through the mediations was like working up the pyramid in Maslow's Hierarchy of Needs. During the first mediation, I was concerned about the basics—the key components. By the last one, I was concerned with self-actualization for the participants—helping them resolve their conflicts and helping them to feel empowered by the process. I very much enjoyed each of these respective mediations despite feeling out of control on a couple occasions given the mental state of the parties that I was mediating for. ■

Using the evaluation form in Example 3.2, each of the professors provides formal evaluative feedback to the student following the mediation.

■ Example 3.2: Mediation Evaluation Form

1. Preprocess strategies:
   Were there any used?
   If so, what?
   How effective were they in the student's opinion?
   If none were used, why not?
2. Student's initial contacts with participants:
   Room arrangements?
   Parking facilities?
   Welcoming behavior?
3. Student's opening:
   Explanation of format?
   Education about process?

Confidentiality?
Role of Neutral?
Joint sessions and caucuses?
Use of other professionals?

4. Student's response to participant's opening:
   Clarification?
   Assessment of and response to emotional tone?
   Interruption?
   Management of process?
   Ability to establish trust, rapport, and competence?

5. Joint sessions:
   Management of analysis?
   Management of emotional expression?
   Reframing, as necessary?
   Reality testing, as necessary?
   Maintenance of future orientation?
   Use of caucuses appropriate?

6. Working toward agreement:
   Use of triangulation?
   Use of flip chart/board/diagrams, as necessary?
   Use of objective data, as necessary?
   Creation of options for participants' consideration?

7. Agreement:
   Clarifying details of agreement?
   Determining drafting process?
   Explanation of "loop back" provision?
   Availability for future sessions to execute agreement?
   Option of seeking professional review of agreement?

8. Mediator presence:
   Ethical issues were identified and addressed appropriately?
   Neutral at all times appeared impartial?
   Parties appeared to trust neutral?
   Neutral treated all parties with respect?
   Neutral identified issues of cultural competency and acted appropriately?
   Neutral created an atmosphere of a safe haven for all participants to address their issues?
   Neutral projected an air of competency and confidence? ■

In the mediation example, application of the five perspectives in Fenwick's (2001) framework is as follows. From a constructivist perspective, the teacher exposes the learner to a mediation experience. Reflective observation following a mediation experience leads to an expanded paradigm that is then tested in future mediation experiences. This process is evident in the student's journal.

From a psychoanalytic perspective, for effective learning to occur, learners need to work through internal conflicts related to the mediation process. The teacher provides the opportunity for questions that may arise from internal conflict and adequate time for the learner to work through the conflict. The conflict of being able to understand the facts while being sensitive to the parties involved is evident in the student's journal:

> After going through some level of fact-finding, my biggest area of opportunity was that I wasn't sensitive enough to the parties' emotions. I worked to understand the facts, although not in such great depth that I was focused on the problem rather than the solution (good). I didn't adequately identify with the emotional frustration (particularly the defendant's), which likely prolonged the issue itself.

By providing expert feedback to the student regarding perceptions of her own performance, the teacher may help the student resolve the conflict she is feeling.

In the situative perspective, learning occurs by the act of doing mediation and is specific to that situation. The role of the teacher is to facilitate an authentic mediation experience, to help the student discern meaning from the experience, and to coach the student toward independently performing mediation. The role of the teacher in the mediation situation certainly applies. The role of the student is to actively participate in the mediation process and to discern its meaning and value as related to self and the parties involved. Each of the mediations presented different experiences for the student who practiced mediation that was specific to the situation at hand.

From a critical cultural perspective, learning is enhanced by understanding the social and cultural capital valued by the involved parties. In the journal following the second mediation, the student wrote, "What made this mediation more difficult was that it seemed the defendant didn't truly care about the outcome." While the role of the student is to be a positive change agent throughout the mediation process, one can see by her statement that she was frustrated because it was difficult for her to accomplish the task without fully understanding the social and cultural values of the party involved. Here, the teacher may need to coach the student to help her better understand the perspective of the party in this situation.

Finally, from an enactivist ecological perspective, learning occurs by the integration of the thought processes and the interactions occurring throughout the mediation process. The teacher's role is to help the student integrate what has been learned about mediation with the act of mediating. The student's role is to actively and consciously participate in the mediation process, recognizing that predetermined patterns may not apply to the current problem, requiring the student to adjust to a somewhat ambiguous situation. In the overall summary, the student makes the statement, "I very much enjoyed each of these respective mediations despite feeling out of control on a couple occasions given the mental state of the parties that I was mediating for." This indicates the student recognizes mediation may be ambiguous based on the situation, requiring her to adjust her practice to serve the needs of the respective parties. One may conclude that each of the five perspectives may assist learners and teachers in better understanding and enhancing an experiential learning activity.

Homelessness

In this example, graduate students participated in a social experiment that was part of their work regarding urban poverty. The class was titled The Nature of Cities, which is a regular course offering for a graduate degree program in public service. The course was taught by Dr. Jill Florence Lackey, a cultural anthropologist. Much of the experiment was filmed as a documentary (Lackey, 2010), *Can We Become Homeless?* The learning objectives for the course were to improve understanding of the effects of poverty on people and to understand how easy it is for people to become homeless when working at low-paying jobs.

Most of the students in the program are working full-time and the mean age is 26. The students were given mock identities of individuals earning seven dollars per hour. All were full-time workers and some were single parents. In their mock identities, their role was to avoid becoming homeless during the semester and to work their way out of poverty, which their identities were born into and had lived with all their lives.

The mock identities had one significant other, someone who cared about them but could not help them financially. They needed to find housing they could afford by actually calling landlords to inquire about vacancies. Some of the identities had pets, which made affordable housing even more difficult to secure. Each month they randomly selected several *life chances*, changes to their identities' situations, written on a piece of paper that was folded and placed in a basket. Some were positive, such as a small raise in wages or a more appealing job. They also needed to cope with negative life chances, such as health conditions, the loss of a job, the loss of housing, or the loss of the significant other.

Their journals included all their housing contacts, their strategies dealing with positive and negative life chances, their monthly budgets, and their significant reflections throughout the process. Many learned about soup kitchens and food pantries and other social services they might be able to access. Some learned to be very resourceful, claiming income tax refunds from the previous year when they had a full-time job. The average refund was $1,100, which helped them immensely. In some instances, individuals' mock identities were forced to stay in a homeless shelter or live on the streets, as they could no longer afford housing. Some students actually visited places where the homeless slept to get a better feel for homelessness.

The following are quotes, strategies, and stories taken from the documentary. The first set of quotes relate to students' search for low-income housing.

Quote 1: I went into the apartment and it was in a very bad neighborhood, so it made me feel really, really bad. And there was actually a prostitute downstairs asking men weird things. But that was the best that I could find. The landlord told me that I would need a $300 deposit and I agreed.

Quote 2: I looked for signs with phone numbers, because I wanted to find something as cheap as possible. I figured that if they (landlords) didn't have money to advertise, the rent might be less.

Quote 3: The areas that you could live that would accommodate your budget were, what I would consider, very questionable. Being a single female, they weren't really areas that I wanted to live in. In fact when I went to look at my apartment building there was a group of individuals congregating in the hallway, which made me feel really nervous and a bit uneasy walking into the place. But you sort of do what you can with the means that you have.

The following are journal entries made about 6 weeks into the experiment.

Journal Entry 1: I feel there is no hope. Every time I look at my budget, I laugh. There is no way that I could keep this up.

Journal Entry 2: How can people live like this? This isn't for a month or two for them. Maybe it's their lifetime.

The following are a few strategies students tried. Some of them were successful and others failed.

Strategy 1: I'm trying to pay back whatever I can when I can. And my strategy right now is just to save, put money in the bank and have a safety net of money in case something should go wrong.

Strategy 2: I had to move and to save on moving expenses I sold my furniture, but now I have nothing soft to sit on or lay on so I developed a medical condition that cost me $350. It's been challenging to come up with this money. I took on some extra work, but it only amounted to about $50 a month.

Toward the end of the semester, the students decided to visit a homeless day center to learn about the services and to hear the following stories of actual homeless people.

Story 1: A brother of mine got murdered. A sister got raped. My mom passed away. My dad was in a house fire while I was in prison and I had to deal with all of that. But today I am a strong person because God has taught me to be strong. But I went through a lot of trials and tribulations in my life and due to all of that one day I had to go to the mental health complex because I was having psychological issues. And they gave me medication and told me about this place [homeless center]. And I have been coming here ever since.

Story 2: I was standing in a warehouse and it was really cold and we didn't have any way to take a bath and I had gone five days without taking a bath and this guy that I met told me there is this place that you can go and you have to sign in when you are there and you can take a shower and get some clothes because I had left everything behind when I came to town because I was in a self-destructive mode and I didn't want to be anywhere anymore. I didn't care about myself anymore. So I came here [homeless center] and signed in.

Story 3: I was so devastated of the stigma of being homeless that the first thing I did was I went to Walgreens and I took a book bag and

I stole deodorant, toothpaste and all the personal hygiene items I thought I would need while I was living on the street and then I went back to the shelter. You had to leave at 5:00 in the morning and you could come back at 5:00 at night and I told a girl what I did because I felt so bad and she told me that I wouldn't have to go into the stores and steal—that she would take me to a place where they would give you a change of clothes and personal hygiene items and that was ten years ago when I first came here [homeless center].

Story 4: I'm not homeless anymore, but I come here to help out. I got myself on my feet.

Students whose mock identities became homeless went through the intake experience at a homeless shelter. They learned about services offered at the shelter and its rules. By the end of the semester, 5 students were on the streets, 10 more students were one month from being on the streets, and 10 students thought they may make it through the summer.

At the end of the semester, students did final presentations regarding their experiences. Taken from the documentary, the following is what some of them had to say about those experiences.

Quote 1: At the beginning of the semester, you know we all started off with similar situations and it was very apparent very quickly how one or two positive or negative life chances could really impact a person's life who is living on or near the poverty level making it appear that there is a thin line between just making it and becoming homeless. Participating in this experiment really forced me to put myself in the shoes of someone else and although as I said, my mock identity didn't become homeless and is seemingly in an ok position now, I struggled to pay her bills and to find education for her child, to file her service paperwork, to pay off her debts and what have you. It just gave me a new found respect for people who do this on a daily basis, especially for someone who has to account for a child. I, myself, don't have children, so I just really respect someone who is able to do this in her daily life.

Quote 2: One of the things that I was really, really stressed out about when I was doing this experiment was that in my real job I was constantly thinking about my mock identity. Every day I would wake up and say, "Oh, my God, what am I going to do for this service or what am I going to do about my food—what am I going to eat?"

Quote 3: It did hit me hard when I heard that some of our class-mates did become homeless. It made me realize that although I was able to get life chances that were very beneficial to myself, that doesn't happen to everyone out there. So I did take the homelessness of other people very hard.

Quote 4: What this experiment made me realize is that we are really only a paycheck away from being homeless. It could happen to any one of us for any number of reasons. I'm in a situation where that is unlikely to happen, but it could.

Quote 5: Just doing this experiment is something that I think everybody should do to get them aware of homelessness.

Quote 6: In real life, I now have a better appreciation of single parents and of sticking to budgets. I've now made donations to food pantries. As a result of this [experiment], I've done some research and I now do volunteer work for my church and I've learned about some of my church resources and where some of my tax dollars go for these programs.

Returning to the five perspectives, from a constructivist view, the teacher has provided the learners with multiple novel experiences regarding homelessness. Learners are expanding their schemata on homelessness through reflective observation of the novel experiences they are living in their mock identities. Keeping a journal is the method of recording their observations and their responses to them. When sharing their reflective experiences with classroom colleagues, learners become teachers. Learners have multiple opportunities throughout the semester to test their new paradigms on future experiences in the world of the homeless.

From a psychoanalytic perspective, throughout the semester the teacher gave students the opportunity to work through conflicts by writing in their journals and by discussing those conflicts during F2F classes. Learners had to continue to work through the internal conflicts that surfaced as they began to realize what it means to be homeless and how it affects the lives of those in poverty who struggle with the fear and daily reality that they are likely to become homeless. By working through these internal conflicts, they were able to learn strategies that kept their mock identities from becoming homeless—at least in the short run.

A situative perspective views learning to occur by the act of doing and that learning is situation specific. In this case, the teacher provides an authentic community experience by having learners assume a mock identity. Students learned about poverty and homelessness from living their mock identities for the course of the semester. By doing so, they become more attuned to the needs of a specific group of individuals in the community. Through their newfound understanding of homelessness, they begin to think about their social responsibility as related to this group of individuals.

Throughout this semester-long experiential learning activity, the teacher has exposed learners to authentic social experiences that are more likely to engage them in future actions that work toward achieving equity and freedom for those in poverty, specifically the homeless. Most evident in this learning activity is that by assuming a mock identity, the learners begin to understand the distribution of power and the dominance of social structures that have affluence. Students begin to view social responsibility toward the poor and homeless in a new light as shown in several of the quotes. In other words, they begin to transform into agents of social change.

Finally, from an enactivist ecological perspective, the teacher has integrated classroom learnings with authentic community experiences, thereby aiding students to seek a better understanding of the world by helping them make sense of unpredictable and complex interactions. The life chances that each mock role had to cope with throughout the experiment taught learners about the fluidity of systems, helping them to recognize that preexisting patterns no longer applied to the life chances they were dealt.

In summary, experiential learning has been and continues to be a vital way of learning for adults. The two detailed examples of how one might incorporate experiential learning into a hybrid course demonstrate how each of Fenwick's perspectives may apply.

CHAPTER FOUR

PLANNING YOUR HYBRID COURSE

Critical Questions to Consider

Creativity takes courage.

—Henri Matisse (1998)

A S MENTIONED IN THE PREFACE, several critical planning questions provide the foundation for the hybrid faculty development program at the Learning Technology Center at the University of Wisconsin–Milwaukee. Faculty enrolled in the program claimed that answering these questions helped them tremendously as they designed their hybrid courses. Although the development program itself is focused on practical application versus theoretical constructs, many teachers respond to the questions by applying pedagogy derived from theory.

Question 1: What is it that students must demonstrate they know by the time they have successfully completed the course?

In other words, what are the student learning objectives for the course? According to experts in course design (Brown, McCray, Runde, & Schweizer, 2001; Fink, 2003; McTighe & Wiggins, 2004; Walvoord, 2004), this question pertains to any course, whether a traditional F2F, online, or hybrid course. As with any course design, addressing this question early in the planning stage is essential for a student-centered hybrid course. Only after we identify what students need to know can we begin to consider how to best help students learn what they need to know. For help on designing student learning objectives, readers can refer to the work of any or all the experts mentioned in this paragraph.

Question 2: What learning activities could students actively engage in to achieve identified learning objectives?

Fink (2003) said that in his years working with faculty on course design, he has observed that the bottleneck in teaching occurs in the design of instruction. He further stated that although teachers know their discipline and most are able to successfully interact with students and manage their courses, they have little or no experience in designing a student-centered learning activity. Figure 4.1, Fink's model with a slight adaptation, illustrates what he has identified as the four components of

Figure 4.1   The Four Components of Teaching

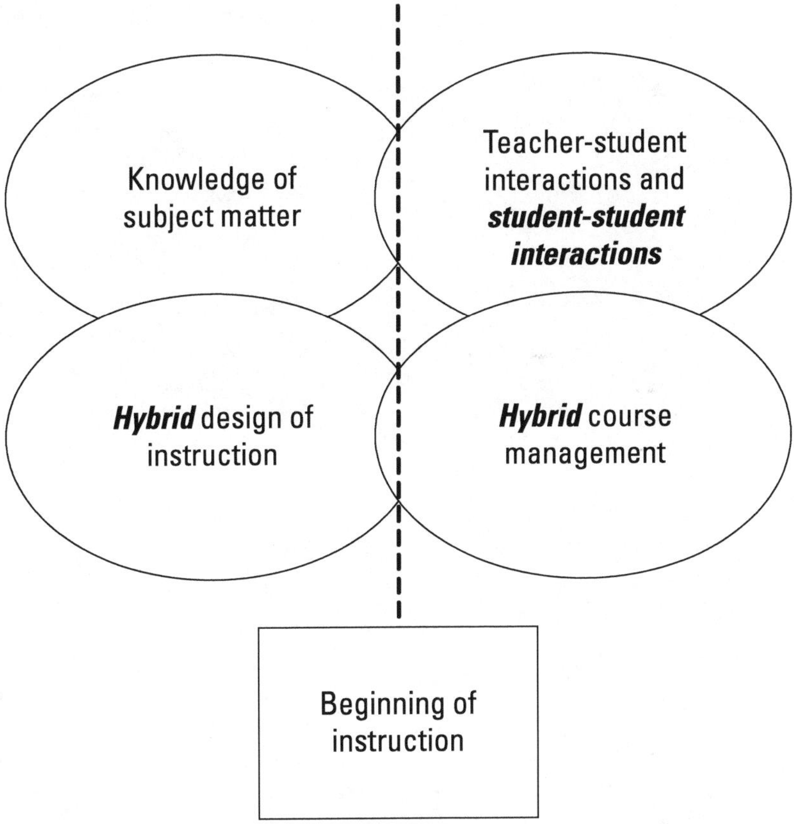

Knowledge of subject matter

Teacher-student interactions and *student-student interactions*

Hybrid design of instruction

Hybrid course management

Beginning of instruction

Adapted from *Creating Significant Learning Experiences*, p. 22, by D. Fink, 2003. San Francisco: Jossey-Bass. Copyright 2003 by John Wiley & Sons. Adapted with permission of the author.

teaching. The bold and italicized print indicates additions made to the model that highlight important components of hybrid teaching.

As previously mentioned, regardless of the mode of delivery, the teacher must know the discipline intimately before beginning to teach a course. There is a distinct difference between knowing facts associated with a discipline, which students often read and memorize, and having tacit knowledge of that discipline. Sternberg (2002) stated that tacit knowledge is implicit versus explicit; it is generally acquired from experience in a specific environment, or in this case, in a specific discipline. Tacit knowledge may only be acquired by applying higher-order cognitive functions in gaining a deeper understanding of the foundational principles and theories of a discipline or area of study. In general, it is our job as teachers to create learning activities that engage students in acquiring that discipline's tacit knowledge. From a constructivist viewpoint, "Learning, even self-directed learning, rarely occurs in isolation from the world in which the learner lives" (Merriam et al., 2007, p. 5). Because of increased opportunities for interaction outside the classroom provided by a well-designed hybrid course, students are given more opportunities to acquire that tacit knowledge.

To illustrate further, for those of you who can remember first learning how to work on a computer, you most likely began by learning a specific software application. You then moved on to another software application and yet another and so forth. While you did this, you began to develop a tacit knowledge of how software generally functions. In fact, when software complies with the general principles that are part of our tacit knowledge of software usage, we refer to the software as being *user friendly*. When encountering a new software program, most of us do not turn to the software user manual and memorize it. We may not even read it, or we may refer to it on occasion for a specific purpose. Instead we begin using the application by applying our acquired tacit knowledge of how software applications function. This is somewhat analogous to how we want students to learn a discipline. Initially they may read a text and recall some of the material, but unless they actively try to understand the material through reflection and guided interaction, it is highly unlikely they will acquire the tacit knowledge of the discipline. Only by repeatedly applying the higher-level functions of analysis, synthesis, and evaluation, as described by Bloom (1956) or Vygotsky (1978), can students acquire the tacit knowledge of a discipline, which they are likely to retain.

If Fink (2003) is correct in his observation that faculty have difficulty in the design stage of a traditional course, then it is highly likely that those same faculty will have difficulty designing a hybrid course. As mentioned in the preface, perhaps this is the reason many faculty who have enrolled in a hybrid faculty development program claim that learning to teach in a hybrid format improved their overall teaching. This makes sense, as the focus of instruction in most hybrid development programs is on course design or course redesign (usually from traditional F2F to hybrid). For hybrid, focusing on design is very important since a significant portion of learning takes place outside the classroom. Therefore, in addition to well-planned learning activities inside the classroom, learning depends upon well-planned activities outside the classroom, and on how well online and F2F learning activities are integrated throughout the course. The importance of integrating learning activities is discussed in Question 3.

Ultimately, the teacher's decisions regarding the most effective learning activities are based on any number of factors, such as student background, time constraints, course content, and class size. In conjunction with identifying the learning activities, the teacher must also decide where the learning activities will take place, which could be any combination of locations, including the F2F classroom, the virtual classroom, or out in the community. Consider one of the learning objectives for a leadership theory and ethics course: Students will demonstrate knowledge of the global impact of leadership by studying a leader whose work has made major contributions to one or more societies. Upon identification of the student learning objective, the teacher constructs activities that help students demonstrate competency in meeting the objective. Examples of student-centered integrated learning activities are an internship with a community leader, reporting observations to the class while relating them to relevant leadership theory, and social responsibility.

In summary, the teacher's job is to involve students in learning activities that require higher-level cognitive functions, and the student's job is to fully participate and share knowledge derived from the experience in one or more interactive formats with the teacher and other students in the class. This interaction, which may take place in F2F and online environments, is an example of what is meant by a student-centered learning experience. The primary responsibility for learning lies with the student. The primary responsibility of the teacher is to engage students in learning activities that achieve the learning objectives, while critically evaluating and expanding upon the knowledge students acquire and share with others in the class. This leads to the next planning question.

Question 3: How will the F2F and time out-of-class components be integrated into a single course?

For me, integrating the in-class and out-of-class teaching and learning activities necessary for a well-constructed hybrid was the toughest to learn. Sometimes I still don't get it right, yet I know it is an essential component of effective hybrid teaching. It is only through disciplined concentration, what Csikszentmihalyi (1990) first described as *flow*, that I am successful in establishing and maintaining this integration throughout the course. To more clearly illustrate what I refer to, here is an example taken from my own teaching.

I teach organizational behavior at the undergraduate and graduate level. Students at both levels often have difficulty differentiating schedules of reinforcement, which is an important concept to understand when designing motivating employee compensation plans. Before I began teaching in a hybrid format, I assigned a reading on schedules of reinforcement and followed with a lecture and discussion, highlighting several short scenarios applying different schedules. After the lecture and discussion on the topic, during class I gave students brief scenarios and asked them to identify the appropriate schedule of reinforcement; they mostly got it wrong. Based on time constraints, I eventually gave them the correct solution (passive learning), explained why it was correct, and we would move to another topic. Then I covered schedules of reinforcement on the next quiz a week or so later. Invariably most students, including the exceptional ones, would again get the questions regarding schedules of reinforcement wrong. I reviewed the quiz results with the students; however, I never felt confident they truly understood the concept. When I retested on a midterm, my fears were generally confirmed.

My hybrid mentor once told me that one of the best ways to begin teaching in a hybrid format is to think of a problem encountered when teaching traditionally and determine whether a hybrid format would help solve that problem. Picking up on this recommendation, when I began teaching organizational behavior in a hybrid format, I changed the way I taught schedules of reinforcement. Now, I assign the same reading, and during the F2F class I explain the concept briefly instead of lecturing on it. Following the F2F class small groups (three to five students) are assigned a scenario, and asked to discuss online what schedule of reinforcement is being applied. I also ask them to provide evidence for their choice, letting them know they will present their findings to the entire class for further discussion during the next F2F meeting. To earn points for the assignment, everyone must contribute to the asynchronous group discussion. I still find that groups sometimes identify the schedule of reinforcement incorrectly online, but in almost all instances, through further in-class discussion, the class will arrive at the correct choice. Using the same questions, quiz responses on the concept have improved dramatically and when retested on the midterm, responses are significantly improved. See Table 4.1 for comparison and contrast of the two teaching methods. Differences are in italics.

By changing the method of teaching schedules of reinforcement to include asynchronous peer discussion involving everyone, students had time to reflect on the problem; referring to the various definitions for each schedule and noting the similarities and differences between them, they could post the results of their analysis. Others in the group could agree or disagree with each other's postings. By identifying each other's flaws in thinking, students were generally able to arrive at the correct schedule of reinforcement. They were then able to present their solution in class, giving other groups an opportunity to evaluate and discuss it.

Table 4.1   Comparison of Traditional Teaching Method to Hybrid Teaching Method

Steps in Traditional Teaching Method	Steps in Hybrid Teaching Method
Preclass reading	Preclass reading
In-class lecture	*In-class brief overview of concept*
In-class scenario discussion	*Asynchronous small group scenario discussion*
	In-class small group presentation and discussion
Out-of-class online quiz	Out-of-class online quiz
In-class review of quiz	In-class review of quiz
In-class proctored midterm taken online	In-class proctored midterm taken online
In-class review and discussion of midterm	In-class review and discussion of midterm

The increased opportunity to interact with the material and with each other outside the classroom helped students to learn the concepts. According to Winn and Snyder (1996), metacognition, which consists of monitoring your own learning process and making necessary changes in your thinking based on interactions with others, encourages students to become more effective learners by increasing self-awareness and independent learning. The time constraints in the F2F class and the immediacy of response required by students during the F2F class would not have permitted time for them to reflect on their own thinking as well as that of their peers, which helped in identifying the correct solution most of the time. The in-class experience of having to present the groups' findings either reaffirmed their thinking or caused them to reexamine their thinking when others in the class challenged the solution presented. In addition to demonstrating how the online interactions increased the effectiveness of learning schedules of reinforcement, this assignment demonstrates the integration of online work with F2F work.

In summary, three things are worth highlighting in this example of a hybrid assignment. In the hybrid methodology, the in-class and out-of-class teaching and learning activities complement one another and are highly integrated. Again, this is crucial when designing a hybrid course as it provides for higher-level learning to continue outside the classroom. The preclass reading introduces the topic to the student who at that point may or may not have understood the material. During class, the topic is briefly explained. Through the small group interaction online following the F2F class students begin to further reflect on the material and apply it to a specific situation. When they come to class, they present their solution to the class for further discussion. By this time students have had multiple exposures to the material and have had the opportunity to apply higher-level cognitive functions through self-reflection and interaction with their group members.

Also note how the assignment has become more student-centered as opposed to teacher-centered. Students need to solve the problem through discussion and presentation. This is intentional, as the hybrid method places the primary responsibility of learning with the learner, and the primary responsibility of creating opportunities and fostering environments that encourage student learning with the teacher.

Finally, the increased use of discussion is a prominent difference between the traditional and hybrid teaching methods. According to Brookfield and Preskill (2005), one of the most important purposes of discussion as a teaching tool is to help students reach a better understanding of a concept. In learning schedules of reinforcement, increased exposure to the concept through online discussion prior to in-class discussion provides all with an opportunity to engage with the material while interacting with one another, adding value, depth, and efficiency to the F2F discussion that follows. Disciplined concentration on making learning activities more student-centered through the use of increased interaction outside the classroom and through the intentional integration of online activities with in-class activities led me to discover a better way to help students learn the concept of schedules of reinforcement.

Question 4: As you consider the characteristics of your class (size, area of study, demographics, length of F2F classes, and class duration), how will they influence your course design?

Through the years I have had the privilege of thinking about this question with several hundred faculty. The hybrid course redesign that many of them achieved as a result of thoughtful planning and implementation was as varied as the courses and subjects they taught. One of the more rewarding aspects of teaching is that teachers can consider class characteristics, the critical concepts of the discipline, and personal strengths and challenges with teaching when considering how to assist students in achieving learning objectives. Some of the unique learning experiences creatively designed and taught by faculty from various disciplines are reviewed in Chapters 11 and 12. Some common considerations when creating a student-centered, engaging hybrid course are discussed next.

Class size is an important determinant in designing learning activities in a hybrid course, or for that matter, any course. Learning activities need to be student-centered, engaging, focused on learning objectives, and practical at the same time. The schedules of reinforcement assignment works well for classes of 12 to 30 students. In the assignment's current structure it would be too time intensive for a class of 100 to review and discuss 20 different scenarios. By modifying the assignment to include only five different scenarios with multiple small groups assigned to the same scenario, groups would discuss the differences in solutions between groups that worked on the same scenario, making the assignment more practical for a class of 100. Adjustments need to be made with varying class sizes.

The area of study may greatly influence the selection of recognized teaching methods and tools in a particular field. As an example, more direct instruction (lecture and demonstration) may be needed for courses such as statistics and calculus, while a more indirect method of instruction (case analysis) may be effective for organizational behavior or communication. This is not to imply that more direct instruction should take the place of creating a student-centered learning environment. Even when using mini lectures as a teaching tool, there is room for engaging students in an interactive learning activity immediately following the lecture. In all cases, it remains the teacher's responsibility to design the learning activities in ways that ensure students achieve the learning objectives. This often means guiding online or class discussion to illustrate an important concept. As stated by Garrison and Vaughan (2008), "Direction may be needed from the subject matter expert to help students become aware of the nuances of the discipline" (p. 43).

The following is an example of how class characteristics, such as content, class size, and duration, may affect the design of a hybrid assignment. I teach a hybrid course in research methods to graduate students pursuing a degree in leadership. For the most part, these are working professionals in their late 20s or early 30s; class enrollment is generally around 20. The class meets eight or nine times in a 14-week semester for a 2-hour period, generally late in the afternoon. When I designed the course, I had three major objectives: help leadership students learn basic research methods and design to better understand empirical research, help leadership students learn an appreciation for good research specific to their field of study so they become better consumers of research, and help leadership students learn that good research is an iterative process that requires a significant amount of planning with great attention to detail.

One of the assignments in the course is to design a Thurstone scale. I begin by having the students visit a website on Thurstone scaling prior to our F2F class. Then we briefly discuss the concept during class. Thurstone scaling is a unidimensional scaling technique predominantly used in the social sciences to assess attitudes regarding some topic or group of interest. Examples include any of the following: attitude toward obesity, attitude toward CEO compensation levels, or attitude toward global warming. The size of this class is perfect for generating a list of about 80 statements that express an attitude about a topic of the students' choice in varying degrees from positive to negative. For instance, if the topic is CEO compensation levels, a very positive statement in support of highly compensated CEO's would be, "Because CEO's work very hard, they deserve to be rewarded with big salaries," indicating a very positive attitude. On the other hand, a very negative statement in opposition to highly compensated CEO's would be, "Because CEO's are motivated by greed, they negotiate exorbitant salaries that do not reflect the quality of their performance," indicating a very negative attitude. After generating the list of 80 statements on a projected computer screen during class using Google Works, the class moves to the online environment. By a designated date, every student in the class ranks the 80 statements online from 1 to 11, using the Google Works spreadsheet designed for that purpose (see Chapter 9 for more on Google as a tool). Again, 20 individuals completing the scale provide the students with a solid median ranking for each statement. Reaching a consensus with a group of 20 students online would take an exorbitant amount of time, so students work online in their small groups of four or five to complete the Thurstone scale. Each designated group leader presents the group's completed scale during the next F2F class. If students worked individually to complete their scales, there would be inadequate class time for each student to present. However, five groups presenting works well, leaving ample time for discussion of the differences between scales and leaving time to move to the next topic for discussion.

In summary, this example demonstrates how the content, size of the class, and its duration can be used to plan the various steps of a hybrid assignment. Again, all steps of the assignment are student-centered, and the advantage of working on the assignment in class and online provides ample opportunity for peer interaction as well as for interaction with the teacher. The activities that can be achieved during class occur there, while activities that may be achieved outside the F2F class occur online. The assignment also demonstrates the integration of online and in-class activities, which is vital to the success of any hybrid course design. When considering time management for the teacher, it takes much less time to evaluate five Thurstone scales versus 20 of them. Although a group grade is assigned for this particular assignment, the course also has a number of individual assignments that help determine students' individual performance. Peer evaluation for group work is a part of each student's grade, lessening the likelihood of shirking. Finally, for emerging leaders, working well in groups is a vital skill that must be learned; thus group work is not only an effective way to complete much of this hybrid assignment, but it is also a way for leadership students to practice a skill needed to become an effective leader.

Another example includes structuring the frequency and duration of F2F classes to complement class demographics. For instance, an undergraduate class, average age of 20, meets 12 out of 14 weeks, but the duration of each F2F class period is abbreviated by 30 minutes as compared to a traditional class. However, a graduate class, average age of 32, meets 8 out of 14 weeks, and the duration of the class is about the same as the abbreviated hybrid undergraduate class. Why the difference in frequency of meeting times? I have found that traditional-age undergraduate students need more frequently structured meeting times of not more than 2 hours to help them effectively learn the course content; my colleagues tell me the same, and the literature on self-directed readiness to learn supports this finding as well (Bryan, Danaher, & Duay, 2005). Additionally, the literature on attention span supports the need for classes of shorter duration (Burns, 1985; Middendorf & Kalish, 1996; Postman, 1985).

As indicated in the preceding example, the demographics of the class, particularly the age of students, may affect the way you structure in-class and out-of-class learning activities. A class of predominantly 18-year-olds who are generally not fully engaged in becoming self-directed learners will require a more structured learning environment than a graduate class of 35-year-old working professionals. To compensate for the general differences in these two populations, undergraduate classes met more frequently but for shorter periods of time. This allowed more frequent F2F interaction with the teacher, taking into consideration the need for more frequent guidance while recognizing that attention span generally tends to diminish significantly after 2 hours.

Although some researchers argue there is no average adult attention span, others disagree. According to Middendorf and Kalish (1996), the average attention span of an adult student is 15 to 20 minutes. A study by Burns (1985) had similar findings. Postman (1985) said the average attention span for literate adults is 10 to 12 minutes, and that attention span decreases as multitasking increases. This is compounded by the fact that many of today's students are coming to class exhausted after a full day's work, with jobs that often include considerable travel. It is a wonder they are able to stay awake during classes that are sometimes four or more hours in length much less comprehend the material being studied. The good news is that if we change learning activities, we can renew attention span, and certainly other factors such as interest in the material, personality of the student, and the amount of interaction may positively affect attention span.

However, as exhaustion increases, attention span decreases. I came across the following comments on course evaluations from students in response to the question, "What aspects of the class detracted from your learning?" One student replied, "The class was three hours long!" Another student replied, "Having a class for four hours after a day in the office." A third student replied, "No class should meet this long." (This class had been scheduled during summer to meet from 5:30 pm until 10:30 pm.) I suspect most of us would agree there is a limit to how many times we can refocus students' attention—and four or more hours in a classroom after a full day's work is likely to be stretching that limit.

Abbreviated course terms warrant adjustments in course design. Experienced teachers know it is impossible for them to teach and for students to comprehend the same amount of material in a 6-week summer session versus a 14-week semester. This holds true for a hybrid course, perhaps even more so. Therefore the course design must take into consideration the time given to teach the course. Designing a student-centered course means more time is spent involving students in reflection and interaction, whether online or in the classroom. Reflection and thoughtful interaction take time, leaving less time for direct instruction. According to Garrison and Vaughan (2008), "Students will have little chance to approach learning in deep and meaningful ways if they are overwhelmed with content and do not have the opportunity to discuss, reflect, and digest the meaning of the material presented" (p. 88). Therefore frugality in course design is essential. Thought in planning teaching and learning activities that meet learning objectives effectively and efficiently is crucial.

For example, when teaching a 6-week hybrid summer course that meets F2F once a week, students may have one major project due at the end of 6 weeks instead of two major projects, one at midpoint and one at the end of a 14-week semester. Asynchronous discussion assignments and course readings are also significantly reduced. This means the remaining learning activities need to assist students in achieving the learning objectives despite a reduced workload. For some teachers who feel obligated to cover the same amount of content in 6 weeks as in 14 weeks, this presents a dilemma. However, reflective practice takes time as it involves higher-level thinking processes; it is through reflective practice that students experience deeper understandings that lead to actions that improve learning (York-Barr, Sommers, Ghere, & Montie, 2001). It only makes sense that less time means less material covered.

In summary, many class characteristics potentially may influence your course design. Those mentioned here are the more common ones but are not meant to be all encompassing. When beginning to plan your hybrid course, you may want to make a list of those class characteristics you believe will influence the way you design and teach the course, referring to that list periodically throughout the design process. Following this approach may help you design with minimal rework, as making course design modifications while the course is in progress may quickly lead to student and teacher frustration.

Question 5: How will you divide the percentage of time students spend in class and out of class, and how will you schedule the in-class time in relation to the out-of-class time?

Teachers who are new to hybrid frequently ask this question. Unfortunately there is not one standard answer, but a number of considerations are worth thinking about. Some may be based on the class characteristics discussed under Question 4. Others include the types of learning activities you intend to employ specific to the hybrid class you are designing.

For example, in some courses I teach, such as an intermediate level course in graduate statistics, students benefit from more direct instruction. Thus, I use mini lectures (no more than 15 minutes) most often containing a critical question or two, followed by interactive in-class small group work applying the material presented during the mini lecture. Groups then report on their work, and we discuss differences, clarifying any misconceptions. We also spend time reporting on work done outside class since the last meeting, including online discussions, quizzes, problems, and simulations.

Out-of-class time is spent doing reading for the next F2F class, completing online simulations or quizzes, solving statistical problems similar to those worked on in small groups during class, and compiling a critical literature review for presenting a statistical topic of interest to the class in lieu of completing a final exam. This course has more F2F time than most hybrid courses I teach. For a full semester, students spend about 3 hours per week in class for 9 out of 14 weeks. Except at the beginning when we generally meet each week for at least 3 weeks, the 5 weeks spent outside class are dispersed fairly evenly throughout the duration of the course. The purpose of this is twofold. First, in addition to providing direct instruction, initial class time is required for students to get acquainted with one another and to review the course plan, including the syllabus, program outcomes, student learning objectives, course materials needed, schedule of classes and assignments, use of the course management system, and formation of work groups. Second, initial F2F time is used to establish social presence for the remainder of the course (social presence is discussed in more detail in Question 8).

In summary, the time spent inside the classroom, online, and in the community or within an organization is dependent upon a number of factors, including demographics of the class, course content, and the preferences and skills of the teacher. The data from faculty interviews discussed in Chapters 11 and 12 further address this question from multiple perspectives.

Question 6: Faculty tend to require students to do more work in a hybrid course than they might normally require in a purely traditional course. As you design your hybrid course, how might you lessen the likelihood of creating a course with an excessive workload?

Failure to redesign an existing course that has been previously taught in either F2F or online mode is a major contributor to the excessive workload challenge. Rather than focusing on how to redesign a course by identifying the learning objectives during class and the learning objectives outside class, teachers have a tendency to add learning activities without subtracting from the previous design. Putting it simply, instead of redesigning a traditional course to make it hybrid, they simply add online work to the traditional design. Students then become overwhelmed by the workload, and higher-level cognitive learning diminishes. To avoid this, identify learning activities for each learning objective; then decide whether the work would be more effective online or F2F.

Although the concept of a hybrid course is relatively simple, designing an effective hybrid course is more complex when integrating classroom activities with out-of-class activities. The focus must be on designing a student-centered class with heightened interaction despite reduced F2F time. To achieve true integration, time must be spent discussing past out-of-class activities in addition to discussing new concepts, identifying critical questions, and preparing for future out-of-class activities. The challenge becomes one of accomplishing these critical components in the time allotted without minimizing student interaction. Time management and organization are critical skills needed to orchestrate a well-planned student-centered hybrid course.

A simple way to manage class time is creating an agenda with time estimates for each learning activity planned for F2F classes. It also serves as a reminder to include any review of online work that was completed after the previous F2F class. Other simple planning measures such as sending an e-mail to students reminding them of the activities for the F2F class the next day will help them better prepare. This is especially beneficial when students have not met F2F for more than a week.

Question 7: How will you effectively communicate what will occur during class and out of class, including how work in both of these environments will be evaluated?

Students who are new to hybrid and a student-centered learning approach may feel overwhelmed during the initial few weeks of class. Therefore frequent and careful communication is vitally important. Do not be overly concerned about repetition. Most students appreciate it when the same instructions occur in multiple places in addition to the teacher's verbal instructions during the F2F class.

For hybrid courses, students need a calendar and a course plan so they can see the dates and times of the F2F classes and immediately distinguish out-of-class versus in-class work and when assignments are due. Beginning each F2F class by asking if students have questions and posting a discussion forum for questions between F2F classes may be very helpful in reducing the stress that accompanies any new learning experience. According to Garrison and Vaughan (2008), students who have a clear sense of what the course plan is will be more likely to actively and positively engage in learning activities. An example of a calendar and schedule of assignments for a graduate leadership theories course is provided in Table 4.2. In almost all cases, the student has 1 week to complete online assignments. The statement at the top of the right column, "Assignments due on Sundays by 11:59 pm unless otherwise stated," gives the last available date and time for posting an assignment. In this case the student had from Monday after the F2F class until Sunday evening to complete online work.

So that students recognize the importance of completing all learning activities assigned, a breakdown of the portion of their grade determined by each major learning activity is helpful. Grading rubrics save grading time, help in providing objective feedback to students, and assist students in learning (Stevens & Levi, 2005). More detailed information regarding grading schemes and rubrics is presented in Chapter 5.

Question 8: How will you develop social presence in your hybrid class?

Social presence theory was first proposed by Short, Williams, and Christie in 1976. According to these researchers, social presence is the

Table 4.2   Course Calendar and Schedule of Assignments

August/September	
Mondays 5 pm–7 pm	Assignments due on Sundays by 11:59 pm unless otherwise stated
Class	*Assignment*

	Class	Assignment
8/27	**F2F (face-to-face)** • Introductions • What are you looking forward to learning about in this class? • Review of syllabus • Review of major course assignments • Review of assignments for this and next week • Review Desire to Learn (D2L) Course Site • Establish groups • Begin discussion on Northouse • Assign theory	**Read:** • Northouse: Chapters 1–3 • Useem: "Roy Vagelos Attacks River Blindness" & "Wagner Dodge Retreats in Mann Gulch" • Building the Emotional Intelligence of Groups (Link to reserves on D2L content page) • "The Lonergan Reader" (Link to website on D2L content page) • Beauchamp: "Peer Review of Grievances" ***D2L Discussion Assignments:** • D.1.1 Establish Group Ground Rules • D.1.2 What Makes a Profession a Profession? • D.1.3 Recruiting for the Bank • D.2.1 What Makes a Theory a Theory? • D.2.2 Advocating for a Profession **Self-Assessments & Journal Entries:** • Complete the Learning Trait Questionnaire (LTQ), (p. 33 of Northouse & D2L content page) & have five of your coworkers complete it on your behalf • Complete the LTQ grid (D2L content page) • Complete journal entry and upload it to the D2L dropbox. Include the completed grid. Instructions for journal entries are located in the "Getting Started" folder of D2L, which is located on the D2L content page. • Complete the Skills Inventory, p. 65 of Northouse along with journal entry **Complete Introductory Survey in "Getting Started" on content page of D2L.**

Table 4.2 (Continued)

Class	Assignment
LABOR DAY HOLIDAY	

9/10 **F2F**

- Begin theory presentations
- Report on D2L discussion assignments
- Review key concepts from readings
- Review next assignment
- Vote for profession
- Video: "No Smoking Employees"

Read:
- Northouse: Chap 4 & 5
- Beauchamp: "Introduction: The Use of Cases"
- Beauchamp: "Drug Testing at College International Publishers"
- Useem: "Eugene Kranz Returns Apollo 13 to Earth"

*D2L Discussion Assignments:
- D.3.1 Analyzing a Theory
- D.3.2 Eugene Kranz Returns Apollo 13 to Earth

Self-Assessment & Journal Entry:
- Complete the Style Questionnaire; Northouse, 86 & D2L
- Have five of your coworkers complete the Style Questionnaire on your behalf. (D2L content page)
- Complete the grid as well
- Complete a journal for this self-assessment

9/17 **F2F**

- Continue theory presentations
- Review key concepts from readings
- Review next assignment

Read:
- Northouse: Chapter 6
- Beauchamp: "Managing the Crisis at Mitsubishi Motors"
- Nash: "Ethics Without the Sermon" (D2L)
- Bandura: "Selective Moral Disengagement" (D2L)
- Smith: "Educating the Human Subject" (D2L)
- Carley: "Bernard Lonergan and the Catholic Teacher" (D2L)

*D2L Discussion Assignments:
- D.4.1 Applying Nash and Bandura
- D.4.2 Understanding Lonergan
- D.4.3 Interview Questions

Self-Assessment & Journal Entry:
- Complete the Least Preferred Coworker (LPC) Measure located on pages 124 &125 of Northouse
- Complete a journal for this assessment & upload to dropbox

	Class	*Assignment*
9/26	**F2F** • Conclude theory presentations • Report on D2L discussion assignments • Review key concepts from readings • Review next two weeks' assignments	**Read:** • Northouse: Chapter 7 • Beauchamp: "The Reluctant Security Guard" • Useem: "Alfredo Cristiani Ends El Salvador's Civil War" ***D2L Discussion Assignments:** • D.5.1 Another View • D.5.2 Evaluating an Empirical Study Applying Path-Goal Theory • D.5.3 Alfredo Cristiani and El Salvador's Civil War **Self-Assessment & Journal Entry:** • Complete Path-Goal Leadership Questionnaire (Northouse, 146 & D2L) • Have five coworkers complete on your behalf • Complete grid (D2L) & journal; upload to dropbox
	October 2007	
10/1	**Virtual**	**Read:** • Northouse: Chapters 8 & 9 • Beauchamp: "Ellen Durham's Dilemmas Over a Customer Base" • Useem: "Arlene Blum Ascends Annapurna" ***D2L Discussion Assignments:** • D.6.1 Bringing It All Together (discussion board for your final project; use as needed for remainder of course) • D.6.2 Students Dig It (based on Northouse case, 197) **Self-Assessment & Journal Entry:** • Complete the LMX 7 Questionnaire; Northouse, 169 • Complete a journal for this assessment & upload to dropbox
10/8	**F2F** • **Guest speaker** • Report on D2L discussion assignments • Review key concepts from readings • Review next assignment	**Read:** • Northouse: Chapter 11 • Beauchamp: "Accountants as Consultants" **Leadership narrative paper to dropbox by 10/14** ***D2L Discussion Assignments:** • D.7.1 Another View **Self-Assessment & Journal Entry:** • Complete Psychodynamic Approach Survey; Northouse, 261 & D2L • Have five of your coworkers complete the survey on your behalf • Complete the accompanying grid as well. • Complete journal and upload to dropbox with grid.

Table 4.2 (Continued)

Class	Assignment
10/15 **F2F** • **Guest speaker** • Bring hard copy of leadership narrative paper for submission • Report on leadership narrative papers • Review key concepts from readings	**Read:** • Northouse, chapter 10 • Beauchamp: "Violent Music: Sony, Slayer, and Self-Regulation" ***D2L Discussion Assignments:** • D.8.1 Ellen Durham's Dilemmas • D.8.2 Team Video Assignment **Self-Assessment & Journal Entry:** • Complete Team Excellence and Collaborative Team Leader Questionnaire; Northouse, 233 • Complete a journal for this assessment & upload to dropbox
10/22 **Virtual**	**Read:** • Northouse: Chapter 12 • Beauchamp: "Corporate Campaign Contributions" • Bogle: "What Went Wrong in Corporate America?" (D2L) • Bok: Excerpt from "The Cost of Talent: How Executives and Professionals Are Paid and How It Affects America" (D2L) ***D2L Discussion Assignments:** • D.8.2 Team Video (Part II) • D.9.1 Corporate Campaign Contributions • D.9.2 Executive Compensation **Self-Assessment & Journal Entry:** • Complete the Gender-Leader Implicit Association Test; Northouse, 288 • Complete a journal for this assessment & upload to dropbox
10/29 **F2F** • *Final Guest Speaker* • *Final Theory Presentation* • Report on team assignment • Review next assignment	**Read:** • Northouse: Chapter 13 • Beauchamp: "AIDS, Patents and Access to Pharmaceuticals" ***D2L Discussion Assignments:** • D.9.1 Corporate Campaign Contributions (Part II) • D.10.1 Lack of Inclusion & Credibility **Self-Assessment & Journal Entry:** • Complete Dimensions of Culture Questionnaire; Northouse, 334 • Complete a journal for this assessment & upload to dropbox

Class	Assignment
November	

11/5	**F2F** • *Report on journalism assignment* • *Contingency Theory* • Review next assignment	**Read:** • Northouse: Chapter 14 • Ellen Moore in Bahrain (Harvard Case Pack) • Beauchamp: "H. B. Fuller in Honduras: Street Children and Substance Abuse" • The Parable of Sadhu (Harvard Case Pack) ***D2L Discussion Assignments:** • D.10.1 Lack of Inclusion & Credibility (Part II) • D.11.1 Ellen Moore in Bahrain **Self-Assessment & Journal Entry:** • Complete Perceived Leadership Integrity Scale; Northouse, 365 • Complete a journal for this assessment & upload to dropbox
11/12	**Virtual**	**Read:** • Beauchamp: "How Reserve Mining Became Cleveland-Cliffs" • Beauchamp: "Regulating Emissions: From Acid Rain to Global Warming" • Orr: Excerpt from "Earth in Mind" (D2L) **View:** • *An Inconvenient Truth* ***D2L Discussion Assignments:** • D.12.1 On Environment
11/19	**F2F** • Cape Town Video • Report on D2L discussion assignments • Review key concepts from readings • Review next assignment	**Enjoy the holiday!**
Thanksgiving Holiday, Nov 21–25	
11/26	**Virtual**	**Prepare for final group presentation** **Final Peer Evaluation to Dropbox**
December	
12/3	**F2F** • *Course evaluations* • *Final "Good Work" Presentation* • Celebrate completion of course—munchies welcome!	**HAPPY HOLIDAYS!!**

*When completing discussion assignments, please refer to the "Rubric for Discussions" located on the content page of D2L.

degree to which we perceive we are interacting with other persons versus inanimate objects. If the perception of social presence is high, we tend to interact in a collaborative manner that increases group cohesion and free expression of emotion, building trust among group members. Conversely, if we perceive social presence to be low, we feel disconnected, and group cohesion and trust is nonexistent. We know that social presence helps build a community of inquiry (Garrison & Vaughan, 2008). Finally, we know from constructivist theory that adults learn from relating past experiences to new concepts and from interacting with one another. Thus, the challenge in any learning environment is to involve students in learning activities that encourage a high degree of social presence. One of the advantages of hybrid teaching is that we capitalize on creating social presence when students meet F2F, and social presence then continues to develop in an online environment. Thus, when designing a hybrid course, including F2F and online activities that have the potential of enhancing social presence may positively affect learning. Creating social presence is illustrated in the discussion examples in Chapter 5.

In summary, this chapter contains eight critical questions to help in planning a hybrid course. If planning and designing a student-centered learning experience is a relatively new concept for a teacher, having adequate time to do it is vitally important. If student-centered learning and hybrid course design are new concepts, requesting the assistance of an experienced course designer may be a good idea. Most teachers say it took them several months to plan and design their initial hybrid course. The following chapters provide many more ideas about designing, teaching, and evaluating hybrid courses.

DESIGNING AND TEACHING YOUR HYBRID COURSE

CHAPTER FIVE

DISCUSSION AS A WAY OF LEARNING IN A HYBRID COURSE

> Knowledge cannot be developed and sustained adequately by individuals experiencing and reflecting in isolation.
>
> —Lee Shulman (1998)

THIS CHAPTER PRESENTS IDEAS about creating, participating in, and evaluating discussion as a means of learning. The focus is on asynchronous discussion online and F2F discussion in the classroom. Topics include setting the tone for discussion, preparing students for meaningful discussion, creating logistically clear directions for discussion assignments, evaluating discussion work, and defining the roles of students and teacher when engaging in discussion. In a hybrid course, the use of discussion as a means of learning is available in several modes. An asynchronous discussion is a delayed-response format similar to the usual delay in receiving a reply to an e-mail message. It is the most common form of online discussion in hybrid course design.

Usually synchronous or real-time chat is an available feature in course management systems (see Chapter 9). Real-time chat is frequently used for virtual office hours when the teacher is available online to address specific student questions. Real-time chat also seems to work well for small groups wanting to discuss the logistics of a group assignment. It does not work well for reflective in-depth discussion for a number of reasons, including the time it takes to type responses, inadequate time to reflect on others' responses, and confusion resulting from multiple simultaneous postings.

Finally, discussion occurs during a F2F class. Sometimes video or teleconferencing may be used to bring together people from different geographic locations for a real-time discussion. Regardless of the type of discussion tool, as with any assignment, the goal is to create engaging discussions so the conditions for effective learning to occur are good. For an in-depth review of discussion from a theoretical and applied perspective, Brookfield and Preskill (2005) and Bender (2003) provide helpful information, as well as listing many additional resources related to discussion-based teaching.

To repeat, hybrid course design is dependent on a number of variables, including size of the class, content, student demographics, and teacher preference. Discussion is a flexible learning tool easily adaptable to different class dynamics and demographics. There are many ways to use discussion as a learning tool and any of them may be successful. The examples in this chapter are meant to generate ideas about designing discussion for a hybrid course versus trying to impose or even recommend any specific discussion design.

Setting the Tone for Discussion

Whether in class or online, discussion may be formal or informal. If the teacher is the facilitator for the discussion, role modeling what is expected is very effective in helping students understand how to participate in discussion. Regardless of where the discussion occurs, the teacher needs to decide the level of formality required for each discussion assignment. As an example, I tend to keep asynchronous discussion relatively informal; however, when I ask students to post an essay assignment to the discussion area for others to read, which I often do in preparation for F2F discussion, the request is more formal. For asynchronous discussion, I want students to focus on idea generation and idea analysis during a discussion instead of focusing on communicating those ideas in perfect written or oral format, which can be done when formally presenting or writing essays or research papers. For essay assignments, students are asked to critically reflect on and interact with the content assigned so that when they participate in a future F2F discussion with their colleagues and with me, they are fully prepared to do so. For discussion assignments, inclusive of preparatory work, I explain that using well-understood words instead of industry jargon and acronyms will help everyone communicate more effectively. I am quick to respectfully ask a student to explain the meaning of any jargon or acronym, regardless of whether I know the meaning.

Furthermore, I want students to feel safe in saying or writing anything as long as it is said or written clearly in a way that is respectful of all individuals. I also want students to learn to respect views that are different from theirs. Thus, they are expected to attentively listen when novel or opposing views are being expressed. Respectfully challenging any view, including mine, is highly encouraged. In summary, I try hard to create and maintain a democratic classroom environment, whether online or in the F2F classroom.

Planning a Hybrid Discussion Assignment

When properly designed, discussion assignment topics assist students in demonstrating achievement of learning objectives. When planning a hybrid discussion assignment, first think about what part of the assignment would work best online and what part would work best in the F2F classroom, which varies depending on content, student demographics, class size, and other relevant variables. For example, if the content is more technical in nature, the discussion assignment generally becomes more structured. During the initial stages of the work, more pedagogical versus andragogical principles are applied. Discussion assignments are generally based on previously assigned content. The content could be a reading, an interview, a role play, a video, or a simulation. The goal is for students to interact with content by using higher-level cognitive skills, such as application, analysis, synthesis, and evaluation, prior to interacting with other students and the teacher. Why? As mentioned previously, applying higher-level cognitive skills leads to acquiring knowledge of the discipline's core concepts. This knowledge coupled with practice leads to tacit knowledge of the discipline, and it is this tacit knowledge students are likely to retain. Thus, in future discussion, they can further build upon their previous thinking by listening to how others have engaged with the content. Discussion then tends to be insightful versus superficial in nature.

In most instances, ask students to interact with the content in a context they are familiar with. Why? Because learning from experience is the foundation of experiential learning, and adults are master experiential learners (Beard & Wilson, 2006; Knowles, Holton, & Swanson, 2005; Kolb, 1984; Miller & Boud, 1996). The following five examples apply many of these learning principles. For all five classes, discussion was a major component of the course design.

About Example 5.1

This hybrid discussion assignment is taken from a professional graduate class in organizational behavior with enrollments of 20–35 students.

Example 5.1: Mastering Competing Values (Due Tues., July 7; 50 points)

Hello,

The purpose of this assignment is to enhance your skills in building a diverse team of people who work collaboratively toward meeting the organization's strategic goals. In Quinn's article (2006), "Mastering Competing Values," located in Chapter 2 of your text, he describes a conceptual framework that may help you better understand how culture determines strategy within organizations. In an *APA*-formatted document, please write a short essay (2–3 pages, not including title page and reference page) that applies Quinn's conceptual framework (see Figures 1 and 2 in the article) to the culture within your organization. If you are currently unemployed, then use an organization where you once worked or a community-based organization where you are a member. How might applying Quinn's framework help to build a more collaborative work environment?

Remember to refer to the rubric when writing your essay. Be prepared to enter into discussion of both the conceptual framework and your application of it when coming to class next week.

Best, JC

Refer to Table 5.1 for action steps with the accompanying rationale. Table 5.2 is a critical thinking rubric used to evaluate the Mastering Competing Values assignment and is intended to better prepare students for F2F discussion. Review rubrics thoroughly with students during the F2F class, explaining what is meant by each of the criteria. Think about giving students access to examples of superior work from previous students; the

Table 5.1 Action Steps and Rationale for Discussion Assignment 5.1

Action Step	Rationale
1. The learning objective is clearly stated within the assignment.	Student recognizes what is to be learned by completing the work. Student assessment of the value of the work can be made. Work that is valuable is engaging, and based on intrinsic motivating factors, is likely to be learned.
2. The due date for the written work and the date for the future F2F discussion are clearly identified.	Integration of written prep work with F2F work is identified in order that the student recognizes that in-class work is a continuation of online work and vice versa.
3. Students are told how much their work is worth in relationship to the total number of points in the course.	Student recognizes the impact of work in relationship to course grade, which is an extrinsic motivator; student thereby has the freedom to decide how much effort will be put into the work based on other relevant variables.
4. The topics for the future F2F discussion are identified.	Better prepares student for F2F discussion.
5. Students are first asked to interact with the contact by writing an essay in which they apply the conceptual framework discussed in the content.	Reflective work in preparation for F2F discussion.

6. In the essay, students are asked:
  a. To apply the content in a familiar context.
  b. How the framework could create a more collaborative working environment.
	Higher levels of cognitive skills are required to successfully complete the essay, specifically application, analysis, synthesis, and evaluation. Experiential learning principles are applied in that the student is asked to think about the framework in the context of past experiences within a familiar work setting.

7. Students are given a rubric that identifies how their work will be evaluated.	Heightens student awareness of important points, which better prepares the students for effective learning.
8. Correspondence to the students includes a greeting and a closing signature.	Actions that assist in creating social presence and a democratic environment that is respectful of others.
9. F2F Discussion	Gives students the opportunity to broaden and perhaps modify their perspectives, which is an application of constructivist theory.

Table 5.2 Rubric for Short Essays

Criteria	Unacceptable	Acceptable	Superior
Is able to correctly apply theory and concepts, identifying important patterns and connections	Fails to identify connections and to perceive implications of the material	Brings together related data or ideas in productive ways	Develops insightful connections and patterns that require intellectual rigor
Is able to identify and understand multiple views	Consideration of multiple views lacking	Discusses strengths and weaknesses of multiple views, drawing reasonable conclusions regarding those views	Evaluates multiple views and draws from personal experience to develop, support, and critique one's own view
Comprehensiveness of work	Does not meet some or all of the criteria requested for assignment	Meets all criteria requested for the assignment	Exceeds criteria requested for assignment
Grammar and spelling	Frequent or serious errors	Less than five (5) errors	No notable errors
APA formatting	APA formatting generally not followed	Less than three (3) formatting errors	No notable errors
Clarity and organization	Content inconsistent for clarity and organization	Fairly clear and organized content	Consistent clarity of thought, appropriate vocabulary, and well-organized content
On a scale of 0 (unacceptable) to 3 (superior), X on line indicates where this work falls	0		3

examples chosen do not have to be from the exact same assignment, however. Note that the rubric is broad enough to enable more specific feedback for any of the criteria, yet specific enough so that students are generally aware of what is expected of them. Again, by interacting with the content, the essay prepares students for the discussion that will follow. Because students have already interacted with the material in a reflective way outside the F2F class, they are better prepared to have an insightful discussion with their colleagues, which may occur either online or F2F.

Consider for a moment the differences in a traditional class as compared to a hybrid class. Typically, in a traditional class students are assigned to read the material and that's what they do, but generally that is all they do. Then they come to class either to hear a lecture on the material they have read (it is hoped), or to hear a lecture on supplemental material. Unfortunately, if they didn't really understand what they read in the first place or didn't read it, they haven't deeply interacted with it and supplemental material may not be at all helpful. They may spend some time discussing the material in class, and time permitting, they may ask a question or two. Because of the size of the class and the limited time, most students will not get answers to their questions because either they are too uncomfortable to ask them or there is inadequate time to do so. Second, without really interacting with the content in any thoughtful way prior to discussing it in class or online, discussion frequently lacks depth, and the critical questions oftentimes are not discussed.

About Example 5.2

Example 5.2 illustrates another way to use asynchronous discussion. This discussion assignment was part of a hybrid graduate class in negotiation; the class had average enrollments of 20 to 30. Students worked in two pairs, with each pair or party receiving important information regarding an entity the pair is representing in the negotiation process. Preparation for the negotiation is conducted online, with each party having a private discussion forum. Prior to beginning the actual negotiation process, the teacher provides feedback regarding each party's preparation.

Then the actual negotiation is conducted asynchronously online, with both parties accessing a third discussion forum designed specifically for that purpose. This time the teacher provides feedback on the negotiation process itself. The negotiation is repeated during the subsequent F2F class. Students observing the negotiation in class complete a formal evaluation on the two parties conducting the negotiation and post their evaluation in the discussion forum.

There are several advantages to structuring a negotiation in this way. Successful negotiation is largely dependent upon the preparation that occurs prior to the beginning of the negotiation. The teacher can see the process unfold and provide feedback as necessary on the preparation and the actual negotiation. Second, students are often quite nervous when initially negotiating in front of a class. Rehearsing the negotiation online and receiving feedback from the teacher prior to conducting the negotiation in the presence of others generally makes it a less stressful experience for the negotiating parties and a more effective learning experience for students observing the parties negotiate. Providing formal feedback to each negotiating party teaches students to listen carefully to the negotiation and to give feedback in a constructive way. The rubric for this example has also been included in Table 5.3 on page 91.

▮ Example 5.2: Process for Virtual Negotiation

Folks,

Below are the steps for the virtual negotiation process that is scheduled for Week 5, April 25th through May 1st. The nine negotiation parties will receive their negotiation information through Study.Net. It will be accessible by Tuesday, April 20th. All offers and counteroffers will take place in the private discussion created for that purpose.

Please read the steps below carefully, review the timeline and the rubric. Let me know if you have any questions or concerns regarding this assignment, which represents 10% of your final grade in this course.

Virtual Negotiation Process Steps

We will be using a three-part series of negotiations for the Adam Baxter Company from years 1978 through 1985. Parties 1 through 6 will be negotiating the 1978 settlement. Parties 7 through 12 will be negotiating the 1983 settlement, and Parties 13 through 18 will be negotiating the 1985 settlement. Party A and Party B will receive information respective to each party's role in the negotiation process.

The negotiation process will follow the timelines indicated in the calendar to follow. Please note that these are maximum timelines; individuals may post to the discussion forum earlier.

You are encouraged to carefully review the negotiation process in Chapter 4 of Leigh, which provides an excellent model, including an example for negotiating. Parties will post their preparation for the virtual negotiation to the digital drop box *prior* to posting their initial offer on Sunday, April 25.

Both individuals will present their respective opening offers by the same date, giving no one the advantage of a first offer. The same will hold true for the counteroffers. Following the counteroffers, parties may engage in asynchronous dialogue before posting another counteroffer. *All offers should be clearly identified as such in the title of the posting!*

Individuals may reach an agreement following the opening round. There is no definite number of rounds that need to occur; however, within the time constraints allotted, the goal is to reach the highest level of negotiation possible, as described by Leigh.

Any individual who misses a negotiation posting date will lose five points on the assignment. If this occurs a second time by the same party, that party must accept the last offer that was made by the other party.

The final posting to the discussion thread must occur by Sunday, May 2nd at 11:59 pm. That posting should indicate that either a settlement has been reached or that no settlement has been reached. The details of the final or failed settlement should be posted by one of the two parties. You will need to decide who is to do this. Parties will be given 10 minutes to discuss any last-minute details prior to presenting their negotiation in class on either Tuesday, May 4th or Thursday, May 6th.

Virtual Negotiation Posting Calendar
All postings due by 11:59 pm on date indicated!

Sunday, April 25; post initial offers.
Tuesday, April 27; post counteroffers.
Thursday, April 29; post second counteroffers.
Saturday, May 1; post third counteroffers.
Sunday, May 2; final posting due by 11:59 pm
   Those observing negotiations (5 points per observation)

Groups observing will be expected to read the negotiation data specific to *one* of the entities in preparation for the negotiation process that will be presented in class. Fifty percent (50%) of the observation groups will be given data on one of the entities while the remaining observation groups will be given data on the other entity. Groups observing will be given 10 minutes to get together in class to discuss the negotiation prior to observing it. Groups observing will provide constructive feedback on the feedback form posted with this assignment; upload the completed feedback form to the general discussion board within two days following the observation.

Best, JC ■

About Example 5.3

Example 5.3, I Survived Valentine's Day, was designed by an experienced hybrid teacher who is a cultural anthropologist (Aycock, 2006). The assignment is for an undergraduate introductory course in cultural anthropology. Students first need to answer several questions posed by the teacher, uploading their responses to a drop box that is accessible to the teacher only, permitting the teacher to provide them with individual feedback privately before completing the next part of the assignment. Then students are asked to prepare a 10-minute presentation in Power-Point for the next F2F class. Following these presentations, the students participate in an online discussion providing feedback to their peers regarding the presentations. Note that for this assignment, the rubric is contained in the body of the assignment. Directions for each step of the process have been clearly identified.

■ Example 5.3: I Survived Valentine's Day!

The objective of this assignment is to demonstrate your understanding of how cultural norms influence decision making. This assignment is intended to let you apply to your own experience of Valentine's Day what we have been studying and discussing about gift giving and reciprocity. (Please note: I know that not everyone celebrates Valentine's Day! If you don't, pick a comparable holiday festival, such as this past Christmas, that you do celebrate.)

1. To whom *must* you give a Valentine's Day present? Why are these people required to receive presents from you? How do you decide what present to give people in this category?
2. To whom *may* you give a Valentine's Day present? Why do you have a choice about whether to give these people presents? How do you decide what present to give people in this category?

Table 5.3   Rubric for Virtual Negotiation Process

Criteria (each criterion worth 5 points)	Achieved all possible points for criteria when this column is checked. Comments may be included in this column.	One to 3 points deducted per criterion when this column checked. Comments will be included in this column.	Four or more points deducted per criterion when this column checked. Comments will be included in this column.
Preparation clearly identifies BATNA, reservation, and target points for each pertinent negotiating point.			
Preparation identifies and prioritizes the issues.			
Preparation has been posted to the drop box in accordance with the timeline.			
Negotiation process demonstrates a search for adding value to each party's situation versus compromise or leaving money on the table.			
Negotiation process indicates use of one or more of the following tools to expand the pie: unbundling, adding issues, adding alternative and trade-offs.			
Individuals reached a fair-minded negotiation agreement where all added value has been distributed among the parties.			
Final settlement or failure to settle has been posted in the discussion topic in accordance with the timeline.			

3. To whom *must you not* give a Valentine's Day present? What cultural pattern would you violate if you did?
4. Please give an example of a Valentine's present *gone bad* because of what was given or whom it was given to.

Your task is to figure out the underlying rules for Valentine's Day gift giving, and state them clearly. Make sure you give good examples; draw on your own experience and that of your family or friends. The *more specific* you can be about the examples of gifts you use to illustrate these rules for gift giving, the better!

This is one of your project postings, so it's worth 7 points total. Each of the 4 questions above is worth 1 point. You should write two or three sentences to answer each question. You must post your response to the drop box I have set up for that purpose no later than Friday, 8 February, by midnight.

Then, by Tuesday, 12 February, by midnight prepare a 10-minute slide presentation to present your work on this assignment during class on Wednesday, 13 February. This response will be worth 1 point toward the total grade for this project. Then all of you will respond to your group member's presentation given in class by posting to the "I survived Valentine's Day" discussion. Your posting is due no later than Friday, 15 February, by midnight. Your response should take the form of an ethnographic question: What is one additional thing related to our discussion about gift giving and reciprocity that you would like to ask this person that he or she did not already answer in the presentation? Your question should not be a trivial one (e.g., You said that you gave a gift to your girlfriend, have you given gifts to your girlfriends before?), but should attempt to discover an interesting or important pattern in the way this person gives gifts. This posting is worth 1 point.

Your group members will respond to your question no later than Tuesday, 19 February, by midnight. Posting of your response to the question posed is worth 1 point. ■

About Example 5.4

Example 5.4 was designed for a graduate class in research methods for the behavioral and social sciences. In this assignment, students were asked to work together to construct a unidimensional Thurstone scale to measure individuals' attitudes regarding a commonly observed phenomenon.

The nature of the assignment is more technical than the three previous examples, involving some computation completed through the use of spreadsheets. The technical work is predominantly done outside the classroom with step-by-step instructions and a clear example in the reading. Because of the more unfamiliar material contained in the reading and the need to use spreadsheets, F2F discussion occurs during class prior to any written work.

The initial steps of scale construction are completed during the F2F class for two reasons. The first reason is because of logistics. It is too time consuming to generate 80 statements through brainstorming in an online environment. Second, by doing this initial work during the F2F class, students who may be a little anxious regarding the technicalities of the work have an opportunity to ask questions while interacting with each other and the teacher as they generate the statements needed for scale construction. Students then scale the statements individually using a spreadsheet created in Google Docs during class. They then work in small groups to download the Google Docs data into an Excel spreadsheet where they complete the scale. They upload the completed scale to the drop box, receiving feedback on their work before they present it during the next F2F class. Again, because the work is more technical in nature, errors can be highlighted in the feedback. The groups then correct the errors before presenting their work during the F2F class.

Following class presentations, students discuss online the differences in the scales. Students are then ready to apply their new knowledge to a familiar setting. They are asked to give examples of how a Thurstone scale might be used in the work setting to get a better idea of employees' attitudes regarding important workplace phenomena, such as a change in a benefit package.

▨ Example 5.4: Developing a Thurstone Scale (100 points)

Folks,

The purpose of this assignment is for you to learn the concept of unidimensional scaling by developing and evaluating a Thurstone scale.

Assignment Plan: Please go to http://www.socialresearchmethods.net/ kb/scalthur.php and read the information on Thurstone scaling. Contained in the reading is a step-by-step example of how to create a

Thurstone scale. Pay close attention to these steps. Then think about what attribute we could measure using a Thurstone scale. The attribute should be one that is familiar to you and the class, and one that would be worthwhile in measuring. As examples, a few topics chosen by previous classes included the perception of diversity on campus and using cell phones while driving. *During our next F2F class* we will do the following:

1. Vote on ideas presented for Thurstone scale development, selecting the idea with the most votes.
2. Brainstorm to identify the 80 statements needed for the scale.
3. Create a spreadsheet within Google Docs and enter our 80 scale statements into the spreadsheet during class.
4. Address questions concerning scale development.

Before the next F2F class, we will do the following:

1. By June 15, each person will go into the Google Docs spreadsheet and assign a scale number from 1 to 11 to each of the 80 statements.
2. Groups will work together privately in this discussion forum on the logistics of completing the scale. *Be sure to follow the guidelines provided to you in the reading. These guidelines will be used as the rubric for this assignment.*
3. Each group uploads its completed scale to this discussion forum by June 20.
4. I will provide feedback on each group's scale in the discussion forum.

During the June 25 F2F class, group designated members will present the group's completed scale.

By June 30, an online wrap-up discussion regarding scale similarities and differences will take place. You will be asked to provide an example of how a Thurstone scale could be used in your workplace. ■

About Example 5.5

The discussion assignment presented in Example 5.5 was designed by an experienced hybrid teacher who is a fine arts professor (Mangrich, 2006). She teaches an upper-division class titled "Site and the Public Space."

Class enrollments are 15–20 students with majors in visual art or in architecture and planning. Note that the teacher provides a synopsis of a discussion that occurred during a F2F class. She is interested in furthering that discussion online. It is clear by what she states in the summary that the intent of the discussion is to prepare the students to make a major decision regarding the artwork they will be creating as their final project during the semester-long class. Note the democratic tone demonstrated throughout the teacher's summary of the class's discussion.

■ Example 5.5: Continuing the Ideation Discussion

(At least one posting due by Tuesday, Nov 4; 5 points.)

The goal of this discussion is to further the ideation discussion that we had in class, to continue to discuss and identify themes and to come closer to a group decision concerning how to determine content. Please refer to your notes from class regarding major themes discussed. Here is a synopsis and my thoughts thus far.

As several of you have mentioned, the visual display for our project must be quite large and clear so that it may be read from a distance. Smaller details are definitely possible, but the main visual elements should be clear and concise. Finding a main idea that we want to talk about will help our project be "read" by as many people as possible.

If the main goal of our project is to inform the citizens of Parksville about the experience of being a citizen of Parksville, then what elements will help us talk about this?

Yes, landmarks give us a symbol for our city and its neighborhoods. People become much attached to these symbols because they are a visual representation of their own identity—the place where they live.

History is also important because these past events created the city of the present. Many people are unaware of the history of their city. It is true that it is important to understand the history of a place in order to fully understand that place. However, if we are to create a clear "picture" of the experience of living in Parksville today, history may be less effective in creating that image than other potential content.

One thing that we want to do is to create a "picture" that is an accurate representation of the experience of Parksville. It seems that stories are one way to achieve this. Maybe these stories include history and landmarks, but maybe they do not for some citizens. I think we should think about ways to get the stories and experiences of individuals into our project. The stories of people may help determine the role of history and landmarks in our project.

Many of you are interested in neighborhoods. Interviewing within neighborhoods has the potential to get a somewhat accurate "cross section" of the population. Also, contemporary stories (as compared to historical stories) have the potential to be an accurate portrait of the thoughts and feelings of the population that lives in the neighborhood *now* rather than a hundred years ago.

We talked on Thursday about this project being a voice for a city that is ever-changing and in flux. How can we show this? ■

Summary

Although these five discussion assignments are designed quite differently, they also have several important similarities. First and foremost, they apply adult learning theory by inviting students to draw from a familiar context, emphasizing experiential learning. Second, students are given multiple opportunities to interact with the content, their colleagues, and the teacher, applying constructivist theory. The degree of multiple modes of interaction in and outside the F2F classroom is the primary benefit of a hybrid course. This intensity and frequency of interaction creates the potential for effective adult learning. Third, most of these assignments require higher levels of thinking, including application, analysis, synthesis, and evaluation, thereby assisting students in developing tacit knowledge leading to sustained learning. Finally, the integration of what goes on in and out of the classroom is clearly evident. There are no parallel tracks in these assignments; instead F2F learning is interwoven with online learning and vice versa.

Other similarities are more logistical in nature, but nonetheless very important. Each assignment has clearly stated deadlines. In each case, students know how their work will be evaluated and how many points are associated with the assignment or in some cases with each portion of an assignment. Finally, the purpose of the assignment is made clear from the onset.

One last thing worth mentioning is the teacher's role in discussion assignments. Just as students need to know what their role is in any discussion assignment, they also need to know the teacher's role. In each of these assignments, the teacher's role is clearly identified. Students know when and how they will receive feedback from the teacher, whether online, during the next F2F class, or in both environments.

Discussion is clearly a versatile and important learning tool in many hybrid environments. Rather than being prescriptive, the examples in this chapter are intended to help you generate ideas about how you would like to design engaging discussions in your hybrid class.

CHAPTER SIX

PROVIDING AND SOLICITING
STUDENT FEEDBACK

Feedback is the breakfast of champions.
—Rick Tate (as cited by Ken Blanchard 2009)

S IMILAR TO THE DIFFICULTY I have in separating my professional
life from my personal life, I also have difficulty separating my role
as a teacher from my role as a learner. I see both as occurring
simultaneously, in concert with one another. For example, if I teach ethics
in my professional life and behave unethically in my personal life, I lack
integrity professionally and personally. The same relationship is true with
teaching and learning. As I teach I learn, one experience is intertwined
with the other. The primary difference between professional teachers and
students in my mind is that teachers have current and advanced knowledge of the discipline being taught and advanced knowledge of learner-
centered teaching practices, which helps students to learn effectively. Just
as students learn a discipline by receiving formative and summative feedback on their work, teachers advance their teaching practice by receiving
formative and summative feedback from students and from colleagues.

Formative feedback occurs as a result of a student's applying new
knowledge. Nursing students who are learning how to take an accurate
blood pressure reading receive feedback from the teacher while they practice taking blood pressures, often on each other. This is formative assessment. The key is that the feedback is immediate, and students have the
ability to use the feedback immediately to improve their technique. The
primary purpose of the assessment is to improve performance rather than

to evaluate performance for the purpose of earning a grade; many times performance is not graded at this stage. Summative assessment occurs periodically when students have or should have learned a skill set, and should have achieved acceptable or more than acceptable performance. Using the same example, students may be asked to demonstrate the correct way to take a blood pressure as part of a practical exam. In this case, the feedback is a grade that informs students of their mastery of a particular skill set. Just as important, however, is that summative assessment in aggregate informs teachers of their mastery in teaching the skill set and informs the program organizers whether the program is achieving its stated outcomes.

This chapter is about feedback, specifically assessing student learning and giving formative and summative feedback to students in a way that is most likely to improve and sustain learning. Second, it is about purposively generating formative feedback from students regarding their actual learning experience. Their feedback, when given constructively and taken seriously, is an assessment of teaching meant to improve practice. Significant changes in teaching may be the result of feedback from students on anonymous surveys or during F2F meetings.

The Importance of Feedback to Enhance Learning

There are three major reasons feedback is important to learning. The first is that immediate feedback when learning a difficult concept or skill is necessary to gain understanding, and should occur throughout the learning process (Thalheimer, 2008a). Learning a difficult skill or concept often takes place in stages, and learning the next stage is dependent upon successfully learning the previous stage. This principle is made clear by a somewhat humorous story my favorite ski instructor, Tom, told me many years ago. In skiing terminology *moguls* are commonly referred to by skiers as *bumps*. These bumps, or mounds of hardened snow, are found on steep terrain; they result when fairly advanced skiers jam the edge of their skis into the snow to make a series of rapid turns to control their speed as they progress down the mountain. As with most sports, it takes a significant amount of practice before becoming an expert. Tom once told me, however, that his students often wanted to be taught to ski moguls during their first week of lessons. The problem, he said, is they don't know how to ski. How can I teach them to ski moguls when they haven't learned to ski a moderate slope without losing control? The point of the story is this: Learning how to ski moguls is dependent upon learning to ski the basics. If you can't ski less challenging terrain, then you can't progress to moguls, which is an example of how multistage learning works.

The second reason feedback is important is that effective learning depends heavily upon retrieval mechanisms (Howard, 1995; Thalheimer, 2008a). If you can't retrieve something you learned from memory, you will need to relearn it. Effective feedback triggers retrieval mechanisms. Telling stories to illustrate a principle is an effective form of feedback that triggers retrieval of the associated principle. The ski instructor story is an illustration of this. I heard the story at least 15 years ago and associated it with multistage learning at the time and still do until this day. The story is the retrieval cue, the concept is multistage learning.

The third reason feedback is important to learning is that it corrects misconceptions (Howard, 1995; Thalheimer, 2008a), which is why meta-cognition is an effective feedback tool. Metacognition has two major components: the first is being conscious of your progress in learning, and the second is evaluating and perhaps modifying your learning strategies to assist in improving your learning (Winn & Snyder, 1996). One advantage that online learning tasks have for teachers is that the learning process becomes more transparent for all students in the class. Thus the teacher may provide formative feedback to students based on misconceptions, which often become quite apparent when reading discussion posts, for example. In the F2F classroom, however, not all students have the opportunity or desire to participate in discussion; thus, the learning process for many students is invisible to the teacher who does not have the opportunity to provide feedback regarding any misconceptions.

How to Provide Effective Feedback

Providing effective feedback requires an accurate assessment of the status of the learner, which is true for a number of reasons. First of all, providing specific feedback is always a good practice, but the type, timing, and comprehensiveness of feedback is dependent upon where the student is in the learning process. As just stated, multistage learning depends on getting the previous stage right before progressing to the next stage, so the timing of the feedback is important. The teacher needs to assess the learning that has occurred and correct any misconceptions before the student repeatedly retrieves incorrect mental models, which negatively impacts learning the next stage.

Retrieval mechanisms are very powerful. The more frequently the student retrieves incorrect mental models, the more difficult it is to correct them. This is quite apparent when learning motor skills. If you hold the tennis racket incorrectly when you swing, the more times you swing, the more difficult it is to correct the bad habit, as each swing enforces the retrieval of an incorrect mental model.

If students get it right, positive reinforcement, or feedback in this case, becomes important for three reasons. It reinforces the correct mental model and retrieval mechanism (Howard, 1995; Thalheimer, 2008b); it increases self-efficacy specific to what is learned, thereby improving performance (Bandura, 1977); and it affects future learning by clarifying future expectations. One of the benefits of teaching in a hybrid format is that feedback may be received online shortly after a F2F class and prior to the next assignment. Upon reviewing feedback, students have the opportunity to contact the teacher with any questions. For instance, Example 6.1 is feedback to a small group that presented a case analysis and needed to present additional case analyses for the class. The feedback was posted electronically in a course management system within 48 hours following the presentation.

▪ Example 6.1: Feedback to a Small Group

Dear Group 1 Members,

The strengths of your analysis are as follows. Your purpose statement is clearly stated as is your root cause. Both are reasonable for the case content. You identified three plausible strategies. Your visuals were free of grammatical errors and illustrated the main points in your presentation, and your conclusion summarized major points that you made during the presentation. Your presentation was well organized and well presented.

The weaknesses of your analysis are as follows. Your snapshot of the current state of affairs lacked comprehensiveness. Remember that most of your audience has not read the case. Thus, you need to concisely address major points affecting your analysis. As an example, the type of compensation plan plays a major role. You did not identify it in your snapshot. Second, you need to clearly lay out the strengths and weaknesses of each of your strategies. Although requested on the rubric, you did not do this. How could the rubric be made clearer in this area? When you identify weaknesses of a strategy, be sure to address what proactive action steps should be taken to compensate for those weaknesses. As an example, when you recommended changing the compensation plan, a weakness that could have negatively affected this strategy is that it is likely to increase compensation costs. What measures would you take proactively to combat this weakness? Last, I asked you to consider how you could have applied concepts you were exposed to in the readings or that we discussed in class. As an example, emotional intelligence could have been discussed in the context of this case.

In closing, I enjoyed listening to your presentation, and I look forward to listening to your next one. Please refer to the accompanying rubric for the number of points earned on each criterion. Don't hesitate to contact me with any questions you may have regarding the feedback given or the points you received.

Best, JC ▓

The positive feedback (strengths) is to the point and specifically addresses what the group did well, which helps clarify expectations for future case analyses.

When students get it wrong, immediate feedback is important for two reasons: to correct misconceptions before they become ingrained mental models and to improve future performance. Classes with few assignments give students little opportunity to improve based on feedback. There is nothing more frustrating to students than receiving feedback on the first assignment after they have submitted the second. What is even more frustrating to students is receiving initial feedback at the close of the course.

The weaknesses addressed in the feedback example identify a need for improvement in specific areas of the case analysis. The feedback is designed to correct the mental model of what should have been included in the analysis, and is likely to lead to a stronger case analysis next time, which leads directly into the next section.

Why Aren't You Hearing Me?

Sometimes feedback is not well received; students disregard or appear to disregard it. Unfortunately this may occur for any number of reasons, including but not limited to lack of understanding because of inexperience with the assignment or with the process; complexity of the task; disinterest in the content or method of learning; language barriers related to diversity factors, including cultural differences, and differences in educational background, age, and life experiences; anxiety related to fear of failure; fatigue related to life imbalance or physical well-being; time constraints based on numerous priorities; and defensiveness related to differences in style and opinion. To illustrate, I requested students submit an essay conforming to the *Publication Manual of the American Psychological Association (APA)*. My written instructions were as follows: "For this assignment, submitted in APA format, please write a short essay, two to three pages, excluding title page and reference page." And that is exactly what I got from one student, a three-page essay without a title page and reference page.

The best teachers can do is provide feedback in a way and at a time that increases the likelihood that it will positively affect learning. Duplication of critical points is good. The importance of correcting misconceptions by providing specific and timely feedback has already been emphasized. Despite our best efforts, however, ineffective feedback is a common occurrence. If this weren't so, everyone would be achieving all possible points on every assignment.

Let's return to the case analysis assignment with the example of feedback given to Group 1. Prior to completing the case analysis, the class read a brief article on the process of case analysis, which was then discussed during the following F2F class. A rubric designed for case analysis was posted online for review prior to class, and each criteria listed on the rubric was discussed during the following F2F class. Finally, a practice case applying the rubric was completed in small groups during the F2F class, and a report on the analysis immediately followed. Feedback on each rubric criterion was given as the report on that criterion was made. So why didn't each group earn all points associated with its initial case analysis? In fact, because of the number of variables involved in learning, rarely does any group earn all points on any case analysis. However, through incorporation of adult learning principles in our teaching practice we increase the potential for students to learn effectively.

Emotion Is Important Too

Until a few decades ago, research primarily focused on behavioral and cognitive aspects of learning with little focus on the emotional aspects.

Now several researchers (Bandura, 1977; Goleman, 1995; Harter, 1990; Lawson, n.d.; Weiner, 1994) agree that emotions significantly affect learning. Bandura stated that our perceived level of self-efficacy regarding learning a skill influences our performance for that skill. Goleman said that lack of emotional competence leads to a reduced attention span; increased thinking problems, such as acting without thinking; and nervousness interfering with the ability to concentrate. Weiner linked emotions to behavioral consequences that affect learning, such as choice of behavior, level of effort, and persistence. Finally, Lawson stated, "Learning requires thinking. Our thoughts influence how we feel. How we feel influences how we think. The connections between emotion and learning are bi-directional and complex" (Conclusion section, para. 1).

In returning to the feedback example one last time, the reason the heading, brief final paragraph, and closing are included as part of the feedback is to demonstrate respect, encourage future learning, and further the idea of social presence and democracy in the virtual and F2F classrooms. When receiving feedback in a democratic, safe, and supportive learning environment, students are less likely to become defensive and anxious and lose confidence. Creating the most effective conditions for students to receive feedback increases the likelihood of improved future performance on learning tasks.

Student Feedback

Receiving student feedback is equally as important as giving student feedback. Each time students submit an assignment, they are providing feedback about learning that *is or is not* occurring. However, in regard to improving future learning, specifically soliciting formative student feedback regarding foundational concepts and perceived learning experiences are invaluable. This is evident when considering the following survey findings from over three decades of work as reported by Miller, a political scientist at Northwestern University.

+ Twenty percent of Americans believe the sun revolves around the earth;
+ Less than one third of Americans link DNA with heredity;
+ Only ten percent of Americans understand what radiation is. (as cited in Dean, 2005)

Somewhere along the way, incorrect mental models led to ingrained misconceptions regarding these basic principles taught in elementary school. Miller's example demonstrates the importance of frequently assessing what is being learned.

Soliciting Student Feedback to Improve Learning and Teaching

Student learning can be actively and regularly assessed in a number of ways. The classic work of Angelo and Cross (1993) provides comprehensive coverage on classroom assessment techniques (CATs), a method to assess how well students are learning key concepts, enabling the teacher to provide immediate feedback to students regarding their performance. Common qualities describing CATs include learner centered, anonymous, formative, novel, discipline specific, and brief. As of this writing, the following websites are good resources for CATs:

- ♦ Angelo and Cross website at the University of Hawaii, http://hono lulu.hawaii.edu/intranet/committees/FacDevCom/guidebk/teach tip/teachtip.htm#assessment
- ♦ Iowa State University, http://www.celt.iastate.edu/teaching/cat.html
- ♦ Vanderbilt University Center for Teaching, http://www.vanderbilt .edu/cft/resources/teaching_resources/assessment/cats.htm

Table 6.1 provides several examples of CATs (Angelo & Cross) and how they may be used. Although teachers may not call them CATs, my guess is many teachers already include classroom assessment techniques in their practice. The examples in the table are specifically designed for a hybrid environment.

Student Feedback Regarding the Overall Learning Experience

Teachers may also be interested in assessing the overall learning experience of their students. To do that, most course management systems have an anonymous survey function. I generally use a survey developed by the faculty from the Learning Technology Center at the University of

Table 6.1 CAT Descriptions and Applications for Hybrid Classes

Title of CAT	Description of CAT	F2F Class Application	Online Application
Muddiest Point	At the close of class, student is asked to identify in one paragraph or less what was most unclear about a principle discussed during class.	Today we discussed how we could apply Bandura's ethical framework to the HIV case scenario. Identify in one paragraph or less, what point was most unclear about this discussion. Please take five minutes to do this and submit your work to me on your way out of class.	Teacher reads the muddiest points and posts a summary online to further clarify student points identified and to correct any misconceptions, inviting any follow-up questions.
Minute Paper	At the close of class, ask students to identify something new that they learned along with a question they may still have.	What's one thing that you learned today that you didn't know when you walked through the door? What's one question that you would still like to ask about what you learned? Please take five minutes to answer these questions and submit your work to me on your way out of class.	With an online posting, teacher has an opportunity to read what students learned and correct any misconceptions. Questions submitted may also be addressed.
What Is the Principle?	Asks students to identify what specific principle is being applied.	Today we discussed five rules of probability. I have posted several probability problems in the discussion area. As you consider each problem, please identify which rule of probability applies.	As students post which rule of probability applies in considering the problem, the teacher may clarify any evident misconceptions.
Background Knowledge Probe	Used to assess the competency of students as they begin a course.	Within a few days following the initial F2F class, students are asked to complete an anonymous online quiz related to the course content.	Students complete the quiz, giving the teacher an idea of what students know about course content and what differences exist among students' knowledge base.

Wisconsin–Milwaukee. I have modified it slightly and frequently administer it anonymously online after the first 3 to 4 weeks of class. The aggregate results of the survey are given to students during the following F2F class. I do this for three reasons: to demonstrate that I take student feedback seriously and to thank students for providing it; sometimes I'm unclear what certain comments pertain to, and many times students are willing to clarify feedback upon further review during class; and students see the diversity of responses, thereby gaining a better understanding of why it is difficult to accommodate everyone all the time. When students provide this type of formative feedback, I generally am able to make small improvements to the class almost immediately. Example 6.2 contains the questions for the survey. For years I was surprised at the depth of valuable student feedback and I was curious about why they would take the time to give me feedback. Conducting an empirical study regarding this question (Caulfield, 2007), my findings indicated that students were willing to provide feedback for two statistically significant reasons: to improve the value of the current class and to improve the value of future classes.

▧ Example 6.2: Reality Check Survey

Hi Folks,

You will need about 20 minutes to complete this short-answer anonymous survey. Please answer at least 10 of the questions. The purpose of the survey is to let me know how you think this course is going thus far. Please know your feedback is very important to me as most of the changes I make in how I teach a course are based on what you have told me about your experiences.

Best, JC

1. Does the way this course is being taught make sense to you? If so, why? If not, why not?
2. Does the course cover enough ground? If not, what else should we be doing?
3. Are we trying to do too much in this course? Would it be better to focus on just a few things? If so, what might they be?
4. What do you think of the textbook(s) required for this course?
5. Are you getting enough out of the course related to practical application to your life?

6. Would you like to suggest a quick fix—some little thing that would make the course better?

7. Do you find the online resources helpful? Why or why not?

8. Do you think that having a D2L course site makes this a better class? Why or why not?

9. Does what we do online appear to be integrated with what we do in class?

10. Has this course made any difference in the way you think about your profession?

11. There's a lot of emphasis on active student participation in this course, and as a result our class time is almost entirely spent on these activities. Are you learning enough from the professor?

12. Does having you and your colleagues take a leading role in our class make the class a better one from your point of view?

13. If you could change the way the grading in this course works, what would you change? Why?

14. Take a look at the learning objectives listed at the beginning of the syllabus. If you could remove one or more of them, which would you take out? Why?

15. At the end of the course, if we had accomplished only some of these learning objectives, which ones would make you feel good about having taken the course? Why?

16. What else do you think I need to know about the way this course has been set up? ▪

Regardless of course design and mode of delivery, feedback is a very important learning tool for students and teachers in any classroom environment. It assists in increasing student understanding of difficult concepts, in forming retrieval mechanisms, and in developing correct mental models. In a hybrid environment, it is possible to use the F2F and online environments to give and receive feedback. To use feedback wisely, it is important to frequently assess student learning and to provide the feedback when and how it is most likely to be beneficial to learning and positively received. Receiving feedback regarding students' overall learning experience is valuable in improving teaching. Students are willing to provide significant feedback if they know it will be used to make course adjustments when possible and to improve future classes.

CHAPTER SEVEN

USING SMALL GROUPS AS A LEARNING STRATEGY

Would you rather work as a part of an out-standing group or be a part of a group of out-standing individuals? This may be the key question in thinking about the premises behind participation.

—Max DePree (1989)

T HIS CHAPTER FOCUSES on using small groups to create effective learning environments. The terms *group* and *teams* are often used interchangeably, which tends to mask differences between the two concepts. Although some researchers tend to treat the concepts of group, team, and small group similarly (Parks & Sanna, 1999), more researchers identify distinct differences between the two (Hayes, 1997; Katzenbach & Smith, 1993; Levi, 2007). The literature indicates that the need for inter-active skills in college graduates entering the workforce today is of paramount importance (Robinson, 2001; World Bank, 2007). Based on the abundant cultural and group dynamics research (Goleman, 1995; Hayes, 1997; Hofstede, 2007; Katzenbach & Smith, 1993; Levi, 2007; Michael-sen & Knight, 2004; Myers & Anderson, 2008), students will not learn interactive skills simply by working in small groups for several hours a semester; interactive skills must be taught. Small group work may be structured in a way that either begins to develop or further develops needed workplace interactive skills, which will only increase students' marketability in today's global workforce.

Groups or Teams?

Levi (2007) distinguishes groups from teams based on several characteristics. He identifies a team as a subcomponent of a group; in other words, a team is always a group, but a group is not always a team. A group may vary in membership from a few to several thousand, such as membership in a local garden club or in a political organization. Generally, membership in a group is voluntary, based on some common interest or characteristic such as shared religious beliefs, shared professions, shared hobbies or shared disabilities. The group has a defined purpose, identifiable group norms, and certain benefits members derive from interacting with each other on a regular basis. Examples of groups include the American Medical Association, Boys & Girls Clubs of America, and Alcoholics Anonymous.

According to Levi (2007), a team generally consists of 4 to 20 individuals who rely heavily on one another to achieve a clearly defined outcome, therefore team members hold each other accountable. Successful teams have the autonomy, skills, and resources necessary to achieve their goal. Teams can exist for a number of reasons. A senior management team is responsible for managing and controlling the business activities of an organization. A college basketball team is primarily organized to learn effective team behavior by winning basketball games. A customer service team maintains a high level of satisfaction among its customers. A small group is defined as 3 to 15 people working together on a specific task, with the ideal group size for effective small group work being 5 to 7 (Myers & Anderson, 2008).

Because the small group description tends to fit the characteristics of a learning group more than that of a team, the term *small group* will be used throughout the remainder of this chapter. Although the literature is vague on estimating how long it takes to form a productive small group, experts in group dynamics generally agree it takes a considerable amount of time (Levi, 2007; Myers & Anderson, 2008; Tuckman & Jensen, 1977). In part, that vagueness is related to a number of variables, such as group size, diversity, clarity of the task, and probably many other variables. Group dynamics researchers frequently use stage models to study and explain group behavior and group development. Probably the most commonly known model is Tuckman and Jensen's, although there are several other development models and not all are stage models (Gesick, 1988; Marks, Mathieu, & Zaccaro, 2001; McGrath, 1990). Because of its applicability to learning groups, Tuckman and Jensen's model is briefly described as an example.

Tuckman and Jensen (1977) name five stages of development in small groups: forming, storming, norming, performing, and adjourning. The forming stage involves getting to know one another, the storming stage is characterized by conflict as members define what needs to get done and assign who needs to do it, the norming stage consists of coming to an agreement with what needs to be done and who is going to do it, the performing stage focuses on completing the work, and the adjourning stage is completion of the task and possibly ending the existence of the group.

Because of the limited amount of time students have to work together for a course, they are not likely to experience in any depth the group development process in which members are comfortable with their roles, know each other's strengths and limitations, and have learned to trust the working relationships. Therefore, it is important for teachers to structure and coach small groups in ways that promote effective behaviors while decreasing the likelihood of ineffective group behaviors. The goal for learning groups is twofold: to develop the social skills necessary to work effectively in the group and to accomplish the learning task, both of which are equally important and interdependent.

Advantages and Disadvantages of Working in Small Groups

The advantages of working in small groups include gaining multiple perspectives in accomplishing the task (increased creativity), a shared workload, access to diverse skill sets, learning through peer interaction (applied constructivism), increased risk taking (Levi, 2007), and fulfillment of social needs. Disadvantages include ineffective group behavior; increased time commitments to arrive at a consensus; a need to establish meeting times, and other group logistics; and increased time to communicate in ways other than F2F. Each of these factors are discussed in the following section.

Creating Conditions for Effective Small Group Work to Occur

By structuring the group process to accentuate the advantages and minimize the disadvantages commonly attributed to small group work, it is more likely that students will benefit from rewarding group interactions and successful group outcomes. One of the greatest advantages of small-group work is that group members learn from each other by sharing knowledge gained through formal learning and diverse life experiences. Through this process they achieve outcomes superior to those achieved by working alone. In a hybrid class, groups have the advantage of meeting F2F as well as online, giving them the opportunity to establish social presence in both environments while accomplishing the task on hand. One of the disadvantages associated with online communication, however, is the increased time it takes to receive replies, commonly referred to in the literature as *transaction costs*. Increased transaction costs may occur with telephone communication as well. To decrease transaction costs, group members may be encouraged to establish ground rules that incorporate specific deadlines for e-mail responses and discussion postings. To avoid missing telephone calls, telephone conferences may be scheduled in advance.

Early in the class, multiple opportunities exist to increase social presence in the F2F and online components of the hybrid class. In the initial F2F class, groups may be given time to interact by members' introducing themselves and by establishing ground rules, which may be posted in the course management system by a group member following the class, such as in Example 7.1. The group in this case had also listed contact information for each member, but for confidentiality reasons it has been removed. The comprehensiveness of this group's example shows that its members took their work together very seriously.

▨ Example 7.1: Learning Team Goals

Our learning team agrees to the following goals:

- ♦ To provide each member of the team with the support and help needed to ensure that the team project will obtain the highest grade.
- ♦ That each member works hard individually and collaboratively to make sure the level and quality of the teamwork is in line to help us achieve a high grade.
- ♦ That we used each person's skills and experiences to the full advantage of the team.

- Each individual's goal should be to contribute wherever possible to make this team successful. It should be a primary goal to help the team where we can and ensure a high level of quality in the work and deliverables of the team.
- Each individual's goal should be to produce quality work on behalf of the team and ensure that we work together as a group and achieve a grade reflective of our efforts and abilities.

What are potential barriers to the achievement of these goals?

- Failure of a team member to complete a portion of the work on time or of substantially less quality.
- Team member not alerting the rest of the team that work will not be completed on time.
- Timely and open communication is critical, and if not present, will constrain the team and its effectiveness.
- A team member not clearly understanding the goals or expectations of the week or the assignment.

Ground Rules

- We will need to work together via e-mail to ensure that team assignments are broken up equally and that clearly set goals and deliverables are developed with deadlines that are achievable by each member.
- A defined set of tasks and deliverables assigned to individuals that leverage their strengths. First step is to establish the individual deliverables, assign them, and set milestones for completion.
- John will be able to procure a meeting room if necessary for our discussions.
- Each week define the task and what needs to be accomplished by the end of the week and complete those assignments in a timely manner.
- Have a point person, who can be one person or the members can rotate, who is responsible for collecting the information and putting it together so that it reflects the work of a team and not that of four individuals.
- Remember the "grandma rule" when posting or sending e-mail. Treat each message as though it could be read by anyone in the world, including your grandmother.

Conflict Management

♦ We need to work well together and rely on each person to complete the assigned work on time. If a situation arises that will cause a deadline to be missed or provide lower than expected quality of work, the person in question should e-mail the team immediately so that we have time to restructure that portion of the work and still meet the homework due date.

♦ Communication is key, and if a deliverable cannot be accomplished it needs to be communicated early. We all lead hectic and unique lives that don't always align well with the demands of school and specific assignments.

♦ In addition we should use both e-mail and discussion boards to communicate with team members according to agreed upon timelines. ■

Groups may be asked to post an introduction in a discussion board. Although brief introductions may take place during the initial F2F class, the posting, which may include photos and links to websites, Facebook, and so forth, helps students associate names with background information in the posting. To role model desired group behavior, begin the discussion by posting your own introduction (Bender, 2003), which should focus on developing online social presence as well as promoting a safe and democratic learning environment. Example 7.2 is a portion of one of my introductions.

■ **Example 7.2: Introduction**

Hello & Welcome to LEDR 250,

My name is Jay Caulfield and I am an associate professor for leadership studies. The most enjoyable part of my job is teaching. I learn so much from the students in my classes and my goal is to help them become thoroughly engaged in learning. I look forward to working with all of you over the course of the semester.

My research interests are primarily in two areas. One area is in organizational behavior, specifically leadership . . .

We have three grown children and a Chi named Bruiser. She is pictured above. Our oldest son . . .

Now it is your turn. Please share with the class some things about you. What are your interests? If you are employed, what do you do? What do you hope to learn from this class? Share anything about your personal life—family and friends—that you feel comfortable in sharing. Pictures are welcome.

Best, JC ■

During the F2F class, you may use a fun activity that demonstrates the effectiveness of small groups such as, What's In the Box? For this activity, place 25 commonly known items in a box with a cover. These items can be Post-it notes, a safety pin, a toothbrush, a penny, and so on. Then ask each group of four to five individuals to circle around the box, one group at a time. Before removing the cover, tell them they have 30 seconds to study the items in the box. *They cannot talk with one another.* Immediately after 30 seconds, cover the box while the students return to their chairs and each individual lists as many items from the box he or she can remember. Everyone is then asked to report individually. In classes where I've used this activity, the highest number of items any one person has remembered thus far is 17; most remember about 10. Following individual reports, groups are asked to combine their lists. Frequently at least one group lists all items. The point of the activity is to create social presence in the F2F class while demonstrating that working together achieves a better outcome than working alone.

Finally, multimedia assignments regarding effective group behavior, such as a short video on gender differences in communication or an article regarding the emotional intelligence of groups, may be given to heighten students' awareness of the importance in developing interactive as well as intellectual skills. F2F or online role play helps students learn to provide constructive feedback regarding effective and ineffective group behaviors.

Group size affects small group performance in a number of ways. First, the larger the group, the more time it takes to arrive at group consensus and to work out group logistics (who does what when); in larger groups, it is easier for certain group members to avoid responsibilities (Levi, 2007). Although researchers believe small groups of five to seven members are ideal (Myers & Anderson, 2008), small groups in the classes I teach and have observed others teach generally do not exceed five, and in many instances have only three members. Based on the content taught and the type of students, this smaller group size may work well, as it tends to decrease transaction costs for students. With a smaller group, shirking responsibility is rarely a problem since it becomes clearly evident if it occurs.

Random assignment to a group is preferred for a number of reasons. Unfortunately, for the most part, individuals can't choose their colleagues in the workplace; therefore students need to learn to work with many different personalities. Second, letting students choose who they want to work with is often viewed by other students as inequitable because of preexisting relationships between group members. As evaluation of small-group work is often based on group interaction as well as outcomes achieved, student choice of group members could result in an inequitable situation. I make exceptions to using random assignment in two instances. The first is when random assignment results in a more homo-geneous group than would be beneficial, such as a group of all women, all engineers, or all individuals working in one department. In these cases, I repeat the random selection process until I achieve more diversity. The second instance is when a course assignment involves a significant research project. I do let students who have a similar research interest work together. Deciding how to select groups is somewhat dependent upon the criteria deemed relevant to the learning experience. In the inter-ests of maintaining a democratic learning environment, it is important, however, that students are aware of the criteria used and the rationale for using it.

Complex assignments work well for small groups in that these assign-ments require frequent interaction, which assists in group development and in completion of the learning task. The task should be sufficiently complex to warrant the extra transaction costs associated with group work. The additional time required to complete a group assignment when it could have been done faster individually will not be time well spent and is likely to annoy most busy students. Providing timely feedback to groups on process and outcome is important as it helps the group development process, leading to group cohesiveness (Michaelsen & Knight, 2004), and group cohesiveness leads to development of trust among group members (Fujishin, 2007). Peer feedback when evaluating group behavior versus criticizing an individual's personality trait or appearance increases group motivation and overall group effectiveness (Harris, 1988; Quaglieri, 1980). Example 7.3 is a simple technique devised to assist students in providing effective peer feedback following a group meeting.

▧ Example 7.3: Peer Review of Small Group Behavior

Today your behavior was especially valuable to the group when you _____

_____.

During group work, I would like you to do more of _____.

During group work, I would like you to do less of _____.

Example 7.4 is a rather complex, multistage hybrid assignment designed for a team-taught undergraduate class in small group behavior (Caulfield & Waldschmidt, 2004). Note the characteristics of the assignment and the accompanying rationale in Table 7.1. ▧

▧ Example 7.4: Small Group Problem-Solving Exercise: Devil's Advocacy

Assignment Overview

Much like dialectical inquiry, the process of devil's advocacy for problem solving and decision making relies on constructive conflict to better ensure that a high-quality decision is reached. In this approach, a solid, well-supported argument is made for a set of recommendations and then subjected to an intense evaluation by another group taking a different perspective. Those who use devil's advocacy assume that only the best plans will survive such a thorough critical review and evaluation. The following procedures will help your group prepare for a round of devil's advocacy:

1. Groups will do an initial analysis, Group 2 will serve as Group 1's devil's advocate; likewise Group 1 will serve as Group 2's devil's advocate.
2. Each group develops a plan to solve the problem, making sure to list all key assumptions and the facts that support those assumptions.
3. Group 1 then submits the recommendations and a list of the assumptions that underlie them to Group 2. Likewise, Group 2

Table 7.1   Detailed Instructions for Part 1 of This Assignment (35 points)

(Postings to Devil's Advocate are group versus individual postings.)

Group 1 Task	Group 2 Task	Completion Date	Points
You have decided to hire Mary Rogers. Using Group 1 Discussion Forum 5.1, develop the strongest possible rationale for hiring Mary Rogers. Be sure to include the use of at least one of the problem-solving techniques Levi discusses in Chapter 11 of your assigned reading. All members must participate.	You have decided to hire Bill Cook. Using Group 2 Discussion Forum 5.1, develop the strongest possible rationale for hiring Bill Cook. Be sure to include the use of one of the problem-solving techniques Levi discusses in Chapter 11 of your assigned reading. All members must participate.	Nov 5	8
Post your 500–550-word rationale to the Main Discussion Board 5.1 in order that your devil's advocate, Group 2, may evaluate your rationale. Please title your posting, "Group 1's Rationale for Hiring Mary Rogers."	Post your 500–550-word rationale to the Main Discussion Board 5.1 in order that your devil's advocate, Group 1, may evaluate your rationale. Please title your posting, "Group 2's Rationale for Hiring Bill Cook."	Nov 11	9
Try to uncover everything that is wrong with the recommendations and any inaccurate assumptions that Group 2 has made; post your 500–550-word rebuttal to Group 2 in Main Discussion Board 5.1. Please title your posting, "Group 1's Rebuttal."	Try to uncover everything that is wrong with the recommendations and any inaccurate assumptions that Group 1 has made; post your 500–550-word rebuttal to Group 1 in Main Discussion Board 5.1. Please title your posting, "Group 2's Rebuttal."	Nov 14	9
Post a 200–250-word response to Group 2's rebuttal in Main Discussion Board 5.1. Please title your posting, "Group 1's Final Remarks."	Post a 200–250 word response to Group 1's rebuttal in Main Discussion Board 5.1. Please title your posting, "Group 2's Final Remarks."	Nov 16	3
For our next F2F class, prepare a brief PowerPoint presentation (no more than 10 minutes) to present challenges that your group experienced and strategies devised to overcome those challenges.	For our next F2F class, prepare a brief PowerPoint presentation (no more than 10 minutes) to present challenges that your group experienced and strategies devised to overcome those challenges.	Nov 18	5

submits the recommendations and a list of the assumptions that underlie them to Group 1.

4. Both groups subject each other's plan to an intense evaluation, trying to uncover faulty recommendations based upon inaccurate assumptions.

5. Each group then adjusts its recommendations based on valid criticisms of its devil's advocate group.

6. Each group submits its adjustments to its devil's advocate group for final review.

Purpose of Assignment

There are two equally important purposes for this assignment. The first purpose is to assist you in successful *within* group and *between* group interaction. This is accomplished by having you reflect upon group process after concluding the actual group work. The second purpose is to help you develop skill in becoming a devil's advocate. One of the main things you need to master is the ability to *critically analyze an argument regardless of whether it supports or undermines your own position*—to be objective about argument quality. Please read the following case scenario and the assignment details that follow.

Part 1: Problem Scenario

A medium-size manufacturing company located in a medium-size city is looking for an office manager. The employees to be supervised are 15 female and 8 male computer operators, and an administrative assistant. The function of the department is to process all accounting, financial, production, and sales documents for the firm.

The current supervisor, who has been in the job for two years, has been promoted, creating the vacancy. He has practical accounting experience and an associate's degree in personnel management from a community college.

It is company policy to promote from within the firm whenever possible. Two employees have applied for the manager position, and each knows about the other's application.

Mary Rogers is currently the administrative assistant in the office. Mary is 28 years old and has been in the office for 5 years—2 as a computer operator and 3 in her present position. She is thoroughly familiar with the requirements of the department and gets along well with most of her coworkers. A few of them disapprove of her because she has been living with her boyfriend, George, on and off for 5 years; now a rumor is going around the office that she is pregnant and intends to keep the child even though she has no intention to marry George.

Mary had applied for the position of office manager at the time that the current manager was hired. She was told that he was selected over her because of his greater experience and better knowledge of personnel administration. Since then, Mary has completed an associate's degree in accounting from the local community college and is taking a course in supervisory skills there.

Mary has told her friends that if she does not get the job this time, she will probably file a discrimination complaint with the regional office of the Equal Employment Opportunity Commission.

Bill Cook is the other applicant for the office manager's job. He has a bachelor's degree in business administration from a nearby university and is 23 years of age. He has worked in the accounting department of the company for 18 months and has obtained a thorough understanding of company operations. Consequently, his line supervision experience is limited, but he has studied supervision and personnel management in his university program and is considered to have outstanding management potential.

Bill is married and the father of one child. He is a Rotary Club member and coaches Little League baseball. He considers himself to be in the center of the political spectrum and is against abortion. Bill is generally well regarded and has demonstrated an ability to get along with people. He sees the office manager's job as a significant step to a higher managerial position in which he could demonstrate his managerial potential, and therefore does not anticipate spending more than two or three years in this position.

Bill's current supervisor, Martin Jones, contacted you to tell you that Bill is currently being offered a comparable position with another firm. Jones urged you to hire Bill so he will not leave the company.

This problem scenario was retrieved from Penn State a web page that is no longer available. However, many team tools can be found at Penn State's Building Blocks for Teams website, http://tlt.its.psu.edu/suggestions/teams/student/index.html.

Part 2: Individual Small Group Reflection Essay (35 points)

To reflectively evaluate your ability to work within a small group, write an *individual* group reflection essay, using the devil's advocate assignment as context for your experience. In the essay, please address the following points:

1. Identify the strengths that each group member brought to the group, including your own (5 points);
2. Identify the challenges that each group member brought to the group, including your own (5 points);
3. Identify the challenges that the group experienced as a whole and the group strategies devised to overcome them (5 points);
4. Identify your personal challenges in working with the group and the strategies you devised to overcome them (5 points);
5. Identify the challenges faced when working with your group's devil's advocate group and the strategies your group devised to overcome them (5 points);
6. If you could repeat the group process, what is one thing you would have done differently? Explain (5 points).
7. Your essay should be written using *APA* format and should not exceed five pages, not including the title page and reference list (5 points). ■

Coaching to Curb Ineffective Group Behaviors

Commonly occurring ineffective group behaviors include conflict, domination, competition, social loafing, and group think. Applying specific small group strategies that address each of these behaviors is likely to make group work more enjoyable and more productive.

Conflict. Conflict may be constructive or destructive, and groups experiencing no conflict have most likely never entered the storming stage of group development (Tuckman & Jensen, 1977). Although it produces anxiety, conflict that centers on the evaluation of ideas can be very constructive, adding to the quality of decision making (Levi, 2007; Myers & Anderson, 2008). Conflict that is personally attacking, however, is destructive and can permanently damage group cohesiveness. Coaching behaviors modeled by the teacher may lessen the likelihood of destructive conflict. Treating everyone with respect, creating a democratic classroom environment, evaluating ideas expressed during F2F and online discussions rather than evaluating the individual expressing them, and addressing any disrespectful behavior immediately will help group members understand the behaviors expected of them.

Domination. Domination by one or more group members lessens the likelihood of equal participation. A major strength of group work is the diversity of thought and shared experiences of each member, but the advantage becomes nonexistent if some members never have an opportunity to be heard, which may also lead to a mentality called *group think*, a term coined by social psychologist Janis (1972) who said that when the desire to avoid conflict is greater than the desire to make good decisions, group think may become a problem. Ways to control domination and potential group think include establishing, defining, and rotating group member roles, such as leader, time keeper, and note taker. Another tactic is to encourage students to search the literature for multiple views on any topic being studied. Finally, the group may assign the devil's advocate role to one of the members during each discussion.

Competition. Competition is prevalent in individualistic cultures such as that of the United States and Australia (Hofstede, 2007). In fact, external competition is the driver for many economic systems. Competitors view situations as an opportunity to win. The individual goal of winning becomes more important than any of the group's goals. The difficulty with this type of thinking in a group is that if a competitive group member wins, other group members may lose the opportunity to collaborate with the entire group to achieve stellar outcomes. Competition within a group leads to a lack of group cohesiveness (Levi, 2007), which ultimately destroys trust and the overall effectiveness of small group work. One of the most effective ways to decrease the likelihood of internal competition is to make it clear to the group from the onset that group work will be evaluated as a group versus individually, emphasizing that the advantage of group work is the diversity of skills and experiences that lead to achieving superior outcomes. Another strategy to control internal competitiveness is to require peer evaluation and to use that evaluation to determine a portion of each student's course grade.

Social loafing. Social loafing occurs when a member lets others in the group do the work and refrains from putting forth one's best effort (Sexton, 2008). Social loafing is more common within individualistic cultures where the needs of the individual often take precedence over the needs of the group (Zorn & Tompson, 2002). A number of strategies may be employed to lessen the likelihood of social loafing. The most effective one is to define every group member's role and to clearly delegate a specific responsibility to each group member (Sexton, 2008). Other strategies include keeping the size of the group small enough so the workload makes social loafing apparent. It can then be addressed through peer evaluation. Based on extrinsic motivation, peer review that affects an individual's grade may be very effective in curtailing social loafing. Finally, explaining the value of the assignment is likely to increase interest, thereby decreasing the likelihood of social loafing.

When social loafing is suspected by the teacher, group members may be requested to list their contributions to a project and sign the list, indicating agreement with every group member's stated contribution. If it is discovered a group member contributed nothing, in addition to the impact of peer review, the teacher can take appropriate action, including assigning another project to social loafers who have done minimal or no work on their own.

Summary

The purpose of this chapter is to identify the advantages and disadvantages of small group work as a learning strategy when used in hybrid class design. I have used small groups extensively in my teaching and my experience has been decidedly positive. I would argue that the benefits of group work, especially related to improved social interaction skills, are well worth the risks. Small group work applies constructivist and experiential learning theory in that group interaction expands mental models and invites sharing experiences in the context of the course content. Hybrid course design invites observation and evaluation of online group process as well as group outcomes. As with any positive learning strategy, there are negative aspects as well. However, being aware of ineffective small group behaviors and proactively addressing them through coaching while appropriately structuring small groups is likely to decrease their occurrence.

CHAPTER EIGHT

MEETING STUDENT EXPECTATIONS

> We can only serve that to which we are pro-
> foundly connected, that which we are willing
> to touch.
>
> —Rachel Naomi Remen (2006, para. 5)

S TUDENTS, LIKE TEACHERS, are busy people. Historically, one of
the primary characteristics in defining traditional college students
has been age; more specifically, Wirt et al. (2002) define traditional
students as those being 18–24 years of age. In the United States, the
majority of traditional students have been from white middle- or upper-
class families, and in the past many have had the luxury of living in a
dorm on campus or in nearby housing while focusing primarily on their
education. However, based upon data from the National Center for Education Statistics (NCES; Wirt et al., 2002), 43% of college students are
now older than 24, and the percentage of older students is projected to
continue to increase. According to data from NCES 75% of students are
nontraditional students, meeting one or more of the following
characteristics:

- did not enroll in college during the same year as graduating from
  high school
- enrolled part-time for at least part of the academic year
- worked 35 or more hours per week
- were classified as financially independent as defined by federal
  financial aid eligibility criteria

♦ have one or more dependents other than a spouse
♦ are single with one or more children
♦ lack a high school diploma

Wirt et al. (2002) report that 56% of those attending colleges today are women, about 33% of all college students are minorities, and 80% of college students are employed. This increase in nontraditional students means an increase in students who are working full-time, are married, and parenting while attending college. Students are very busy people, which is one reason a hybrid course design is preferable to many of today's college students (Boyle, Bradley, Chalk, Jones, & Pickard, 2003; Cottrell & Robinson, 2003).

Multigenerational Classrooms

The increasing age span of college students means that the classroom of today is likely to comprise traditionalists, baby boomers, Gen Xers, and millenniums. Depending upon the source, traditionalists are 64 to 82 years old, baby boomers are 45 to 63 years old, Gen Xers are 33 to 44 years old, and millenniums are 11 to 32 years old (Kane, 2009). For each of these generations, the characteristics and values differ. In creating functionally effective classrooms, teachers and students benefit from being familiar with these multigenerational differences, just as managers do in the workplace when interested in optimizing the productivity of their workers. In other words, teachers need to know their learners just as employers need to know their workers.

Table 8.1 lists traits and values of the different generations and relates them to likely preferences in learning environments. As reported in a study by NCES (1997), the average age of full-time faculty in 1997 was 48, which means most faculty today are baby boomers while the majority of college students are Gen Xers and millenniums, and to a lesser degree, baby boomers and traditionalists. Thus, teachers need to understand how to navigate across generations in their classrooms.

If an instructor is willing to be flexible and variable with course design and demonstrate sensitivity to different generational preferences in the hybrid classroom, many of the students may be satisfied most of the time. Disparity in learning preferences were quite apparent in a study (Caulfield, 2010) in which graduate students enrolled in seven hybrid

Table 8.1   Generational Differences as Related to Learning Preferences

	Traits	Learning Preferences
Traditionalists Age 64–82	Hard working, loyal, submissive, and tech challenged; value safety, security, consistency, conformity, hierarchical structure, and F2F communication.	Comfortable with lecture-based classes and F2F communication in a structured classroom environment. Will do work assigned without complaining. May not be comfortable with or like to engage in web-based education.
Baby Boomers Age 45–63	Workcentric, define themselves by their position, motivated by money and power, not afraid of confrontation, tech friendly, independent, confident, goal oriented, and competitive; value lifelong learning, want to make a difference in the world, see retirement as a new career geared toward giving back to the community.	Comfortable with online learning and accessing information on the Internet. Like to engage in provocative discussions. Work hard to achieve academic success. Not afraid to learn independently and informally by visiting websites and participating in blogs. Tend to view the teacher as a facilitator of learning rather than an expert.
Gen Xers Age 33–44	Formally educated (60% attended college), self-reliant, individualistic, tech competent, and adaptable to alternative lifestyles; accept diversity; dislike authority and structure; value independence, freedom, responsibility, flexibility, and humor at work; environmentally friendly; value work-life balance.	Comfortable with online education based on the flexibility and the independence it provides. Comfortable in multicultural classrooms. Teacher is viewed as a facilitator of learning. To achieve or maintain work-life balance, will expect every learning task to have recognizable value. May expect teachers to lighten the workload based upon valuing work-life balance.
Millenniums Age 11–32	Tech savvy, family centric, confident, ambitious, achievement oriented, team oriented, celebrate diversity, and are not afraid to question authority. Value new challenges, meaningful work, a green environment, team relationships, frequent affirmation, and reassurance.	Online learning is not perceived as something extraordinary; rather online learning is perceived as a useful commodity to enhance learning. Comfortable in multicultural classrooms. Excellent customer service from the institution as well as its teachers is an expectation. Tech competence is expected at the institutional and instructional levels and may be a critical factor in making enrollment choices.

classes were asked to identify three learning tasks that were the most engaging and three learning tasks that were the least engaging. The learning tasks some students found most engaging were the ones others found least engaging. While some of those differences may have related to the content itself, it was clear by what students said that many of those differences related to generational preferences. Awareness of the student demographic, understanding learning preferences, and offering learning tasks that vary in structure may help engage diverse students in learning.

Being respectful of students' time and somewhat flexible with scheduling appointments also demonstrates an understanding of diverse needs. While earning my doctorate I was working an average of 50 hours a week and parenting three children. One of the professors who facilitated an independent study I was doing, repeatedly asked me to leave my job in the early afternoon to meet with her; it was a very bad time for me to leave the office, and I made her aware of it. Nonetheless the professor insisted on consistently meeting at this time, and as my goal was to get through the learning experience and achieve my targeted graduation date, I complied. Each time I would arrive on time, only to sit outside her office waiting at least 20 minutes while she conducted personal business on the phone, including discussing with her interior designer the drapes she wanted in her living room, scheduling routine doctor's appointments, and so on—all very audible to me directly outside her office in plain view of her. This particular professor was convinced that successful doctoral students needed to be full-time students who were not employed full-time, and she made this very clear to me. The problem with this type of thinking today, however, is that it excludes many students from doctoral work. Based on her behavior, I made a point of not recommending her as a teacher to any of my full-time working colleagues, which included nearly everyone in the program. More important, however, her behavior taught me to be respectful of my future students' time. Again, today's students are very busy people.

Multicultural Classrooms

Having a multicultural classroom adds value to discussions and the overall learning experience. However, it also means that teachers must make some thoughtful decisions regarding how to successfully engage multicultural learners. According to Brookfield (2006):

Contemporary teachers now work in truly multicultural classrooms. Newly arrived immigrant groups, communities of color that have been part of this country for centuries but rarely seen as college-level material, indigenous peoples that traditionally have been excluded from higher education, students for whom English is a second or third foreign language—all are now present in college classrooms in ever greater numbers. (p. 154)

Assessing work in multicultural classrooms also presents a challenge in that English is often not a first language, and the discussion continues among teachers on whether focusing on assessing writing in standard English diminishes the ability of multicultural students to freely express themselves. This topic is of particular importance in a hybrid or totally online class because much of the dialogue is written. However, the discomfort international students experience related to differences in pronunciation, cultural views on active learning, perspectives on participation in discussion, perceptions of the role of the teacher and the student, and the use of colloquialisms and unfamiliar analogies is detrimental to effective verbal and written communication. Stereotyping, or categorizing people based on false perceptions, may also severely damage learning environments. De Vita (2000) wrote, "Of the identified barriers to intercultural communication (culture-specific non-verbal cues, faulty attributions, perceptual biases, etc.), stereotyping is undoubtedly the one which, in the educational context, holds the most destructive connotations" (p. 169).

When creating effective multicultural classrooms, teachers and students must be receptive, respectful, and always ready to listen to and learn about cultures different from their own. When teachers model these behaviors, which are foundational to creating a democratic and safe learning environment where trusting relationships are encouraged, the likelihood of having an engaging learning experience for all students is increased. My personal fear in this regard is my own ignorance, which could cause me to offend a student without my knowledge or intent. Thus, in multicultural classes, I often begin by telling students that through social interaction we will learn to better understand and appreciate multicultural perspectives and sensitivities, but I emphasize that communication and multicultural knowledge is far from perfect, and there may be times when misunderstandings or unintentional biases may occur. I further stress to students that the only way to improve multicultural understanding is to identify and explore those biases as they occur through continued thoughtful and respectful dialogue. To my knowledge, behaving this way has generally worked as students have not told me otherwise; however, I realize that students may choose not to tell me otherwise. Therefore I continually reflect upon what may work best based on my teaching style, classroom demographics, the hybrid nature of the course, and my assessment of students' comfort level with certain aspects of multicultural diversity. What I have found to be true for the most part is that Gen Xers and millenniums welcome multicultural environments and are quite comfortable in multicultural classrooms, which is in agreement with the literature (see Table 8.1). According to Miller (1992):

> What the multicultural classroom needs ultimately are new paradigms that negotiate cultural transactions rather than cultural assimilation. What students tell us can and probably must be fundamental to how- and whether-these transactions occur. (p. 10)

Hybrid course designs are advantageous to multicultural classrooms in a number of ways. First, when designed as intended, they represent active teaching and learning environments. Lengthy lectures, which may be difficult for students when English is a secondary language, are not a predominant learning tool. Second, the focus on student-to-content interaction as an initial step in the learning process (see Figure 8.1) serves as a form of rehearsal whereby international students whose first language is not English have an opportunity to engage in internal dialogue in preparation for future dialogue with others. Third, small group work is a major part of many hybrid course designs, which provides a more relaxed environment for dialogue to occur, again especially for those students who do not speak English as a first language. Finally, because written dialogue is often another form of rehearsal prior to dialogue in the F2F classroom, international students may read the online work of colleagues in a nonthreatening environment and benefit from having the time to think about the different perspectives expressed, especially in regard to comparing and contrasting cultural norms, before engaging in F2F classroom discussion.

Interdisciplinary Classrooms

The interdisciplinary nature of many classrooms adds yet another dimension of diversity to the learning experience. Certain degrees in areas such

Figure 8.1   Continuous Learning Cycle

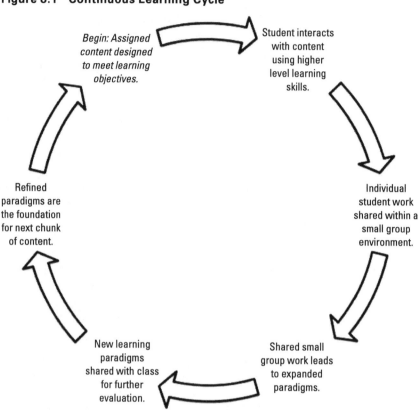

as dispute resolution, leadership, and business draw professional students from varied disciplines. As students from many professions approach the same situation in different ways, this dimension of diversity, which becomes even more apparent in active learning environments, adds value to learning experiences. For example, the following statements from an online discussion in a leadership and ethics class that I taught were made by a number of professionals from different fields when asked whether a photojournalist should put down the camera and intervene when viewing an atrocity involving terminating a human life.

> Journalist: How can I save a life *and* tell the story? Does the story need to be told exclusively by photos? Perhaps a first-person eyewitness account could be just as riveting. A picture may be worth a 1,000 words

but is it worth a life? In essence, I wonder if there was a way to meet both goals.

Community worker: I simply cannot imagine sitting on the sidelines and watching someone die for the sake of my job.

Law enforcement officer: A gang fight or shooting does not have to be filmed to know that it happens and that it is not right and if it is going on, the moral thing is to try to stop it. In this case, my job as journalist has been discarded in favor of my higher moral responsibility to save human life.

Management professional: I think it is important to evaluate who is affected and what is the global impact of the decision. In other words, who is injured? Is it possible more are injured by not taking the photo? I believe there might be scenarios where this is true.

Clergyman: Our inaction to prevent evil in our own little ways becomes the cause for the triumph of evil.

Health care professional: What a photographer is prepared to do and what he actually does in a crisis is entirely different. We are human after all, not robots taking pictures without feeling or emotion.

I seriously doubt whether these different approaches to the same scenario would have been expressed in a classroom where all individuals were photojournalists or law enforcement professionals or health care professionals. The diverse ethical views we share are likely to influence the professions we choose. With the emergence of multidisciplinary work groups in global work environments, including multicultural and intergenerational classrooms, having the knowledge and skill to better understand interdisciplinary and intergenerational viewpoints may lead to a more collaborative workforce and a more collaborative global society as a whole.

Meeting Student Expectations by Paying Attention to Logistics

Although being mindful of logistics in your hybrid course may be a bit easier to manage than intergenerational and multicultural classrooms, logistics are nonetheless very important to student satisfaction as indicated by the following comments taken from student course evaluations.

The instructor was well organized and presented clear expectations early on.

The instructor helped by breaking down the course content into "do-able" chunks.

Too many assignments at the beginning and end of the course made the workload uneven, adding to my stress.

For the purposes of the remainder of the chapter, it is assumed that a hybrid course is hosted by a course management system, a website accessible to students enrolled in the class that hosts course content (see Chapter 9, pp. 144–146, for further discussion on course management systems).

Class Structure

The demographics of the class play a role in structuring F2F and online work. For example, most of the professional graduate students I teach work full-time jobs that require frequent travel. What I have learned from them is to avoid requiring multiple postings on a discussion board within one week, as it is difficult to accomplish this when being on the road or in the air. I have also learned from them that they prefer to do content-to-content interaction outside the classroom followed by in-depth student-to-student interaction and student-to-teacher interaction during the F2F classroom, which is how I design most of my hybrid assignments now.

In developing a hybrid design, think of hybrid assignments as a circular approach to learning as illustrated in Figure 8.1. The cycle is repetitive throughout the course, and for that matter, throughout the program. New learnings are derived from those that have already occurred. Each stage of the learning cycle may occur online or F2F or in both environments, depending upon the characteristics of the class, many of which were discussed in Chapter 4.

Workload

As mentioned earlier, workload can be a big problem in a hybrid class when the teacher has created a course that is unmanageable because of too much content. This leads to a lack of time to discuss all the work completed by students. Being an overachiever is a common trait of boomers. Unfortunately, that may negatively affect a boomer's course design especially for Gen Xers and millenniums who value work-life balance. Moreover, unreasonable workloads may lead to superficial learning. As discussed in Chapter 4, students learn more effectively through reflective practice requiring higher cognitive skills, which often requires social interaction. Students will be unable to learn in meaningful ways if they are overwhelmed with content. Working on designing classes with less content may be challenging for teachers because knowing the problem exists does not make it easy to rectify. Deciding what content should be studied to meet program outcomes and what can reasonably be achieved by students requires extensive thought.

Also, workload may be a student-perceived problem in a hybrid class because of the number of assignments. Generally, hybrid course design depends on *chunking* (breaking down into smaller assignments) smaller doable bits of learning instead of constructing two or three lengthy assignments. For example, short reflective essays can prepare students for F2F discussion. Student perception, however, equates the *number* of assignments with the *amount of work* required for the class. To illustrate, a graduate hybrid course may require a two- to three-page essay each week and a 12- to 15-page paper in lieu of a final exam. This means about 50 pages of written work for a full semester graduate course. However, because of the frequency of writing assignments, students perceive the workload to be excessive, which leads to the next topic of discussion.

Stating Expectations Clearly

Most individuals are uncomfortable with ambiguity because it is likely to decrease the ability to plan, unexpectedly disrupting set schedules and making life more hectic. Students are no different. Thus, explaining the rhythm of a hybrid course during the initial F2F class is very important. Students enrolled in a hybrid course for the first time often feel disoriented for the initial three or four weeks of the semester. Scheduling the F2F classes on the same day of the week is helpful. Although the syllabus may be extensive, listing program outcomes, student learning objectives, course expectations, course calendar, and the semester's assignments with due dates, students are often still confused. They don't know what questions to ask. They see the number of assignments on the course calendar and they become overwhelmed. They may be unfamiliar with the course management system. For all these reasons, clearly explaining the assignments and the flow of the F2F and online learning tasks is paramount. For visual learners, a diagram similar to the one in Figure 8.2 may be helpful in understanding the rhythms of a few assignments.

Figure 8.2   Rhythms of Two Hybrid Assignments

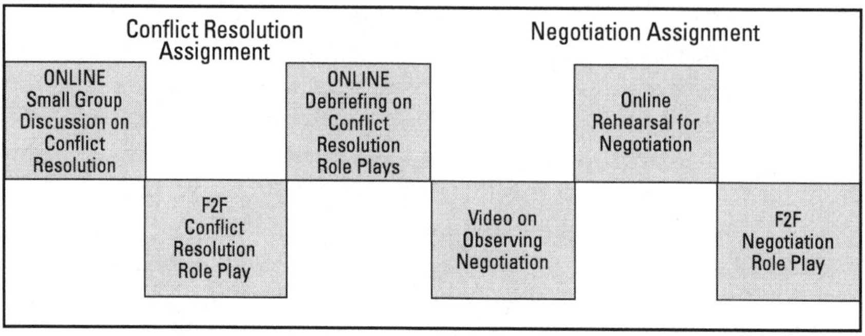

Conflict Resolution Assignment		Negotiation Assignment		
ONLINE Small Group Discussion on Conflict Resolution		ONLINE Debriefing on Conflict Resolution Role Plays		Online Rehearsal for Negotiation
	F2F Conflict Resolution Role Play		Video on Observing Negotiation		F2F Negotiation Role Play

Duplication of important information is good. For example, the course calendar gives discussion posting due dates. At the discussion site, the due date is repeated. Major assignments are explained at the beginning of the class, and as the class progresses, references to those assignments are made repeatedly. Announcements are posted on the course website and e-mailed to students.

At the completion of a hybrid course, asking students to post a list of recommendations may be helpful to future students. The recommendations may be posted at the course website the next time the course is offered. According to student feedback, the listing has been very helpful in understanding course expectations.

Standardized Display of Content

Using a standardized format or template is helpful for students to locate information on the course's website. For every discussion assignment I post, I use a picture related to the content (see Figure 8.3). The picture is easier to locate when scrolling through discussion forums than text alone. The discussion assignment has a coding that I explain to students. The letter *D* indicates a discussion assignment, the numeral 3 indicates Week 3 of the course, and the numeral 1 indicates the first discussion assignment for Week 3. Next the title is listed, followed by a set of parentheses with the due date for the posting and the number of points associated with it. After that is the salutation, the assignment, and the closing. Every discussion assignment has this same format.

Figure 8.3: Why Work-Out Works: The Underlying Principles

Image from http://office.microsoft.com/en-us/images/results.aspx?qu = exercising&origin = FX10 1741979#pg:2

■ Example 8.1: Why Workout Works

D.3.1 Why Workout Works: The Underlying Principles (Posting due Tues, July 21 by 11:59 p.m., CST; 50 points)

Folks,

OK. In Ulrich, Kerr, and Ashkenas's article, they aren't exactly talking about a physical workout, but there are certainly several similarities between a physical workout and the process described in their article.

Identify a professional situation you believe would benefit from a workout. Take leadership of the situation and describe how you would conduct the workout, applying the principles that Ulrich and colleagues describe in their article. Post to this forum your 2- to 3-page essays in the form of a Word document, using *APA* formatting. Be prepared to discuss your work during our next F2F class.

Best, JC ■

Standardized Request for Submissions of Assignments

In addition to using templates for assignments, a standard request for submission is also helpful. For instance, students in my classes know that all short essay assignments should be submitted in *APA* format and posted to the appropriate discussion forum. I remind them of this in the instructions (duplication is good). Making due dates standard also helps students remain oriented to the flow of the class. For example, if the F2F class meets on Wednesday evenings, then discussion assignments in preparation for that class are always due by 11:59 pm on Tuesday evenings.

Decide on How to Organize Your Course Website and Stick With It

To help students locate information quickly, keep the course site organized. Develop a system that works and stick with it. The system will be somewhat dependent on the course management system's functionality. For organizing, modules may be used to categorize content and assignments. A module may have a predetermined length, such as one week. Thus, students may go to the module and know that all needed media for that week is listed there. Another way of organizing a course is by grouping certain types of media. For example, all rubrics used for the course may be listed in one area of the site. In any case, the way the course site is organized and the rationale for doing so should be explained to students during the first F2F class. Example 8.2 illustrates the modular method of organizing course content. Content listed for each course appears in the course management system as a hyperlink, making the materials immediately accessible to students.

Example 8.2: Modular Approach to Organizing Course Content

Module 1. Work for January 19th Class

i. Researcher Predilections—Due January 24th by 8 pm CST
ii. Guide to Reading Research Articles

Module 2. Work and Readings for January 26th
i.   Interviewing in Qualitative Research
ii. Literature Review Handout from NC@Chapel Hill
iii. Critical Thinking and Transferability–An example literature review

Module 3. Module 3 Readings for Feb 2nd
i.   Writing Qualitative Research

Example 8.3 illustrates the categorical method of organizing course content. Again, the hyperlinks make the content available to students immediately. Readings have been hyperlinked to the library's electronic reserves system.

▇ Example 8.3: Categorical Approach to Organizing Course Content

Getting Started Module
- ◆ Syllabus, class calendar, and schedule of assignments
- ◆ Purdue's page on *APA* format
- ◆ Example of a well-written case analysis
- ◆ Example of a well-written fictional case

Rubrics for Assignments
- ◆ Rubric for case analysis
- ◆ Rubric for discussions
- ◆ Rubric for fictional case study

Course Readings to Supplement Text
- ◆ The place of the heart in Lonergan's Ethics
- ◆ Nash and ethics without the sermon
- ◆ Bandura and selective moral disengagement

Slides for Mini Lectures
- ◆ Case analysis
- ◆ Behavior modification
- ◆ Cognitive dissonance ▇

Timely Feedback on Work

Regardless of the level of the student or the mode of course delivery, andragogical and pedagogical principles indicate that timely feedback is very important to students. Unfortunately, teachers are also busy people and this sometimes causes a conflict in priorities. As mentioned earlier, students find it very frustrating to receive feedback on an initial assignment following submission of another similar assignment. It is particularly important to provide timely feedback (maximum within 1 week of submission) on the initial 3 weeks of hybrid assignments, so that students understand course expectations. While providing timely feedback to students for the duration of the course is an important goal, unexpected demands on teachers' time may delay feedback; communicating expected delays to students may help.

Sometimes a major project for a large class may take longer to assess. In these instances, being able to provide feedback for a smaller portion of the work (chunking the assignment) may help students get a better sense of whether they are meeting expectations, and it may help teachers provide more timely feedback. For example, one of my classes requires a critical literature review of 12 empirical research articles; students may choose the topic within the context of their professional interests. First I ask the students to post the research topic, and I post feedback within one week regarding their topic selection. Next I ask them to post their research question, giving them feedback on their questions within 1 week and discussing them further during the following F2F class. Then they are requested to post a critical review of two studies, for which they receive timely formative feedback from me. Finally, they submit the entire critical literature review. Providing feedback on the entire review generally will not occur within 1 week. Having said that, based on the feedback students have already received, they should have a very good idea of what is expected.

Accessibility

Students need to know when the teacher is available for questions and for F2F meetings; that information that may be listed in the syllabus. Second, students need to know where and when they can receive technical support; the syllabus and the course site may list the type of technical support available and the hours. Letting students know how long a delay they may expect when sending e-mail messages is helpful. I generally tell students they should receive a response to e-mail messages within 24 hours; I also ask students to send the e-mail to me again if I have not responded within 24 hours. For the most part, the system works. You will need to develop a system that works well for you and your students and communicate that system to them.

Use Simple Technology That Consistently Works

Nothing is more frustrating to students than not being able to access course materials because of failed technology. This is especially true when immediate technical support is unavailable. When 24-hour tech support is unavailable to students, the technology *must* be simple and *must* be dependable (see Chapter 9 for more on technology).

Conclusion

Student expectations in hybrid courses are not much different from those in traditional F2F courses or fully online courses. Students want and deserve to be treated with respect; they want and deserve to be treated fairly. Most students want the opportunity to safely express their views and to know they are being heard in a nonjudgmental environment, they want prompt responses to their questions and concerns, they want to access course content conveniently, they want timely feedback, and they want the technology to work. When teachers are able to meet students' needs, the time invested in doing so results in less time dealing with frustrated students, and the satisfaction in teaching an effective hybrid course is in itself significantly rewarding.

CHAPTER NINE

ENHANCING TEACHING THROUGH THE USE OF TECHNOLOGY

> I never use technology that is smarter than I am.
>
> —Alan Aycock, University of Wisconsin–Milwaukee (personal communication, 2002)

TECHNOLOGY IS ONE OF THE BEST TOOLS we have to enhance teaching, and it is especially valuable in hybrid teaching and learning environments. It is highly likely that the Internet will go down in history as the most useful innovation of the past century. Yet learning how to use new technological devices and software that is continuously updated and often becomes obsolete may take an inordinate amount of time, and teaching students how to use technology takes even more time. When technology fails because of user error, incompatibilities, or other reasons, even more time is lost. Thus, making technology choices wisely is one of the most important skills needed in creating effective and efficient hybrid courses.

It is interesting to note that of the 15 faculty members I interviewed for this book, all expert hybrid or online teachers, every one of them reported they routinely use no more than a handful of fairly common technologies when designing and teaching their courses. They select their technological tools carefully and they continue to use them for as long as technology or their university permits. The 11 students interviewed named only a few technologies used in their classes as well. Consider that an hour spent learning new technology is an hour that could be spent in acquiring new knowledge in your discipline. This holds equally true for students. Choosing technologies that are time savers as well as effective teaching and learning tools means more time to attend to other tasks.

The primary purpose of this chapter is to provide user-friendly information about frequently used categories of technologies that are likely to be around for a while. For experienced hybrid teachers, these technologies have the capabilities of enhancing hybrid teaching and learning environments.

The chapter contains a brief overview of specific types of technologies that faculty and students interviewed used most frequently. Pedagogy related to the technology is also discussed and is indirectly evident in many of the examples provided. Instructions on how to use the various technologies are found on the websites provided. In some instances, specific products are mentioned as examples; however, the information contained in this chapter is not intended to promote any specific product.

Accessing Information Through Library Databases and Search Engines

The most commonly used technologies are search engines and databases. The challenge in teaching students how to access high-quality information from databases and search engines is a significant one. According to Yannie (2000), a reference librarian, "The prevailing mindset must be changed from searching for an easier, better means of information retrieval, to finding better material, and the gaining of a better understanding of that material" (p. 43). Most students entering college do not know how to use technology to create an effective literature review on a specific topic, and fewer still know how to evaluate the quality of the information they do find. Because an important goal of hybrid teaching and learning is to create a highly active and interactive student-centered teaching and learning environment, learning how to access, evaluate, and share relevant high-quality information is an extremely important skill for students to learn; one that will help them become more effective learners long after they graduate. Yet Head and Eisenberg (2010) analyzed 191 handouts voluntarily submitted by faculty from colleges and universities in the United States and reported the following: "Few of the handouts (14%) that directed students to use the library's online scholarly research databases (such as those provided by EBSCO, JSTOR, or ProQuest) specified which database to use by vendor or file name from the hundreds that tend to be available" (p. 3). Reference librarians are a critical resource for assisting students in learning how to search and retrieve information. Teachers are critical resources for assisting students in evaluating, processing, and sharing information. When working with reference librarians, providing information that will assist them in helping students access the information needed to complete a particular assignment is often beneficial. For example, I sent the following message to the reference librarian designated to assist the students with a discussion assignment titled, "What Makes a Theory a Theory?" The assignment follows the message.

Hello Sue,

I so appreciate your helping students with this "theory" assignment as most of them find it challenging to access and to retrieve relevant information. Mostly, I think this relates to their unfamiliarity with graduate school (this is generally their first course), their unfamiliarity with the library, with *APA* formatting, with D2L and with my expectations for the assignment—though I try to make them as clear as I can when we discuss the assignment during class.

The assignment's purpose is threefold. First students should learn to understand the meaning of *theory* from a scientific perspective. Secondly, students should learn the *context of theory* within their respective disciplines and within the discipline of leadership—which crosses most every other discipline. Finally, students should begin to learn how to use the library, including the databases and the consulting services available to them. I have attached a few completed assignments that I consider good examples, and I've attached the rubric for this assignment as well. Below is the assignment, itself. Please don't hesitate to contact me with any questions you may have regarding any of these materials. Again, thank you for assisting students with this assignment.

Best, JC

D.2.1 What Makes a Theory a Theory? (Posting due Tues, Feb 2; 50 points)
Hi Folks,

Throughout this course, we will be studying leadership theory. Before we begin our study of leadership theory, however, we need to have a common understanding of the qualities of good theory, in general. *In other words, what characteristics does an effective theory generally possess?* Most of you have probably not thought much about the word "theory" in this context previously. Oftentimes we use the word "theory" in an informal way. For instance, if someone asks us a question, we may say, "I have a theory about that." Used in this context, theory may mean we have a "hunch" about something. However, for this assignment, we want to use the word "theory" in a scientific context.

To answer the question, "What are the qualities of an effective theory?" you will need to do a literature search using the library's electronic databases. In a Word document submitted as an attachment to this discussion forum, please post a scholarly response to the question, "What are the qualities of an effective theory?" with a *minimum of three credible references*. APA formatting should be used for this assignment. When I use the terminology "scholarly response," it means that you need to seek the help of outside references to complete the assignment. Examples of credible resources include peer-reviewed journals; well-referenced texts; newspapers such as the *New York Times* or the *Business Journal*; or magazines such as *Newsweek, Forbes,* or *National Geographic*. For this assignment, credible resources would *not* include such references as *Wikipedia* or *People Magazine*. Your response should minimally include *five* qualities that good theory possesses. On average, responses should be 2–3 pages, not counting the title page or reference list.

Best, JC

To my surprise and delight, a short time after the librarian received my message, I received a link to a learning object (electronic bits of information used to assist learning) the librarian created to assist students in locating resources for the assignment. The learning object is accessible at http://libguides.marquette.edu/LEDR6000theory.

Another way to assist students in learning how to do effective searches is by holding a F2F class in a library conference room or computer lab and inviting a reference librarian to be a guest presenter. The librarian can demonstrate searches on specific topics and explain additional library resources available to students. Students have the opportunity to ask questions specific to assignments they may be working on or they may ask questions about library resources in general.

A number of helpful tools are available to assist students in learning how to evaluate the quality and relevancy of a reference, including websites, articles, books, and simulations. Although not an exhaustive listing, the following are several good and currently available resources:

1. *How to Evaluate the Information Sources You Find*, Cornell University Library, http://www.library.cornell.edu/olinuris/ref/research/evaluate.html (Engle, 2008)

2. *Critically Analyzing Information Sources*, Cornell University Library, http://www.library.cornell.edu/olinuris/ref/research/skill 26.htm (Ormondroyd, Engle, & Cosgrave, 2009)
3. *How to Evaluate Research Materials After You Find Them*, University of Arkansas Library, http://www.uark.edu/libinfo/refdept/ instruction/evaluation.html
4. *Evaluate Web Pages*, Widener University, Wolfgram Memorial Library, a tutorial and exercise, http://www.widener.edu/libraries/ wolfgram/evaluate
5. *Evaluating Research in Academic Journals: A Practical Guide to Realistic Evaluation* (Pyrczak, 2008)

Course Management Systems

A course management system (CMS) is somewhat analogous to thousands of houses that look identical from the outside, but are furnished differently in the inside. In this analogy, the external construction is the CMS template that provides the framework for the internal furnishings, or course content, for the thousands of different courses in the CMS. Along with a course syllabus and schedule of assignments, that content may include links to blogs, simulations, readings, discussion forums, video clips, podcasts, and other websites. CMSs have changed dramatically over the past decade, becoming more and more versatile. Since I began teaching hybrid courses over 11 years ago, I've used five different CMSs.

The pros of CMSs include ease of use and access to course materials in any place and at any time as long as Internet access is available. Most CMSs provide a fair amount of flexibility in creating course sites and most provide somewhat standard functionality, such as places to upload files for students and teachers, a discussion area, a quiz area, and a grade book. The unfortunate thing about CMSs is that teachers usually don't have much control over CMS selection. When the university decides to change its CMS because of price, support issues, availability of new products, and so on, teachers have little control over that decision either. Because CMSs are generally incompatible with one another, course sites will likely need to be rebuilt if the CMS changes. For that reason, it is very important to maintain electronic folders with all course content on a hard drive, which will greatly reduce the time it takes to rebuild a course site in another CMS. What's more, it provides immediate access to materials, should the CMS become dysfunctional for any period of time.

Another important consideration is that teachers are subject to the competency or incompetency of the CMS administrator and to the service philosophy of the information technology department and of the institution in general. Whatever policies and practices the CMS administrator and the institution have in place are what teachers are forced to abide by. The university's level of commitment to online learning and its comfort with risk greatly influences these factors. I have had wonderful experiences with administrators who give faculty freedom over who enters their course sites as well as free access to virtually all the functionality the CMS has to offer. And, unfortunately, I have worked with CMS administrators who restrict access to such a degree it is impossible to take full advantage of a CMS. This is particularly problematic when technical support is limited or not immediately available. Immediate tech support demands a highly skilled and well-functioning technical support staff, which requires a significant resource commitment from the university. According to e-learning research (Kaleta, Skibba, & Joosten, 2007; Ross & Gage, 2006; Wiesenmayer, Kupczynski, & Ice, 2008), accessibility to effective technical support for faculty and students is vital to the success of online programming.

Functions vary somewhat with the type of CMS. However, most have an area where the instructor may post the files needed for the course, such as the syllabus, calendar, rubrics, and examples of past students' work. Other common CMS functions include an asynchronous discussion area; a quiz function that generally has an array of question formats, including essay formats; a survey function with an anonymous response feature; an electronic drop box where students may upload an assignment in a particular file format; an area for journaling; a synchronous chat function; a small group function that permits breaking students into small groups for small group work, reporting group grades, providing group feedback and group discussions; giving them a place to upload portfolio contents; a place to store links to websites and other learning objects, such as simulations or YouTube productions; and a grade book where grades and individual and group feedback may be provided specifically to each assignment. Some of these functions can be somewhat duplicative, which provide opportunities to meet individual preferences. For instance, a student may upload a file to the discussion area as well as to the drop box. It is likely that others having access to the discussion area can review the student's work, but generally only the instructor may review the work that is sent to the dropbox. As long as Internet access is available and the server maintaining the CMS is functioning, the student and the instructor have access to all CMS functions 24/7.

Asynchronous Discussion Boards

Asynchronous discussion boards are highly versatile teaching tools that are a part of most every CMS. As demonstrated in Chapter 5, discussion boards may be used in countless ways, including conventional asynchronous discussions on specific topics, formal debates and negotiations, inviting guests from other countries to participate in a discussion, and for analyzing a case study. Posting links to other learning objects to help clarify points is a feature usually available to teachers and students. Most discussion boards permit the teacher to make all posts anonymous, so the discussion board may also be used as a way to evaluate a specific teaching and learning experience or to provide anonymous peer review. Discussions are one of the easiest ways to create social presence among students and teachers. Because immediate responses are not required, asynchronous discussion also provides the opportunity for reflection and inquiry, enhancing the likelihood for deep learning to occur. If designed well, asynchronous discussion gives everyone in the class an opportunity to become involved in the discussion. Finally, asynchronous discussion is easy for teachers and students to use.

Twenty-six people—15 experienced hybrid teachers and 11 hybrid students—were interviewed for this book. Every one of the teachers and students reported using asynchronous discussion as a major teaching or learning tool in their hybrid courses. Discussion is likely to be the most frequently used interaction tool for any form of online teaching and learning. See Chapter 5 for several examples of asynchronous discussion assignments. The following are several more examples:

■ Example 9.1: Lia Lee, John McKnight, and Care

Assignment written by Cheryl Coan
Course: Communication Management in Public Service

This assignment is due on Monday, April 12 by midnight.

For this question I am asking you to read an online excerpt from a book by John McKnight titled *The Careless Society*. In the book McKnight addresses his concern about the "undoing" of community by the professionalization of care.

After you read this piece (only pages 36–52), consider applying his ideas to Lia Lee's case. Would McKnight's outlook have helped in this situation? Think of the outcome of McKnight's outlook on all the stakeholders in Lia's case so far—the Lee family, the doctors, the hospital, child protective services, and any other stakeholders you might see. What is the impact of care, as McKnight explains it?

Link to the reading: http://books.google.com/books?id = 86hceYOU 2DQC&lpg = PP1&dq = the%20careless%20society&pg = PA49#v = one page&q = &f = false

In addition to reading two excerpts, Example 9.1 requires students to synthesize components of these two readings, thereby developing and communicating a deeper understanding of how professionalized health care may have an impact on community. ■

■ Example 9.2: Travel Insurance

Assignment written by Heather Salisbury
Course: International Travel

Many people debate whether travel insurance is necessary and whether it is worth the cost. Your assignment is to read the handouts provided in class and compose an argument either for or against the purchase of travel insurance for the hypothetical traveler, "Backpacker McGee." Your response should be at least 600 words, and should include a minimum of three solid, supported arguments. This assignment is due at 5:00 pm CST on Tuesday, October 17, 2006.

By Sunday, October 22, 2006, you must respond to one of your classmates who argued the opposite point. In 300 words or less, you must choose one of his or her three arguments and critically evaluate it. In your response, include whether you are swayed by this argument and why.

This assignment is worth 10 points.

3 points for a well-structured argument

2 points for quality writing—grammar, punctuation, and spelling

3 points for a critical, substantial evaluation of the argument

2 points for a quality reason why you were/weren't swayed ■

Note the very specific directions. Students should have a very good idea of what they need to do for the assignment, when they need to do it, and how their work will be evaluated.

■ Example 9.3: Shopping Assignment

Assignment written by Dr. Alan Aycock
Course: Introduction to Cultural Anthropology

Branding sells ideas that the product you buy will make you sexier, happier, healthier, etc. Database marketing sells socially relevant distinctions whereby buying a product affiliates you with a particular image or tribe. Neither the idea represented by the brand nor the distinction exploited by the database necessarily precedes the commodity at hand. Ideas are created when you prefer a brand; distinctions, when you affiliate as an identifiable database entry. Although we are subjects when we choose one item over another, we are also subjected to them and subjectified through and through by the things we acquire.

By contrast, poaching and bricolage are tactics of resistance in which we attempt to fashion ourselves uniquely, despite the efforts of marketers to persuade us otherwise. As long as we buy, of course, instead of stealing or making what we need, we are limited in our ability to step aside from the world of consumer capitalism.

Either way, sellers try to create an ambience that is suited to their purposes. If stores are selling a brand, the store has to present itself in a completely focused, coherent manner that underscores the desired look and feel of the brand. If you are targeted by database marketers, the catalogs you get in the mail or the sites you browse online tend to play upon a certain set of social codes that contribute to the lifestyle of your image tribe. Even if a store features an alternative lifestyle approach intended to attract poachers and bricoleurs, the store has to be consistent throughout.

This is your task: identify a store's ambience and the specific codes or cultural patterns that underlie it. First, choose a store where you will be comfortable and not too conspicuous if you hang around for a while. Tip: Going with a friend or partner can make you less visible. Choose a store that is clearly branded (e.g., Disney, Gap, the museum store) or that caters to a very clearly identified clientele (e.g., in a ritzy neighborhood) or that represents a countercultural movement (e.g., a resale shop, the Outpost, Altera).

Second, visit the store more than once to make sure that your visits are at least somewhat representative. I would say that two visits, lasting about an hour apiece, should be sufficient. If a store clerk asks what you're doing, it's fair to say that you're shopping, as long as you're in a store where you might conceivably buy something. If you're ever asked to leave a store for any reason, just smile, say "thank you," and walk out. Stores (and malls) are private property!

Third, identify *ten* features of the store that contribute to its ambience. Examples: packaging, leaflets, or other promotional materials at the counter, co-branded items, music, lighting, sales staff, posters, window displays, etc.

Fourth, after—and only after—you have left the store, make some notes to yourself so you don't forget what you've seen.

Fifth, add some visual materials (this is the tricky part) such as a brochure that you've taken from the store, advertising or a catalog for this store that you received in the mail, stuff from the store's website.

Sixth, put together a PowerPoint presentation with a title slide and two visual slides as before (i.e., scan in some of your visual materials), plus one or more slides that include bulleted points that correspond to the features you have identified that contribute to the store's ambience. Then post the entire PowerPoint presentation—title slides, picture slides, bulleted slides—to the discussion forum.

Your deadline for posting your PowerPoint file to the first discussion forum is no later than midnight on Wednesday, 20 February!! This part of your work is worth 10% (out of a total of 15%) of your first assignment.

Finally, between Thursday, 21 February, and Sunday, 24 February, I would like you to choose one of the postings (other than your own) to analyze. Write approximately 200 words explaining how Veblen, Bourdieu, Brooks, Hall, Fiske, or de Certeau would perceive the ethnographic situation you have chosen. Use the original posting to give concrete examples to support your case. You will be graded on the persuasiveness and analytical vision that you bring to bear on the data available. If you are familiar with the particular situation described, you may adduce evidence in addition to that which the original poster used but your main focus must remain on the original observations.

Your deadline for posting your commentary to the discussion forum is no later than midnight on Sunday, 24 February!! This part of your work is worth the remaining 5% of your first assignment. ■

Example 9.3 is likely to be a very engaging assignment in that it encompasses an experiential learning experience, specifically two trips to a store, that can include another student or two. The initial part of the assignment provides a good context for the work. The assignment clearly identifies what is expected of students and when each part of the work must be completed. Prior to assigning this work, the teacher demonstrated how to use the technology required for completing the assignment. At this university, the technology is available for student use in computer labs located on campus.

■ Example 9.4: Emotional Intelligence (EI)

Assignment written by Dr. Jay Caulfield
Course: Leadership Theory
Initial posting due Sat, Jan 23 (30 points); final postings due Tues, Jan 26 (20 points)

Hello,

Prior to participating in this discussion forum, please review the mini lecture on emotional intelligence. To *hear* the mini lecture, click on the *PowerPoint audio file* and listen to the presentation by placing the file in Slide Show view. Be sure you are in the Slide Show view and your volume is turned on.

To read the mini lecture, click on the Adobe PDF file. You will need to have Adobe Reader 9, a free upload, to open this file and other pdf files contained in this course. Second, make sure you have read the stories about river blindness and Mann Gulch contained in the Useem text.

Now that you have reviewed the lecture contents and read the stories, please participate in the discussion described below.

Due Sat, Jan 23

Based on the story you read about finding a cure for river blindness and based on what you know about EI, how would you rate Roy Vagelos' EI as he contemplated the decision that he and his company faced? Please cite evidence from the story and from what you know about EI that substantiates your view.

Next think about Dodge Wagner in the Mann Gulch situation. How would you rate his EI? Again, please cite evidence from the story and from what you know about EI that substantiates your view.

Finally, think about the interrelatedness of leader, followers, and situation in these two leadership moments. Compare and contrast the two leadership moments by comparing and contrasting each of the three components of leadership. What influence did each of these three components have on the outcome of each situation?

Be sure to refer to the discussion rubric when completing this assignment.

Due Tues, Jan 26

Then, post a thoughtful response to two of your colleagues' postings. Thoughtful response means adding value to the discussion by citing an example that further clarifies a point made by your colleague, by further applying leadership theory or principles, or by respectfully disagreeing and substantiating your view with evidence from materials read or from a specific life experience. Be prepared to discuss your work during our next F2F class.

Best, JC ▪

Example 9.4 begins with exposing students to the concept of emotional intelligence by listening to a narrated lecture or reading a mini lecture on the concept that has been posted to the discussion. They are then asked to apply the concept of emotional intelligence in a comparison/contrast posting of the behavior of two different leaders. Next they are asked to post a comparison/contrast of these two leadership situations by applying a leadership model. Students then respond to two of their colleagues' postings, synthesizing their thoughts with their colleagues' thoughts. Finally, they are reminded they must report on the assignment during the next F2F class. The rubric for the assignment is linked to the discussion, students know how much each part of the assignment is worth in the way of points, and due dates for each part of the assignment are clearly identified. All this work takes place in one asynchronous discussion, again demonstrating the versatility of discussion boards.

Blogs

The term *blog* is a shortened form of the word *weblog*. A blog consists of a chronological journal or diary posted on a website for the public to view. The author of the journal is called a *blogger*. Depending on the expertise of the blogger, some blogs can be educational. Usually, visitors reading the blog may post comments.

Some blogs are excellent and some bloggers can be very creative. *Time* magazine published a list of what it considered the 25 best blogs in the world in 2009 (http://www.time.com/time/specials/packages/complete list/0,,1879276,00.html).

Edublogs (http://edublogs.org) at the time of this writing had 625,645 educational blogs posted by teachers, students, librarians, researchers, professors, administrators, corporate trainers, government departments, universities, and colleges. The three blog options include one that is free of charge in which the blogger can create several blog themes, but space is limited (20 megabytes), as is functionality, and privacy options. Educators may purchase blog space for up to 50 blogs, which includes 10 gigabytes, significantly more functionality, and full privacy options. Campus sites can also be purchased by universities and colleges. Technical support is reported to be available for all options.

An Edublog site can be used in addition to a CMS, and some features may make it better than a CMS. For instance, controlling whether blog content is private or public increases the utility of the site. An online course promotion can be made viewable to the public, including a course description, learning objectives, and a few learning activities. Evaluative comments from past students might also be posted in the public content area. The private content area could contain discussions and posting links to media from those enrolled in the class. To view a simple Edublog page I created, go to http://jcaulfield.edublogs.org/. To read questions and answers from people using Edublog, go to http://edublogs.org/forums/.

Several other websites are helpful in creating a blog. If you create a Google account, you may sign on to Blogger (http://www.blogger.com/start) and create a blog free of charge in about 5 minutes.

Google Docs

Google Docs (http://www.google.docs), designed for collaborative work, permits uploading almost any type of file, which may be made accessible to others by e-mailing an invitation with a link to the shared document. With permission from the owner of the document, participants may collaborate, editing and adding to it. According to Google Docs support (http://docs.google.com/support/bin/answer.py?answer = 37603&topic = 15119), the following are the size limits:

♦ Docs: Each doc can have a maximum size of 500K, plus up to 2MB per embedded image to be converted to Google Docs format.

- ◆ Spreadsheets: Each spreadsheet can be up to 256 columns, 200,000 cells, or 100 sheets, whichever is reached first, to be converted to Google Docs format. There's no limit on rows.
- ◆ Presentations: Files in .ppt and .pps formats can have a maximum size of 10MB or 200 slides to be converted to Google Docs format; files uploaded from the Web can be up to 2MB.
- ◆ Stored files: Files that you store but don't convert to Google Docs can be up to 1GB each.

As mentioned in Chapter 5 (Example 5.4), I use Google Docs in the research methods class I teach in which we construct a Thurstone scale. The class identifies the construct we want to measure, and during class students generate 80 to 100 statements that have the potential of becoming part of their final Thurstone scale. As students generate the statements, they are typed directly into a Google Docs spreadsheet projected on a screen. Students are given access to the spreadsheet so individually they can score the statements after class. They then download the spreadsheet to their computer to complete the work on the scale. Prior to using Google Docs, students would send an Excel spreadsheet from person to person for scoring purposes, which from a time and efficiency standpoint was cumbersome. Now anyone can access the spreadsheet at any time, to make scoring entries.

Google Docs can also be used in collaborative group work for presentations. A draft presentation is uploaded by a group member, and each group member can edit it, or the group may actually build the presentation in its entirety within Google Docs. Once the presentation is finalized, it can be downloaded to any group member's computer.

Narrated Mini Lectures

When doing narrated presentations in the past, compression software to reduce the size of the narrated file was necessary for uploading to a CMS. However, now many CMSs permit uploading fairly large files. If narrated presentations are less than 30 minutes and with a file size less than 20,000 kilobytes, chances are that the CMS will accept the uploaded file without any type of compression software. Narrated mini lectures are helpful to students who have missed class or for material that is a bit more complicated and warrants repetition. For hybrid classes, F2F time is premium, so narrated lectures may be a way to preserve more F2F time for discussion rather than lecture.

Videos

One of the difficulties of using educational videos in online instruction is fair use regulation. These videos tend to be quite expensive, often priced at $1,000 or more and production companies strictly enforce fair use guidelines. However, thousands of videos are now available to all web users for free. YouTube (http://www.youtube.com) provides a way to produce and publish a video for little cost or experience. Many of the productions are for entertainment purposes; however, thousands of educational videos are available as well, including lectures by faculty from several prominent universities. YouTube videos are fairly simple to produce and require a webcam or video camera, Windows Movie Maker, and a YouTube account (http://www.ehow.com/how_4847418_make-youtube-videos.html). To produce high-quality educational videos, however, the assistance of technical support services at your institution may be an invaluable asset.

Clickers

Clickers are remote personal response systems some teachers require as part of the materials needed by students enrolled in a course; generally they sell for about $20. Each student purchases a clicker and the students' clickers are registered to them. As a teacher asks objective questions during a lecture, the students respond to the questions with clickers. The teacher is able to immediately tally the results. Clickers have been around for over 10 years now, and one of the teachers interviewed for this book uses clickers extensively for the F2F portion of his large lecture class. He finds them to be an excellent tool that encourages student interaction in the classroom. The immediate feedback that he gets from students using clickers informs him whether students understand the material. He then uses small group interaction during class to encourage group members who responded correctly to a question to help those in the group who responded incorrectly. Ohio State University (http://telr.osu.edu/clickers) lists the following uses for clickers:

- ◆ Facilitate Class Discussion—Facilitate discussion by polling students' opinions and discussing the reasons for their opinions.

♦ Guide Lectures—Collect immediate feedback about students' understanding of lecture topics so confusion can be addressed quickly.

♦ Encourage Peer Instruction—Allow students to share, discuss, and change their opinions before answering a question.

♦ Collect Data and Perform Formative Assessment—Collect data on course topics or learning preferences throughout the cycle of a course.

♦ Offer Quizzes and Exams—Decrease grading time by using clickers to collect student answers to quizzes and exams.

♦ Take Attendance—Record attendance in large lecture courses.

Clickers are inexpensive and easy to use. They can be an asset for the F2F portion of hybrid courses, especially with large enrollments. Clickers are a way to enhance student interaction during class, and they provide teachers immediate feedback on whether students understand major concepts being discussed.

Use of Imagery in Teaching and Learning

Cognitive researchers have been studying the use of imagery in relation to learning for several decades now (Bower, Karlin, & Dueck, 1975; Kosslyn, 1994; Larkin & Simon, 1987; Schwartz & Heiser, 2006). Without getting too far into the specifics of the science, images double the chance of retrieval by yielding a perceptual and a verbal code in memory (Schwartz & Heiser). Later research indicates that students often feel disoriented in a CMS (Mazza, 2004). One way students can more easily locate text materials in the CMS is by associating them with images. For example, if a discussion assignment involves studying a particular model, putting an image of the model near the text at the discussion site helps students quickly locate the assignment.

Images may also help students to remember a key concept. Figure 9.1 illustrates how most authors of organizational behavior textbooks organize the study of organizational behavior. First, authors usually write about topics such as motivation and perception, which are generally associated with an individual's behavior in an organization. Next, authors focus on topics such as internal politics and team building, which are associated with group behavior. Finally, authors write about organizational culture and organizational structure, which addresses behaviors

Figure 9.1   Organizational Behavior

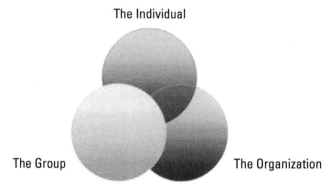

The Individual

The Group

The Organization

that are inherent to the organization as a whole. Although these topics are frequently discussed using this progression, many of the concepts from one of the three areas (individual, group, organization) influences the two remaining areas, indicating some overlap. It has taken me about 153 words to explain what the image depicts when a student is able to see it instantaneously once he or she has been exposed to the concepts involved.

Use of imagery as a technology is for the most part free and easy to use. Because much of the content for a hybrid course is available online, using imagery can be an effective learning tool, assisting students in locating course materials quickly and helping them better recall and understand key concepts. Images are a way to complement read-and-write learning materials, which dominate our educational system. Finally, use of imagery makes the learning materials more aesthetically engaging.

Learning Object Repositories

In the context of this chapter, learning objects are digital pieces of educational information learners can access and use repeatedly, including simulations, short articles, videos, presentations, and blogs. Learning object repositories are websites that contain a large number of links to these learning objects. Merlot (http://www.merlot.org), a large learning object repository, has been in existence for about 10 years. At the time of this writing, Merlot provides access to 22,277 learning objects categorized by discipline. If I search the Merlot site using the word *leadership*, 145 learning objects are listed by title, which is an active link to the material. Using Merlot is free.

Another example of a learning object repository is Podcast (http:// www.podcast.com). A podcast is a digital recording of a radio broadcast or similar program that could also include video. The digital information is available on the Internet, and it can be downloaded to a computer or some other audio device. A podcast titled "The Official Barack Obama Video Podcast" includes a series of 44 videos of some of President Obama's speeches made during his presidential campaign. Finally, YouTube (http://www.youtube.com) provides thousands of short video productions categorized by topic. When teaching hybrid, it is easy to create links to these learning objects in the CMS. Carefully selected learning objects potentially add valuable learning materials to the online part of the course.

Synchronous Discussion

The synchronous (real-time) discussion function in many CMSs is generally primitive. However, products are designed specifically for synchronous discussions, such as Elluminate and Wimba. What I'm about to describe mostly pertains to fully online courses, but, there is no reason why the blended online model could not be applied to hybrid courses. In fact, one of the teachers I interviewed is already successfully doing so. Several experienced hybrid and online teachers from Canada and the United States spoke of the emerging blended online environment they had been using. These teachers, also active researchers, believed that while the asynchronous online delivery mode may provide an effective learning environment, it was simply too time intensive for them to sustain in the long run. In addition to the time-intensive design of a fully online asynchronous course up front, Power (2008) said, "As faculty began to realize the amount of time and the degree of effort which would be required to bring their courses to completion, the need for a more pragmatic and effective approach to distance education became obvious" (p. 504). Power coined the term *blended online*, which he describes as the blend of asynchronous and synchronous teaching and learning environments. He has found through research that teachers who regularly scheduled synchronous periods for students to interact with each other and the teacher in a real-time structured environment have decreased the time it takes for them and students to participate in a fully online course. What's even more positive is that students and teachers report this model to be a more engaging distance education experience. Each week Power meets with his students, wherever they may be, synchronously for three hours, similar in length to a F2F class. He has encouraged other faculty to engage in this type of teaching and learning, which he finds offers flexibility with his other responsibilities including his research. Power has been using this model successfully for 10 years now, and several of his colleagues are following suit. The synchronous classes are recorded and accessible to any student unable to attend a synchronous session. Time zones do not seem to interfere with scheduling the synchronous component as most students live near the university. Demographic information on students who enroll in online classes indicates that most students live within a few hundred miles of the university (Hershberger, 2008).

The pedagogical rationale for choosing the blended online format over the fully asynchronous online format or a fully asynchronous hybrid format in which students do not meet frequently is derived from the literature, which addresses the importance of real-time interaction in relation to increased student engagement, which leads to increased learning (Carini, Kuh, & Klein, 2006; Caulfield, 2010; Ewell, 2002; Garrison & Vaughan, 2008; Kaleta, Aycock, & Caulfield, 2004). Second, the literature indicates that asynchronous online courses are too time intensive for many teachers and students (Boettcher & Conrad, 2004; Power, 2008), making fully asynchronous teaching and learning models difficult to sustain in the long run when added to other faculty responsibilities, such as research, student mentoring, and committee work. The blended online format may provide nearly the same accessibility for students that the fully asynchronous format provides with the preceding added benefits. Blended online models or hybrid courses using synchronous discussion offer no restrictions on location and give students the ability to access synchronous sessions they are unable to attend. Finally, although video and audio functions are available, initially it may be easier to use the audio function only.

Social Network Tools

Boud and Ellison (2008) define social network sites (SNSs) as "web-based services that allow individuals to (1) construct a public or semi-public profile within a bounded system, (2) articulate a list of other users with whom they share a connection, and (3) view and traverse their list of connections and those made by others within the system" (p. 1). According to Boud and Ellison, there are hundreds of SNSs since the first one was launched in 1997. The following is a brief description of a few large and more highly publicized ones.

LinkedIn (http://www.linkedin.com/home), primarily used for professional networking, allows the user to e-mail others in the LinkedIn network, invite individuals to join the network, post professional information by creating a profile, and post jobs for a fee. Creating a network is free. Users can create groups in a network and join existing groups when invited. E-mails are routinely sent to members of a network, updating everyone on who is connected to whom.

Facebook (http://www.facebook.com) is a social networking site where users can upload pictures and send e-mails to others in Facebook. Membership is free. Users can invite others to join Facebook, form groups, and join existing groups upon invitation. Facebook is one of the largest global social networks. MySpace (http://www.myspace.com) is another large SNS similar to Facebook. Twitter (http://www.twitter.com) is yet another large SNS. Second Life (http://secondlife.com) is a website where one lives in a virtual world by creating an avatar (a digital persona) who engages in a number of user initiated activities. Again, it is considered an SNS, though significantly different from the others.

According to an article in *Chronicle of Higher Education* (Young, 2010), although faculty interest in learning how to use SNSs is on the rise, views are mixed on whether SNSs actually improve learning. Boud and Ellison (2008, p. 8) report that thus far the bulk of SNS research is in the areas of impression management and friendship performance, networks and network structure, online/offline connections and privacy issues. Their article provides an overview of research in these areas. However, some SNS sites have reported breeches in security, and some countries block usage of social network sites.

None of the teachers or students interviewed mentioned using SNSs as part of their hybrid classes; however, most of the students were aware of their existence. A few teachers interviewed were thinking about trying one or more of these tools in the future. Several faculty from the University of Wisconsin are actively using SNSs, however, and are reporting benefits at http://uwmsocialmedia.wikispaces.com/. The categories on the left side of the web page provide significant information regarding social media tools and how they may be implemented.

In conclusion, the Internet and other technologies provide us with multiple opportunities to creatively design interactive hybrid courses. There is no limit to creatively using the multimedia tools that already exist. Libraries provide a wealth of resources in electronic search engines, giving students access to thousands of journals and other forms of media within minutes. CMSs are available at most universities, providing a common place for students and teachers to access online learning materials and engage in discussions. Learning object repositories provide access to thousands of simulations and snippets of valuable information. When technology is chosen thoughtfully, it has the potential to enhance the hybrid teaching and learning environment significantly while making the experience more interactive and time efficient for teachers and students alike.

SECTION THREE

INTERVIEW DATA

CHAPTER TEN

WHAT STUDENTS SAY
ABOUT HYBRID

I'd say that the best thing about hybrid is that it gives students 110% participation opportunities.

—Student interview

T HE PRIMARY PURPOSE of conducting student interviews was to learn from students who had taken several hybrid classes what had gone well and what could have gone better, and to share that information with teachers who may find it helpful when designing or redesigning their hybrid courses. The information from these students may not be transferable to other hybrid students, yet in most instances what these students had to say mirrors findings in the literature regarding hybrid and online learning experiences reported by students in the past. Before delving into what students said, however, a bit of background information about the students interviewed follows, including how and why they were selected. General information regarding class size and structure is also provided.

Background Information

The 11 students interviewed were graduate students purposively selected from a graduate degree program taught in a hybrid format. All interviewed were experienced hybrid students who had enrolled in several hybrid classes. The program was offered by one of the colleges at a university ranked in the top 100 by *U.S. News and World Report.* The university's institutional review board granted approval to conduct the interviews before students were invited to participate, and each voluntary participant signed a consent form. Except in one case, students had not taken any classes taught by the 15 teachers who were also interviewed. Almost all course offerings in the 36-credit applied social science professional master's program were taught in a hybrid format, with the exception of electives or classes that were part of a specialization taught outside the college. Most classes were taught in a 14-week semester; a few classes were offered during a 6-week summer session. Students invited to participate in the interview process had already completed three or more hybrid courses in the program. All interviews were conducted F2F and digitally recorded by me. None of the students were enrolled in my classes at the time the interviews were conducted. Interview data were coded and transcribed by two graduate assistants who were not enrolled in the hybrid program.

The median age of students in the program was 37. Of the 11 interviewed, seven were female, nine were Caucasian, and two were African American. The demographics of the sample closely resembled the demographics of the student population enrolled in the program. The average class size was 12, the lowest enrollment in any class in the program was five, and the highest enrollment was 25. All teachers in the program had taught at least five hybrid classes, and most had taught far more. By college policy, time spent in the F2F classroom for hybrid courses had to equal no less than 50% of the time spent in the classroom for a traditional (fully) F2F class, and most hybrid classes met F2F 66% of the time that a traditional F2F class met.

What Students Had to Say About Enrolling in a Hybrid Program

When asked why they had enrolled in a hybrid degree program, six students reported they did so primarily because it was the degree they were seeking; hybrid just happened to be the format. However, two of the six reported a secondary reason: the convenience of spending less time in the classroom. One of these individuals said, "After [completing] the first course, I'd select [hybrid] almost exclusively. Having a family, I like having less onsite classes and I like the paper trail that exists [online] as a result of team activities." The other student cited flexibility as the second reason.

Another three students reported that the hybrid format was one of the primary criteria that influenced their decision to enroll in the program, with type of degree offered being another primary reason. All three said the hybrid format provided them with more flexibility, especially in relation to their work schedules, and two of them said it was more convenient as well as being more flexible.

Two of the students were not in favor of enrolling in a hybrid program, but said they did so because they wanted to earn that particular degree at that particular university. One said she did not want to enroll in a hybrid program because of a bad experience with hybrid classes as an undergraduate; the teachers were unfamiliar with the CMS and "that first couple of classes that I took were just a nightmare." The second student preferred F2F interaction: "I like people around, to be able to interact; I miss that. I certainly wouldn't want to do completely online, but I don't underestimate the value of it, because I know people learn through online programs, but it's that human and social component I really like."

In summary, the students chose the hybrid program mainly based on the degree they were seeking. Those students specifically seeking a hybrid program did so based on convenience and flexibility. The two reporting they would have preferred a traditional offering versus a hybrid offering either enjoyed the benefits of F2F interaction or pointed to a negative experience with hybrid course offerings as undergraduates. Student data are distinctly different from faculty data in this regard. Teachers report choosing a hybrid format because they believe it creates a more effective learning environment (Bourne & Seamon, 2005; Dziuban, Hartman, & Moskul, 2007; Garrison & Kanuka, 2004; Garrison & Vaughan, 2008), whereas students report choosing hybrid classes based on convenience and flexibility (Garrison & Vaughan, 2008). Graham (2006) identifies the convenience and flexibility of hybrid designs as especially important to working adult students.

Based on what students and teachers reported as advantageous, hybrid designs should provide flexibility and convenience without jeopardizing good pedagogy. This type of design satisfies teachers interested in effective pedagogy while satisfying students, especially working professionals with family responsibilities, who are interested in flexibility and convenience. Simple teaching practices such as giving students a schedule of classes and sticking to it, being flexible with student presentation schedules to accommodate students who must travel, using dependable and user-friendly technologies that are effective learning tools, maintaining consistent due dates for assignments, and making learning materials easily accessible all demonstrate flexibility and convenience for students without jeopardizing pedagogy.

What Students Had to Say About Quantity and Quality of Interaction With Other Students

When asked about the quality and quantity of interaction in a hybrid course as compared to a traditional F2F class, all students interviewed answered the question in the context of asynchronous online and F2F discussion in the hybrid course compared to F2F discussion in a traditional course. Eight students reported a higher quality of interaction in the hybrid course for a number of reasons. The most frequently cited explanation was that everyone in the class was given an equal opportunity to participate in the discussion, which meant that those students who did not have the opportunity to speak during class because of time constraints, absences, or other reasons, frequently made valuable contributions to the online discussion. The second reason cited was that the convenience and flexibility of asynchronous postings improved the quality of the posts because individuals had time to reflect on what they had to contribute to the discussion. The third reason stated was that asynchronous discussion posts tended to stay on topic more than classroom discussions. Several students indicated a higher quantity of overall interactions F2F during class and asynchronously outside class. None indicated less frequency in the number of interactions.

Of the three remaining students, two reported no difference in the quality of the interactions. One of the two stated that regardless of how the class was offered, some students tended to participate more than others. She said she saw no difference in the quantity of interactions either. The other of the two felt that the interactions were of equal quality but the quantity was greater because of the convenience and flexibility of e-mail and online discussion posts. The one remaining student reported increased quantity of interaction for the same reasons, no difference in quality of F2F interactions in a traditional class as compared to a hybrid class, but less quality in the online interactions because of the asynchronous nature of the discussion, which did not allow for spontaneity of response.

Student survey results ($n = 241$) regarding the quality and quantity of student interactions in hybrid courses as reported by Garrison and Vaughan (2008, pp. 197–199) for students enrolled in six different hybrid courses were similar to the student interview data reported here. Likewise, Starenko, Vignare, and Humbert (2007, pp. 177–178) found from surveys at Rochester Institute of Technology that students were mostly in agreement with the interview data reported here. Thus, it seems that students' perceptions of student interactions in hybrid classes are for the most part very favorable. Furthermore, these findings demonstrate the consistent and frequent use of asynchronous discussion as a viable learning tool in a hybrid course design, which implies that students view their asynchronous interactions with peers as a significant part of their overall learning experience in a hybrid course. As one student put it:

> The single most enhancing quality for me as a student in hybrid courses was being able to actually review other people's writing. In traditional courses it was very seldom done; there's not enough time to pass around people's work, review it, and offer comments, and with the hybrid courses, particularly when it shifts to postings, not only is time allocated for students to look at other people's work and respond to what they've written, but you also have the opportunity to look at other people's responses to what you've written. And that's important because it further develops people's writing skills; it also gives you a broader perspective that otherwise you might not have learned, you may not have wanted to discuss in length what the perspectives were prior to reading those posts.

The importance of student interaction as an effective learning tool is frequently highlighted in the adult teaching and learning literature (Garrison & Vaughan, 2008; Kitchener, King, & DeLuca, 2006; Merriam et al., 2007; Oliver, Herrington, & Reeves, 2006; Starenko et al., 2007). Hybrid courses provide a convenient and flexible vehicle for peer learning to continue outside the classroom through asynchronous discussion.

What Students Had to Say About Quantity and Quality of Interaction With Teachers

When asked about the quality and the quantity of interactions with hybrid teachers, nine students reported that the quality and quantity of interactions were better than what they had experienced in most traditional courses. Almost all of them related this to the availability of multiple methods of interaction, including F2F interaction during class and outside class, frequent e-mail interaction, and frequent postings in the CMS, all of which helped build more personal relationships with teachers. As one hybrid student put it, "My communication with the professors is ten times more often in this atmosphere." When assigned papers, many said they received feedback on their work electronically in the body of the document between F2F classes, which helped them to progress with their next assignments. Of the two remaining students, one reported that the F2F interactions in a hybrid course were equal in quality to those in a traditional F2F course, but he viewed online interactions as less valuable because of the loss of spontaneity in having to wait for responses to postings. The final student stated that interactions were dependent upon the teacher versus the method of course delivery.

In summary, lessons learned from students' evaluations of teacher-student interactions in a hybrid environment are very favorable, mainly in the increased accessibility of teachers, the ability to communicate in multiple modes, and receiving timely feedback on student work. From this interview data, it is clear students appreciated the increased accessibility to teachers and the fact they could receive feedback on their work between F2F meetings, all important considerations for teachers when designing and teaching hybrid courses. Once again, the amount of teacher-student interaction that generally occurs in a well-designed hybrid course means teachers need to plan their time accordingly. With regard to teacher-student interaction, the findings from these interviews are more favorable than student survey results reported by Garrison and Vaughan (2008, pp. 197–199) and those reported by Starenko et al., (2007, pp. 177–178). Aggregate findings from those studies indicated a less favorable response related to quantity and quality of teacher-student interaction. One difference in findings may be attributed to the fact that those interviewed were all graduate students while those surveyed were almost entirely undergraduate students. Certainly the method of gathering information, F2F interview versus survey response, may also be a contributing factor explaining the difference.

What Students Say About How They Learned in a Hybrid Course

The two most frequent comments regarding learning in a hybrid format are that students learned to take responsibility for their own learning and that the hybrid environment forced them to reflect on assigned topics before going to class. This reflection occurred primarily through research they did to complete online assignments and through asynchronous discussion, which made the classroom discussion that followed more meaningful and more efficient. This is evident from the following comments:

> Student comment 1: I think with hybrid you need to do more research and work beforehand, before you're responding to others. So if I had to describe what hybrid offers, it is efficiency with your communication. So for me, that is fantastic!
>
> Student comment 2: My ability to learn to self-direct my learning. The journey is mine and the instructors are just setting me up to take it (referring to what hybrid classes had taught him).
>
> Student comment 3: You take ownership of your education. By responding to students' work, you become the teacher at times.
>
> Student comment 4: I have to go and complete assignments rather than passively listening to a lecture and I can see the value there, where you're working through things on your own and you go through that process instead of sitting back and letting it come to you. That is what I see as a key difference in hybrid courses.

These comments indicate that somewhere during the course of their studies students saw the value in becoming more responsible for their own learning. Any method of teaching when it is intended to can encourage students to take more responsibility for their learning. However, this is blatantly inherent in a well-designed hybrid course, which encourages continued learning outside the classroom through reflective online assignments (student-content), including asynchronous discussion (student-student and teacher-student) (Anderson, 2003). Bates (1993) emphasized the idea that computer-mediated education will increase the effectiveness of learning using asynchronous communication between teacher and students and between students. This thinking is also aligned with constructivism and social interaction theory.

What Students Say About Challenges Faced in a Hybrid Environment

When asked about specific challenges students faced when taking hybrid courses, six were mentioned more than once. In order of frequency, they were:

Challenge 1: Technical difficulties with the CMS, leading to inefficiencies and redoing work. At this particular university, the help desk was staffed with personnel who could not address student problems immediately. When students couldn't access the CMS, to preserve the integrity of the class teachers sent students course materials by e-mail. However, prolonged lack of access to the CMS disrupts asynchronous discussion, which is generally a significant component of any hybrid course design. Clearly every student loses out in this situation as students benefit in learning from one another, and the teacher loses efficiency by having to send separate e-mails to students who are unable to access the CMS or are having difficulties with the system's functionality. Institutions lose out when students expect the institution will provide the necessary technology for them to do their academic work, and when this doesn't occur they become dissatisfied. If institutions are to be successful in delivering high-quality hybrid courses, it is critical for the necessary technical support to be available to students and faculty (Kaleta et al., 2007; Ross & Gage, 2006; Wiesenmayer et al., 2008).

Challenge 2: Some group members' noncompliance with completing group work on time, leading to increased stress and inefficiencies for compliant group members. Tactics to help alleviate this challenge include using ground rules and peer evaluation as part of the course grade. Moreover, encouraging students to confront unacceptable peer behavior as it occurs is helpful in two regards: It is likely to curb deviant peer behavior, and it teaches peers to solve group behavior problems by developing collaborative and confrontational skills.

Challenge 3: Misinterpreting or misunderstanding what peers posted. Nonverbal communication can be more powerful than verbal or written communication. Unfortunately, nonverbal expression is absent in asynchronous discussion, which may lead to decreased clarity. Thus, along with a focus on clarity of expression, avoiding the use of undefined acronyms and slang are important writing skills for students to practice. Even for good writers, intergenerational, interdisciplinary, and intercultural differences in classrooms today may make written communication difficult under the best of circumstances.

Challenge 4: Difficulty expressing themselves in postings that won't be misinterpreted by others. This very real challenge is derived from the previous one. In the first challenge, the inability to write clearly may lead to miscommunication, which becomes a liability. In the second challenge, increased self-awareness of the need to improve writing skills often makes students better writers, which decreases the likelihood of miscommunication.

Challenge 5: Lack of immediate response in asynchronous discussions and replies to e-mail. Most of the students interviewed were millenniums. As noted in Chapter 8, although millenniums are technologically savvy and fairly confident in their skills, they prefer frequent affirmation and reassurance when completing tasks. Thus, waiting for replies in an asynchronous discussion and waiting for feedback regarding their work may be difficult for them. If teachers set clear instructions about when they will respond to e-mails or post to discussion forums, students will know what to expect. Furthermore, if students establish group norms, including setting target dates for posting to asynchronous discussions, it helps each group member know what to expect and plan accordingly.

Challenge 6: Lack of consistent organization of course materials in the CMS, which led to inefficiency. A couple of tactics may reduce this challenge. One is to orient students to the course site during the initial F2F class. Several students interviewed said they recognized the value in this. The second tactic is to standardize the organization of course content. For example, consistently placing links to required readings in one area of the course site is better than putting them in the discussion area some of the time and in the announcement area other times.

Getting faculty to agree to a certain level of standardization also may be helpful. I do want to emphasize, however, I am not suggesting a college hire an instructional designer or two to build look-alike course sites that prioritize standardization over pedagogy. Not all content should be presented in the same way, and not all teachers feel comfortable adapting their teaching styles to one standardized presentation. That being said, instructional designers are often extremely valuable in assisting faculty with designing their hybrid courses. Note the distinction being made. Teaching faculty how to design an effective hybrid course versus designing a course for them is significantly more sustainable for faculty and the institution in the long run.

What Students Say About Learning Activities Suited to Hybrid

When asked what learning activities were particularly well suited to hybrid, all the students reported that asynchronous discussion was at the top of their list. Specific reasons included its flexibility with many different types of assignments and the ability to easily share different perspectives on topics in an informal setting. Specific examples included sharing analyses of research, obtaining links to research articles and other valuable information from colleagues and the teacher, and completing small group work, such as case analyses, without meeting F2F outside the regularly scheduled F2F classes. Several students mentioned the value of continuing the discussion asynchronously after F2F classes as well. Listening to narrated lectures on difficult material regardless of whether it was covered in class was mentioned by several students as being valuable. Finally, posting self-reflective journals was also reported to be well suited to a hybrid class.

The students said multiple forms of interaction are the most suitable for hybrid classes and are the most valuable learning experience. As one student put it, "Discussion is huge in a hybrid class; in traditional classes, you're not getting that. I think that any time there's room for discussion, there's more opportunity to be exposed to multiple perspectives, and that increases your learning." This comment is no surprise, considering the literature on adult learning, which identifies the importance of drawing on personal experience and relating that experience to information from the discipline, applying constructs from the discipline to real-life situations, and applying scaffolding techniques, such as group interaction, simulation, and case analysis, to enhance readiness to learn on an individual basis (Knowles et al., 2005). Certainly a traditional class may be structured to allow for these activities; however, they are the core of every well-designed hybrid class. In a traditional class, F2F time is limited and a few students who are comfortable with speaking in a public forum and skilled at thinking on their feet generally dominate the F2F discussion. In a hybrid class, those barriers are removed for the most part by the addition of structured and interactive learning activities outside the classroom, including asynchronous discussion.

What Students Say About Technologies and Their Orientation to Them

When asked what technologies were used in their hybrid classes, in order of frequency students reported features of the course management system, such as asynchronous discussion, the web page where links to course materials were accessed, the electronic drop box, the grade book, and the quiz function; Internet technologies, including electronic journals, search engines, videos, and simulations; PowerPoint slides; e-mail; narrated lectures; digital voice recorders for conducting interviews; digital cameras; and teleconferencing. Listing the technologies demonstrates the relatively small number of fairly common technologies, most of which are available to students through the university as part of their tuition fee.

For the most part, orientation to the concept of hybrid teaching and learning was conducted during new student orientation, while orientation to the CMS took place during the initial F2F class. Orientation to library services, inclusive of electronic journals and search engines, occurred during the first few weeks of the first semester. Generally students reported the orientation on hybrid, the CMS, and library services was very worthwhile and sufficient. A few said they could have benefited from a bit more detail regarding CMS functions. Online tutorials were available for the CMS, but students reported they learned the CMS best by exploring its features on their own.

What Students Say About Major Lessons Learned Specific to Hybrid

The student responses regarding lessons learned are rich and have multiple implications for teaching. Student comments and aligned teaching implications are presented in Table 10.1. Some of the student responses include challenges they mentioned previously, but each response contains new points to be considered. To maintain anonymity, quotes referring specifically to the product name of the CMS have been omitted.

What Students Say Hybrid Teachers Should Do

As mentioned previously, the pedagogical literature indicates that student engagement is generally recognized as one of the better predictors of learning (Brint et al., 2008; Carini et al., 2006; Ewell, 2002). According to Skinner and Belmont (1993), student engagement is defined as involvement in initiating and carrying out learning activities specific to assigned learning tasks, such as writing assignments, discussion, and group work. Thus, creating classroom conditions that enhance student engagement will lead to increased student learning, a primary goal for students and

Table 10.1   Major Lessons Learned as Identified by Hybrid Students

Lessons Learned for Students	Implications for Teaching
Comment 1: There's a ton of due diligence with this. If you're someone who wants to take a class and sit in the back, this is not for you. Because to really get the quality of the program you need quality students that are going to put forth effort. It's hard to make peers think when you're not F2F with them and they can't see your emotion! Strong written communication skills are also essential. Be prepared to maximize your written communication skills because people can't read into what your answers are, so you have to be clear. You have to be very clear. I think you have to have great time management. If you start working on Saturday afternoon because it's due at 11:59 that night, it doesn't work out. With the instructors that I've had, the syllabi are great, so you can work ahead, so I look at the syllabus and my work travel schedule and see when I won't have time to work on the class. Then I start working on the assignment earlier.	• Be clear with students from day one that meeting less in the classroom does not mean less course work. • Review major assignment details well in advance so that students may plan their work based on their schedules. • As nonverbal communication is absent in written correspondence, stress the importance of clarity in written communication and model that behavior throughout the course.
Comment 2: You have to embrace the CMS, and you have to use it to your advantage. Some people get frustrated with it and I think there have been improvements through the three and half years that I have been using the CMS, because a lot of times it hasn't been consistent and reliable. For me, the more I used it, the more frequent of a visitor I became to the CMS, the more I felt it helped me. I think people just need to use it as a tool and take advantage of it, because it's there to benefit you, whether it's for communication, to talk with your professor or changes in dates or assignments. . . . It's there for you. Just really embrace it and visit it often.	• Make certain students have access to a thorough orientation in how to use the CMS. • Insist that students use the CMS versus working outside of it. Group process is invisible to the teacher if the group is working by e-mail. • Insist students report technological problems they experience with the CMS to the appropriate technical support staff.
Comment 3: There are no concerns regarding the online aspect of hybrid, because some people have reservations regarding the online learning, but you're going to learn either way. So figure out which is a good match for you when you enroll in a course.	• Make certain students understand what hybrid learning and teaching environments are like so they may decide whether they wish to commit to this method of learning. • Consider inviting potential applicants to visit a F2F session of a hybrid class.
Comment 4: You can learn a lot online. I wouldn't have chosen initially a hybrid class, but I have gotten a lot out of the online interaction, so there's something that I gained from the experience; it's doable and it can be beneficial.	• Identify to students the benefits and challenges of hybrid learning experiences.

Lessons Learned for Students	*Implications for Teaching*
Comment 5: The major thing I learned is to be timely and respectful of people's time and resources. Completing my work influences how other students get their work done. In a traditional class it never seemed as important, as you seemed to be more on your own schedule in getting your work done, versus when you're in a work environment where other people are impacted by what you're getting done. Another lesson that I learned is don't have a false assumption about work load, because for the most part the hybrid courses that I was involved with took more work. It is a lot of work to read other people's work and to respond thoughtfully. If you didn't respond thoughtfully to others work it wouldn't have been so much work, but if you want to engage and provide extra thoughtful information, it's hard, because you're really thinking hard about a good response, because you don't want people to respond to you in a superficial way. If a student answers my posts in a superficial way I may do the same with my comments to his posts, while if another student always gives me good feedback, I will try to always give good feedback to him as well. So don't come in to this environment thinking that in lieu of class you will have extra time to get done with other activities. For the most part, there was a good amount of work in the hybrid environment.	• Emphasize that highly interactive learning environments take time to establish and maintain. • Clearly identify what is expected in an asynchronous discussion environment. • Let students know privately if their responses in an asynchronous discussion require more depth. • Identify and describe the elements of a thoughtful reply to a peer. • While participating in asynchronous discussions, model what appropriate and timely feedback looks like.
Comment 6: Repeat the assignment back to the teacher. Be sure you understand the teacher's expectations. My time is very important. I am not a young full-time student any longer. I have one window of 8 to 10 hours per week to get my assignments done and if I don't understand it and blow that time I have the risk of staying up very, very late or short my kids or someone in the family. Another lesson is related to group activities. A group of four can survive having three strong contributors, a group of three can survive two, but it has a difficult time to survive having only one strong contributor. And so if you get the opportunity to select your group, select those who contribute.	• Be respectful of the time demands on students by making your expectations very clear. (Recall the earlier example of the student who excluded a title page and reference list for an assignment that required *APA* formatting because the instructions were unclear.) • Encourage the use of frequent peer review as a way of addressing social loafing. • Include peer review as part of each student's grade.

Table 10.1   (Continued)

Lessons Learned for Students	Implications for Teaching
Comment 7: Be considerate of others and post information timely so that they can respond back to your postings as well. And be prepared if there is a technical difficulty to wait for a response from the Help Desk. Sometimes that difficulty can be with your own home computer. Having a back-up computer is good. Stay calm and find a solution.	• Identify some potential backup plans for students if technology fails. For example, if students are unable to upload an assignment to the CMS because of technical difficulties, they might e-mail the assignment instead. • Don't use technology that is smarter than you, as generally you will be the first one contacted when that technology fails.
Comment 8: I think this hybrid opened me up in a way that I probably wouldn't have been opened because I'd not have had all that discussion and interaction outside of our class. I think one of the misunderstandings about hybrid is that you will get less interaction . . . it just opened my eyes to the existence of multiple paths on how to learn things.	• Make it clear that the foundation of a hybrid class includes providing the structure to continue interactive learning outside the classroom.
Comment 9: I think one of the things that apply for everybody is that any procrastination is not good. Hybrid is a really nice blend between online and instructor led discussion.	• Emphasize the importance of meeting deadlines for online work, as it will affect the perceived success of everyone's learning experience. • When evaluating online work, include timeliness of posts as one criterion.
Comment 10: Get organized and familiar with what the instructor wants. Because there are so many places in a CMS for you to go and do assignments and because every instructor does it differently. I think if I didn't do those steps I would never know that I had posted when I should have, so that is the major lesson.	• During the initial F2F class, students should be oriented to how you specifically use the CMS, and how you expect students to use it. • Be consistent where you post course materials in the CMS.

Lessons Learned for Students	Implications for Teaching
Comment 11: It really paid to be organized, know your thoughts ahead of time, because you're commenting on other peoples' postings. The CMS is pretty dependable, but it is technology, and it can fail. So you learn. One bad experience will teach you that you type your text in Notepad and do a copy and paste into the CMS, you don't type directly into the system. What I really liked about the online component was to be able to read the posts of other students and see where they were and be able to make comments. It made me more competitive with my peers; you don't want to feel like an idiot, you watch your spelling, you tend to worry about how you will present yourself online; most people care about how they present themselves online. Also, in the way you give feedback, I think that's another crucial element, because you want to be careful that you're respectful, when you're communicating in writing. It helps to be precise and specific. I'm not good at reading other people's handwriting, but when you type it in, it's right there and you can see it. You think, "Wow, that's a good point; I missed that in my thinking."	• Emphasize that the intensive online interaction between students in hybrid courses is one of the major ways students learn; thus, participation should not be taken lightly. • When determining final course grades, the number of asynchronous discussion assignments required in a hybrid course should be reflected in the weight assigned to them. • Emphasize the importance of being respectful in online postings, which includes using understandable sentence structure while avoiding the use of slang and undefined acronyms and terms that may only be understood by certain individuals.

teachers (Caulfield, 2010). The practices identified by students as they spoke of what they believed hybrid teachers should do to make hybrid classes more engaging included the following.

Practice 1: Make certain the syllabus and assignments are accurate and complete. Clarity of instructions was mentioned many times by different students. Most graduate students are working professionals and they just don't have the time to second-guess what the teacher had in mind for an assignment. This becomes evident in one of the students' statements, "Do not treat your syllabus as if this were a F2F class. You're not there talking to everybody twice a week. People need to have more information about the scope of their assignments, due dates, available materials, references, all of that. Students love rubrics." In survey findings reported by Garrison and Vaughan (2008), over 27% of students surveyed indicated that lack of clarity in instructions was one of the least effective aspects of their hybrid courses (p. 199). This percentage was the highest reported regarding ineffective aspects of hybrid courses.

Practice 2: Impose penalties for not adhering to timelines and word limits. Throughout the student interview process, not completing assignments on time was mentioned many times by different students. The comments were primarily related to assignments involving group post-ings or some other type of collaborative work. Students also mentioned that posts need to be clear and succinct. As one student put it:

> I think if you have a rule but you don't impose a penalty for violation, it really has no impact. There will always be a reason for someone not to get the work done—a dog, a tree, a cat, a hat, some reason that impacts the other students' work. So let there be a penalty for not meet-ing the timeline and the word limits. I believe it communicates an expectation that you should be mindful of your language and eliminate the "fluffy" from your words.

Again, emphasizing the importance of respecting each other's time in the online classroom and making peer evaluation a portion of the course grade may encourage students to complete work on time.

Practice 3: Know and use the functions of the CMS. Students felt that using the functions of the CMS added to their overall satisfaction with hybrid. For example, they liked the grade book feature because they could easily track their progress in the course, but some students reported that not all hybrid teachers used it. As one student put it, "It would be good for students if faculty understood their side of the application [CMS] and used it." Similar to students, teachers need a thorough orientation to the CMS, and many universities offer F2F workshops and online tutorials to assist faculty.

Practice 4: Be consistent with due dates for assignments. Students reported it was too confusing having assignments due at different times of the week. As one student said, "Be consistent; if assignments are due Wednesday night, they're due Wednesday night, always the same, because there's so much going on in people's lives." During the initial F2F class, distributing a schedule of assignments with consistent due dates will help students plan their work and complete assignments on time.

Practice 5: Do a debriefing for online work during each F2F class. Although students found the online interaction meaningful, they wanted closure for the discussions during the F2F class. Some students said the debriefing should not take more than a few minutes, but they deemed it important. This debriefing is what integrates the online component with the F2F component. As mentioned earlier, this integration of F2F and online learning is one of the most important factors to consider when designing a hybrid course. If they are not integrated, students tend to view the online component as unrelated and less important than the F2F component.

Practice 6: Don't let students circumvent the CMS. Students' reasons for making this statement were they wanted a permanent place to store information where everyone from the group or class could access it at any time, and using e-mail did not let the teacher observe the group process, which increased the likelihood of social loafing. As one student said, "If you have team activities, work should occur within the CMS as much as possible, within the view of the professor—and have team participation be part of the course grade."

Practice 7: Focus on the quality and go with the flow. According to what several students said, the quality of F2F discussions as a follow-up to online assignments was usually excellent because students had already interacted with the material. Thus, they appreciated teachers who allowed for flexibility in use of class time so these discussions could occur. Again, this illustrates the importance of integrating the online component with the F2F component.

Practice 8: Provide feedback on online work. Many students mentioned how much they appreciated receiving written feedback on their work before submitting the next assignment so they wouldn't repeat the same type of errors. Teachers need to plan for the amount of time it takes to evaluate assignments online, which generally takes longer than writing comments in the margins on a hard copy. Several students mentioned that the use of rubrics was helpful in identifying expectations and in providing feedback. Any tool that enhances clarity in expectations is valuable considering that lack of clarity in assignments is one of the most frequently cited ineffective aspects of a hybrid course.

Practice 9: Stick to the learning objectives, but be creative. Two students mentioned that some assignments appeared to be busy work and were not related to the learning objectives stated in the syllabus. As one student put it, "Plan your syllabus in a way that complements the learning instead of adding busy work to the students. Most graduate students don't mind working, but we do mind wasting time with assignments that appear to have no relevance to the class." Another remarked, "Prepare teachers to create that online environment that gets the student to want to think deeply without that pressure of F2F. The other piece is the creativity involved in what that online assignment looks like. If those are done right, I'd love to take a hybrid class every time."

In conclusion, there should be no surprises in the teaching practices students say make hybrid classes more engaging. For the most part, they are directly aligned to what the literature identifies as good teaching practices. To the credit of the teachers in this particular hybrid program, most students for the most part believed the practices important to the success of a hybrid program were occurring. In fact, students also emphasized how well most teachers did in designing and teaching their hybrid classes.

Suggestions to Consider for Future Hybrid Students

Most of the points made by students to consider for future hybrid students have been discussed and will not be repeated here. However, the following points had a bit of a different focus.

Point 1: "The flexibility is wonderful and now, in some ways, it may be hard to go back to the F2F class because it would be hard to give up that flexibility—and you still have some F2F interaction. You can make the connection and then enhance it with the online. I'd say to students that you really get the best of both worlds." Again, students are busy people. More than 75% of graduate students work full-time (U.S. Census Bureau, n.d.); in addition, about 50% of graduate students are married (Gross, 2010), many with children, which leaves them with less time and less flexibility for formal education. It is no secret that many students initially choose hybrid or online learning over traditional classes simply because of the increased flexibility and added convenience.

Point 2: "It's important to understand what you are getting into. It's not going to be a shortcut, a quicker way to get your degree." Before enrolling in a hybrid course, many students equate less time spent in the classroom with less work. Unfortunately that is not the case, which is why it is so important they understand what hybrid learning is like before they enroll in a hybrid program.

Point 3: "Invest in reliable Internet services and computer hardware; that may seem very mundane to talk about, but it's important. If your Internet is not responding or your computer hardware is incompatible with the university's network, then that could become very cumbersome." Clearly students enrolled in a hybrid program need a dependable computer; commonly used software such as Microsoft Office and dependable Internet service, preferably broadband access, leads to greater efficiency when accessing and sending materials electronically.

Point 4: "Learn the CMS and don't expect the professor to teach it to you. You should be oriented [to the CMS], but you have to go and play. What does this do? What does that do?" Most universities offer online tutorials to acquaint students to the CMS. Although teachers should orient students to the CMS and how they specifically use it, students will find that the sooner they become familiar with the CMS the easier it will be for them to focus on the content of the course.

Point 5: "I'd say be prepared for work. I think sometimes people think that because it's online, it's academic light. Postings are so important; allow time, because it takes time. It takes time to write your own postings, it takes time to read and comprehend other people's postings, and it takes time to give feedback that is going to help your fellow students; so I would say invest the time to learn the system and to do good work." According to a meta-analysis of online learning studies published by the U.S. Department of Education (2009), "Students who took all or part of their class online performed better, on average, than those taking the same course through traditional F2F instruction, $p < .01$ across 51 contrasts" (p. xiv). However, one of the reasons for this finding may be attributed to the increased time hybrid and online learners spend on task. From that same report, "Studies in which learners in the online condition spent more time on task than students in the F2F condition found a greater benefit for online learning" (p. xv).

Point 6: "Be flexible; be open to a new learning experience, and extract the value out of it before you shut down. If you are not open, if you lack that [openness] in your initial experience, then you won't get that good experience, at least I don't think so." However, getting individuals to adopt new practices often takes years, depending on a number of factors, including knowledge of the innovation and the credibility of the change agent (Rogers, 1995). "There is nothing more difficult to plan, more doubtful of success, nor more dangerous to manage than the creation of a new order of things," said Machiavelli (see http://blog.gaiam .com/quotes/authors/niccolo-machiavelli).

Point 7: "I definitely think the mix is a really good balance for people, especially busy people with so much going on, those who are really committed to continuing their education. It [hybrid] really gives them the opportunity to do so." Again, this very practical comment is aligned with the flexibility students seek in graduate education. If it weren't for this flexibility, some individuals would simply not be able to pursue advanced degrees.

To summarize, the points hybrid students made for people thinking about enrolling in a hybrid program centered around the benefit of increased flexibility, the challenge of rigorous work, the necessity of Internet access and dependable technology, the need to intimately know the CMS, and the importance of having an open mind when engaging in a new learning process. Students who recognize the value in these recommendations are likely to reap more benefits and enjoyment from their hybrid learning experience.

What Students Say About Enrolling in Another Hybrid Learning Program

When asked, most of the students interviewed said they would enroll in another hybrid program or class, but they also had the following valuable remarks:

Student 1: Absolutely, I don't think I'd want to go to a traditional program, just because of the flexibility this has afforded me. I think, as we're all getting busier and busier, it's really neat that I'm able to continue my education and don't have to sacrifice my family. The best part was when the kids were home and I could be sitting home doing homework instead of being on campus for three hours. Especially for an adult learner, I think it's the right setting. For kids right out of high school it's different, but for older students it's great. I love it; in fact I'll probably look for another one [hybrid program].

Student 2: Yes, absolutely. Although I really enjoy F2F the benefits of hybrid are worth it. When you have so many other things going on, when you have Saturday or night classes just that alone is difficult, depending on what kind of other responsibilities you have. So even though I prefer and get the most out of in-class discussion and that atmosphere, I still think that there are huge benefits to having the flexibility of doing things online.

Student 3: I would consider it if the material matched my interest, and I certainly wouldn't dismiss a class because it's hybrid. Because you still do meet, it's not completely online. It would take quite a lot for me to do an entirely online program.

Student 4: I would investigate the instructional styles of the people teaching the classes. So, for example, if I had an opportunity to take a class in either hybrid or traditional format, I would want to compare the syllabi and see what the professor had in mind, because the hybrid really helps me with my personal life, and as a working person this is the way to go. I'm probably getting more out of this format than if I were sitting in a lecture tired after work, week after week. But if you have an opportunity to look at competing syllabi and competing instructors, it's conceivable that the best in a lecture class would beat a weak hybrid program. So, would I enroll in another hybrid program, yes. In fact, after talking with my wife, I am considering continuing to take more classes because I love the course material, I love the course structure and I'm pretty thrilled with the university right now.

Student 5: I definitely would, because it's the best of both worlds. I'm not sure if I'd ever enroll in an online only, maybe I would, depending on the course, but I like the F2F component, seeing all my peers, but I also like to be wearing my pajamas responding to people. I think you see two sides of people in a blended class. The F2F, again, if you are introverted you may not come out as much, but I've seen the introverted just blossom online. That's so rewarding, and they offer many diverse critiques or opinions that I never thought of, or they do a process in a completely different way, and I wouldn't have known that in the traditional class, because we don't see each other that way. You learn so much from your peers and it gives you so much opportunity online. So definitely I would.

Student 6: Yes, I actually prefer it; like I said, I didn't realize it right in the beginning, it was hard for me, but it's totally preferable. I think with adults it's preferable. It's nice to get a little grounding, see other students, see the teacher, you feel comfortable; but it's so nice to have that break. You still have something to do but there's a break. In the online week you still have to think and do the assignment and this was nice. I started talking with people I had not talked with before; people would ask, "Who is that?" "Oh, he's an engineer," and then we'd become friends. So you get that in class too, but you also miss some of the people that are really quiet, and I love that when we are online, we're all in a level playing field.

Student 7: Absolutely. I think that practical learning, what you do in the field, and the discussions, I always connected it to my learning. I remember so much of my peers now, I can go into my reservoir of thinking and say I was in a particular class and this person was discussing this. . . . so I think that the information associated with those classes, I can retain it better because of the healthy discussion. You keep hearing me say that this was huge to me because I was thinking that even though the books are great, the theory is great, and the research is great, but to tie the theory to practice the learning, among my peers in my generation, that's the wealth of knowledge for me. Just to be able to sit down at night, have a cup of hot tea and say I'm going to work for three hours. I own the decision that I'm not constrained; you know leaving work, coming to a class that I won't be present in that moment. So the hybrid worked for my whole life, so I'm definitely open to hybrid now.

Student 8: Definitely! I enjoy hybrid very much.

Student 9: I would be very open to choosing another entire hybrid program, but I think it would depend on the subject. If it is something that is very hands on or something that I think might be very difficult for me, I might want a traditional format.

Student 10: If I had a choice I would prefer F2F learning entirely. My experience had been that I've had the ability to travel to locations without much problem. Now that has changed for me personally and I can see the utility of taking a hybrid course because there would be times in lieu of travel that I could do things out of the comfort of my own home; but the type of learner that I am, I get a lot out of F2F interaction. I rely heavily upon nonverbal communication to either clarify something that I've said or be demonstrative and that's absent in the online environment. In the academic environment [F2F], I'd be more critical than I am in online because of those reasons.

Student 11: I would try *not* to, because I find value in socializing with other people and it depends on what I was trying to get out of the course, and if I just needed a course to get some certification and I didn't put a lot of weight in building relationships with those people, I think I would be ok taking hybrid courses, and I certainly would take it if it was all that was offered, but I really believe that there is some F2F contact that is needed to build relationships. One of the things that I am concerned about regarding the whole online course work in universities is that there is no camaraderie; when the students graduate they will not have stories to tell about the instructors. They won't have any of those bonds and if they don't develop a way to build bonds in school, how are they going to be able to effectively work in the work place. So I think if it was the right instructor, the right time, I would, but it wouldn't be my first choice.

In summary, 7 out of 11 students said they would definitely enroll in another hybrid learning experience. One student said she would consider it. Another student said she would be very open to doing another hybrid program, provided the content was not too hands on or too difficult for her. The remaining two students preferred the traditional F2F class because of increased social interaction, spontaneity, and the importance of nonverbal communication. However, both students said that although hybrid wouldn't be their first choice, they would enroll in a hybrid class again under the right conditions.

In closing, the information gleaned from student interview data has many implications for teachers who are interested in designing and teaching hybrid courses, and for students who are considering a hybrid program. Although the interviews were small in number, the interview data were very much aligned with what the literature tells us about hybrid learning and about good teaching practices in general. Much can be learned about the impact of teaching practices from student feedback if teachers are willing to listen.

CHAPTER ELEVEN

WHAT THE BEST HYBRID TEACHERS SAY

> I think that student engagement is greater in a hybrid course, and that I'm able to be more inclusive in a sense that students are more likely to speak up in class if they're also speaking up online. And I can hear students developing their own voices rather than simply reflecting mine.
>
> —Alan Aycock (personal communication, August 5, 2009)

THE PURPOSE OF THIS CHAPTER and Chapter 12 is to present interview data to help novice and seasoned hybrid teachers when planning, designing, teaching, and evaluating a student-centered hybrid teaching and learning course or program. This chapter focuses on what teachers interviewed say about hybrid courses in general, while the next chapter focuses on specific things these teachers do when teaching a hybrid course. Because of the richness of the data, many quotes are included in both chapters.

Interviews were conducted with 15 experienced hybrid teachers from different disciplines. These teachers' universities are located in central and western Canada, and the eastern, midwestern, northwestern, and southwestern United States. In total, those interviewed have taught over 400 hybrid courses in 18 different content areas. Enrollments in classes ranged from 4 to 500 students.

The semistructured interviews were digitally recorded and transcribed. Interview questions were adopted from the work of Garrison and Vaughan (2008) and from the University of Wisconsin–Milwaukee, Learning Technology Center's faculty development workshops. Table 11.1 provides pertinent information regarding the hybrid courses that were taught. Of those 15 teachers interviewed, eight were men, and participant ages ranged from late 30s to early 60s. At the time of interviews, all were employed as full-time academics and had already spent a substantial number of years in the academy. Thirteen had earned terminal degrees and one had completed all doctoral course work and was working on her dissertation research. Two teachers interviewed taught in a blended online format, which is discussed in Chapter 9.

Reasons Teachers Say They Chose Hybrid

Teachers named eight major reasons why they chose to teach in a hybrid format, and some were mentioned by several interviewees. Increased accessibility was mentioned as the initial reason by nearly one third of those interviewed.

Increased accessibility. Expanding reach to those who may not otherwise be able to enroll in a course if taught in a traditional F2F format was the number one reason teachers chose a hybrid format. However, it is important to note this was not simply a matter of geography, in that many who enrolled in hybrid classes were within 10 miles of the university. Rather, it was mostly related to the excessive demands on students' time. According to teachers, many students have family responsibilities in addition to professional responsibilities, and some of them have jobs requiring frequent travel. As you may recall from Chapter 8 (see Table 8.1), Gen Xers value work-life balance and are very technologically savvy for the most part. For millenniums, online learning is not perceived as something extraordinary, rather as a useful commodity to enhance learning (Kane, 2009; Oblinger, 2003; Thielfoldt & Scheef, 2004). Therefore teaching in a hybrid format is very much in agreement with what the literature states about Gen Xers' and millenniums' values and competencies.

A means to get quiet students to share their thoughts. As stated previously, F2F classroom participation is generally dominated by a small percentage of students, specifically those who are comfortable speaking

Table 11.1 Demographics of Interviewees and Classes

Interview	Subject Area or Discipline	Location of University	Hybrid Classes Taught	Average Class Size	Level of Class
1	Communication, diversity, and Leadership	Midwestern United States	50+	8–20	Graduate and undergraduate
2[a]	Leadership in education	Central Canada	12+	10–20	Graduate
3	Statistics in nursing	Northwestern United States	20+	20	Undergraduate
4	Assistive technology in education	Eastern United States	20+	18	Graduate
5	Psychology	Southwestern United States	10+	400–500	Undergraduate
6	Technology	Western Canada	30+	10–30	Graduate and undergraduate
7	Anthropology	Midwestern United States	50+	20–80	Graduate and undergraduate
8	Art and instructional technology	Midwestern United states	20+	15–20	Graduate and undergraduate
9	Instructional technology and educational research	Eastern United States	30+	8–25	Graduate and undergraduate
10	Biology and instructional technology	Midwestern United States	5+	30–33	Graduate and undergraduate
11	Organizational behavior, management, and leadership	Midwestern United States	90+	4–350	Graduate and undergraduate
12[a]	Instructional technology	Central Canada	30+	8–43	Graduate
13	Software design, executive education, business modeling for blended programs	Eastern United States	30+	20–120	Graduate and undergraduate
14	Health care	Eastern United States	15+	20	Graduate
15	Counselor education	Eastern United States	15+	20	Graduate

Note. [a] = teaching in a blended online format.

in a group setting without having substantial time for reflection. Unfortunately the majority of students in F2F classrooms do not fit this description for any number of reasons, including feelings of discomfort when speaking in a group setting, fear of saying something that may be incorrect, limited discussion time, not having adequate time to think about what they would like to say, and having little experience with the topic being discussed (http://gsi.berkeley.edu/teachingguide/sections/participation.html). When students are able to use asynchronous discussion in addition to F2F discussion, many of these reasons no longer exist. As one teacher stated:

> The first class I ever taught in hybrid was a diversity class. I realized there were a lot of people who were quiet in the F2F classroom, and they didn't want to engage in the class or simply needed more time to formulate their thoughts. Online they had great things to say, but they would not share them in class. One of my strategies was to take the discussion back into the classroom the next week, using this as a way to get those quiet people to elaborate on their thoughts.

A more respectful way to teach adult students. Because adult students have many responsibilities in addition to their student role, they frequently come to the classroom exhausted, which hinders their learning. As one teacher put it:

> So I have a big mix of professionals that work a ridiculous number of hours during the week, and this course was in a traditional format, occurring during the weekends. We met on Fridays from 5 pm to 10 pm and then all day Saturday and Sunday from 8:30 am to 4:30 pm. The truth is, they were exhausted, and I didn't get the learning that I wanted to give them. And they didn't get the learning that I know they signed up for.

By converting her class to hybrid, she was able to reduce F2F time and use the virtual classroom for learning activities when it best fit the students' schedules.

Course content is better taught in a hybrid design. Several teachers said this, particularly concerning the number of learning objects available to students on the Internet. As one teacher stated, "I find I can do more in terms of course content, what I ask students and the kinds of interactivity that occurs. In general the hybrid approach lends itself to active learning." Another said, "There are phenomenal resources online. For my students, having the luxury of time to explore them, to see them, and then to discuss them online, that is a much more meaningful way for them to spend their time. If I only had a F2F discussion, there would be three that would participate." Another faculty member stated, "We run games and simulations [online] twelve times a semester, where students can learn and compete."

From a pedagogical standpoint, the use of a hybrid design enhances learning. One teacher said, "Student engagement is greater in a hybrid course, and I'm able to be more inclusive in a sense that students are more likely to speak up in class if they're also speaking up online. And I can hear students developing their own voices rather than simply reflecting mine." Another teacher stated, "Students are more engaged and passionate in this type of format, which supports a variety of learning styles." The literature is reflecting similar findings. According to the U.S. Department of Education (2009), "Students who took all or part of their class online performed better, on average, than those taking the same course through traditional F2F instruction" (p. xiv).

Gives students a place to collaborate and learn from one another outside the classroom that didn't exist before. As mentioned in previous chapters, in a hybrid course learning continues outside the F2F classroom through continued online interaction. This constructivist approach to learning has proven very effective for adult learners (Knowles et al., 2005).

Brings in speakers from all over the world. Two instructors mentioned having guests from China and from Africa joining their discussions. As one teacher said, "As a guest, we invited the first lady of a country in Africa and we brought her into our classroom in a hook-up [video conference], and we do 300 video hook-ups a year. That's very powerful."

Hybrid enhances technology skills that are needed in the workplace. One teacher mentioned how the use of video conferencing and other technologies commonly used in hybrid courses better prepared students for the workplace: "We've given students the space to develop a five minute pitch on how they started a company and have them practice it on web conferencing, because frankly, when they go into the real world, they'll need that skill."

Teachers' Primary Benefits When Using Hybrid Design

Helps in tracking student progress. With the use of asynchronous discussion, the teacher may see who participates in discussion and the quality of that participation far better than in a F2F classroom. Asynchronous discussion provides an equal opportunity for students to earn discussion points, and it provides teachers with an opportunity to observe the degree of student learning.

Asynchronous discussion becomes a learning tool. Asynchronous discussion serves as a tool for constructivist learning and as a student record to use as a reference at any point during the course. Teachers may also take the opportunity to fill in missing components of the discussion and further clarify any misconceptions.

Asynchronous discussion becomes a writing tool. Much evidence supports a need for improved writing skills in today's workforce, specifically in both grammar and content. Participating in asynchronous discussion provides the opportunity to practice, which develops students' competency in thinking about what they want to say, learning to express themselves clearly when discussing sensitive topics without causing defensiveness in their audience.

Hybrid designs improve teaching. Because the course is planned and designed in advance, the weak spots in course design are more readily visible when teaching it. This increased visibility includes a heightened awareness of aligning content with learning outcomes, thereby creating the potential for enhanced student learning. As one teacher commented, "It brought the content in the forefront in a way that I really can't do in a F2F class."

Best practices become more readily transferable. If someone has done a good job developing a course or a portion of a course, other faculty are able to implement the design without having to spend excessive time creating one. For example, much of my hybrid course development is based on techniques I observed in other teachers' hybrid courses. This highlights the importance of teachers' having the opportunity to showcase and talk about their hybrid courses with one another.

Removes barriers to education for people in remote areas. The flexibility of hybrid course design means that the entire F2F portion of the class may be scheduled for one period of time. For example, two weekends of F2F activities during one semester permit students in remote areas to travel only twice to attend class. As one teacher put it, "I think basically a just society, and a good society is a society that looks at all people, and provides means to everyone. . . . so I think the greatest benefit is one of social justice for society and one of development of human potential."

Students take more responsibility for their learning. Considering discussions in previous chapters, this comment should come as no surprise. It is nearly impossible to design a hybrid class without creating an active learning environment where students interact with one another and thereby assume at least partial responsibility for creating a successful learning experience for themselves and for others enrolled in the class. As one student stated during interview, "To really get the quality of the program [hybrid], you need quality students that are going to put forth effort."

A well-designed hybrid course engages different types of learners. A goal of excellent teaching is to create learning experiences that have the potential of engaging learners across the spectrum (Pritchard, 2009). For example, some students may learn best through F2F interaction, while others may learn best through online simulations or case analyses. As one teacher put it, "The intent is to reach all learning styles so that no person is disengaged for the entire course."

Prepares students for workforce training. Hybrid learning better prepares students for the type of workforce training and development they are likely to experience. According to the American Society for Training and Development, hybrid teaching and learning environments is one of the top 10 trends to emerge in the knowledge delivery industry (Rooney, 2003). As one interviewee stated, "At the beginning of the class, if I frame it as, 'this is how corporations are moving to teach,' it helps them to realize, 'Okay, this is going to prepare me for how I may learn in the future.'"

Requires careful planning. Many teachers interviewed stated that creating a successful hybrid experience requires careful planning, which was viewed by some as a benefit and a challenge. As one interviewee commented:

> I think it is a primary benefit and a primary pain. It forces you to do more planning and work. . . . the key is that you have the pieces together so that nobody gets lost, and so when you do it well, it's truly rewarding and amazing. So this notion of "just in time teaching" goes away. I think as a result of that, you become a better educator.

What Teachers Say About Hybrid and Student Learning Outcomes

Much of what interviewees had to say about how hybrid course design is helpful in achieving student learning outcomes is covered in the preceding sections of this chapter. The points that follow are additional views regarding student learning outcomes.

Ready reference to learning materials. Everything is accessible on the course site where students can refer to it anytime they need to and where it won't get lost. As one teacher said, "They have a stronger repository of the course documents or any additional material that would help them to achieve the learning outcomes." They may learn when they are ready to learn versus being forced to come to class more frequently, which could create a hardship for them to be there. In addition to the course materials, they have the World Wide Web at their fingertips. They may explore and learn on their own and share relevant findings with others, and they may explore and learn with others through blogs, chat rooms, video conferencing, and online discussions.

Distance of time and space grants opportunity for reflection. The ability to reflect upon and evaluate what students are learning in the F2F classroom and what they are learning in the virtual classroom is a unique opportunity offered in a hybrid class. The distance of time and space allows for this type of reflective practice, which is critical in achieving the higher learning necessary when gaining professional competence (McAuliffe, 2006).

Limited ability to opt out. In a hybrid course that requires asynchronous discussion as a significant component of the course and as a substantial portion of the grade, it is difficult to opt out and still achieve success in the course. Moreover, as stated earlier, multiple modes of communication tend to give everyone more of an equal opportunity to participate. One teacher's example clearly illustrated this point.

> I've had some situations in particular with ethnic minorities, where students would not participate in the classroom because it doesn't fit with their understanding of the student-teacher relationship; yet, they have been very forthright online because there's nothing in their tradition stopping them.

This type of meaningful participation is one of the factors leading to increased student engagement, which is positively related to learning.

Role plays are more expressive. One interviewee stated she used role plays frequently in her hybrid course to help students achieve the learning outcomes. When comparing the quality of the role plays, she reported that role plays conducted online were more elaborate and more expressive than those in the F2F classroom. Along that same line, in my own hybrid teaching experience, conducting online negotiation between students has been very effective in preparing them for future negotiation role plays in the F2F classroom.

Creating conditions for a vibrant community of practice. A community of practice is a group engaged in shared activities to obtain knowledge in a specific content area or discipline (Merriam & Clark, 2006, p. 42). The community of practice model is based on creating effective teaching and learning relationships among those in the group so higher-order learning may occur. The community of practice model has been demonstrated to be a very effective one for adult learners (Lave & Wenger, 1991; Wenger, 1998). A hybrid class may be thought of as a community of practice. Thus, activities normally included in a community of practice, such as simulations, case studies, internships, and peer review, are likely to enhance higher learning in members who actively participate in these learning activities. One interviewee said, "In terms of writing, we've done a lot of peer review and peer draft review [as a means of achieving learning outcomes]. I've done peer review in the classroom and online, and it is much more effective online."

Hybrid design prepares students to think like a scientist. According to one interviewee, "One of the key learning outcomes [for his course] is to be able to think like a scientist and that is very hard to do in a F2F class." Thus, students could do the readings and prepare online by taking quizzes that demonstrated their level of understanding of those readings before coming to class, which helped them to achieve higher scores on major exams.

Primary Challenges When Teaching Hybrid Courses

Time intensive. All but two interviewed mentioned that designing and teaching a hybrid course takes a significant amount of time, not only up-front time for design but additional time to learn how to teach differently. In addition to what these experienced teachers say, certainly there is enough in the literature to support their claims (Kaleta, Garnham, & Aycock, 2005; Kaleta et al., 2007; Stanley, 2010). This book is devoted to help teachers design and teach hybrid courses, and what has already been said also supports the time intensiveness of the process. As an aside, along with evidence that supports more effective learning, students also spend more time learning in a hybrid course (U.S. Department of Education,

2009). Many times faculty will want to know how much additional time will be required. Unfortunately there is no easy answer to that question because it depends on any number of variables, including how you design your course and how you taught prior to adopting a hybrid format.

When designing a hybrid course, in addition to such things as the size of the class, learning outcomes, the class schedule, and all other factors associated with course design that have already been discussed, it is also important to consider one's teaching style previous to teaching a hybrid course. As Kaleta et al. (2007) say so well, "Faculty who are preparing to teach hybrid courses must be made aware of the importance of making the transition from acting as a presenter of content to becoming a facilitator of student learning" (p. 125). Basically this means moving from a teacher-centered course to a student-centered one.

It is difficult if not impossible to create a teacher-centered hybrid course, unless the teacher simply places lectures online and gives exams in the classroom or assigns a major paper or two. Teacher-centered classes clearly exist in varying degrees, and some students do well in this type of environment; however, a substantial amount of literature suggests adults learn best in student-centered environments (Brookfield & Preskill, 2005; Brown et al., 2001; Fink, 2003; Knowles et al., 2005; Merriam & Clark, 2006). The act of creating a student-centered learning environment leads to the addition of increased student-to-student, teacher-to-student, and content-to-student interaction; multiple incremental learning opportunities for students with rich and timely feedback from their colleagues and teachers; the use of rubrics that clearly explain what the assignments consist of and how they will be assessed; and all the remaining components of the student-centered approach to learning that have been discussed in the adult learning literature. According to Pegrum (2006), teachers who accept relativism as a positive position versus pedagogy of certainty, "are not disseminators of pre-established facts or the coaches of clearly defined skills; nor can students be viewed as empty vessels, passively waiting for knowledge. Rather, education is an exploratory partnership" (p. 17). For the most part, I would argue that the student-centered approach to learning takes more time for teachers and students to learn versus the hybrid course design, which because of the very nature of its design, applies the student-centered approach to learning to a greater degree than a F2F design is able to do, primarily because ongoing interaction occurs outside the classroom.

Technology usage. Challenges associated with hybrid may also occur in traditional courses but likely to a lesser degree. For example, one interviewee said, "I think the biggest challenge for me is the assumption I have that everybody has a certain level of computer literacy, which isn't the case. I found that especially surprising in an art class that I teach where the students are traditional age [18–20] and some don't use e-mail." Unfortunately what may occur in this type of situation is that the teacher spends additional time teaching technology in addition to course content, and usually that occurs outside the classroom. This point highlights the need for the availability of effective and timely technology support for students and teachers, and it emphasizes the importance of using technologies that are user friendly and less likely to fail. As one teacher who also serves in an administrative role stated, "I think the worst thing you can do is get a gifted teacher who may be uncomfortable with technology and try to turn him into a technologist; that's just bad use of human capital." On the other hand, a teacher using technology must know enough about it to avoid it becoming an impediment to the teaching and learning experience.

Keeping content cutting edge. A few interviewees mentioned that one of the challenges they faced when teaching totally online classes and hybrid classes was the notion of spontaneity, although to a lesser extent in hybrid. Because online and hybrid courses are generally entirely designed prior to the start of the class, bringing in cutting-edge research or current news events becomes a bit more challenging. As one interviewee commented:

> The content, I like to revise the day before I come to class; that's something that technical support and advisors have a hard time understanding because they are in the mode of an asynchronous course where everything is prepared a year in advance. They have a hard time understanding that it is a graduate course; it has to do with cutting edge research, last minute events, ideas, books just read and articles just published.

To overcome this challenge in her online courses, this particular teacher held a synchronous session each week using software that easily permitted her and the students to participate. This example demonstrates the importance of faculty insisting that using technology as a tool to effectively teach is what is needed versus letting technology hinder development of effective learning environments.

Selling the students on hybrid. As emphasized earlier, students are busy people. Thus, to sell them on the idea that hybrid is a more effective way of learning may initially be challenging, especially when they begin to realize that it may take them more time to learn in a student-centered environment that uses technology. From their perspective, they are being asked to intimately learn a CMS (for those new to it), learn how to use technologies that may be new to them, learn in a different way, adjust to the instructor's style of teaching while simultaneously focusing on the learning outcomes. The best way to overcome this skepticism is to clearly explain during the initial F2F class how the class will be structured and why it is structured that way. Invariably some students would rather just hear a lecture and go home. However, as one interviewee stated, "They like it [hybrid] once they get the hang of it."

Over the years I have asked students to complete an online survey anonymously to determine their perceptions of how the course is going. With response rates averaging in the 80% to 90% range, 10% or less of the students tell me they prefer more lectures. (Student-centered course designs generally do contain some degree of lecturing.) While knowing a few students would predominantly prefer to hear lectures, I continue to design student-centered learning environments regardless of whether it may be more time intensive for the students and for me because of the overwhelming evidence that adult students learn more effectively in student-centered environments.

Selling peers on the value of hybrid course design. One interviewee spoke of the need to sell her colleagues on the value of the hybrid course design in relation to effective learning. Scholars are busy people, like students, and there is an up-front time investment in designing and teaching a hybrid course, especially if the scholar has been primarily employing a teacher-centered design. Many scholars also need convincing that technology can be an effective pedagogical tool. Substantially more teachers are using technology today than one decade ago, as indicated by the significant body of research that has demonstrated its effectiveness and the increase in the number of online and hybrid courses being taught at today's universities, including highly ranked ones.

Based on data from over 2,500 colleges and universities, Allen and Seaman (2007) of the Sloan Consortium, a professional organization that focuses on integrating online and hybrid education into mainstream higher education, reported the following: in the United States during the fall term in 2006, 3.5 million students (about 20% of all students enrolled in higher education) took at least one online course, representing a 10% increase over the number reported the previous year. Overall, the average growth rate in higher education for the preceding 5 years had been 1.5% per year, while the average growth rate in online education for the same period in time was reported as 9.7% per year.

One interviewee mentioned that educators often make the assumption that teachers teach more effectively in a F2F class. She made it clear that for her and, she suspected, others as well, that simply was not the case.

> I found the F2F meetings most challenging because I am more comfortable online as an instructor. And very often I hear people on campus express the need for someone to teach a course F2F before teaching it online. . . . and the implication is always that you teach better F2F. And I always suggest that people have different teaching styles just as they have different learning styles and there may be people, and I count myself in this, that teach better online than F2F. . . . so that is the biggest challenge for me [referring to the assumption that teaching F2F is better].

Selling administration on the necessary resources. One interviewee mentioned her struggles teaching her hybrid courses in an institution that did not have the necessary tools or technical support for hybrid courses. In some instances, she was forced to reduce her use of fairly common technologies based on what was available to her and to her students. Successful hybrid and online programming generally takes place in institutions whose administrators have developed a clear vision regarding online learning; furthermore, that vision is not only communicated to staff and faculty but is also financially supported with the necessary technology and support services.

Advice for Novice Hybrid Teachers
Based on Major Lessons Learned

The following suggestions were made by several of the people interviewed. Points repeated here that are discussed elsewhere in the book primarily serve as further justification.

Start small and start early. Don't underestimate the time it will take to design your hybrid course or to redesign your F2F or online class into a hybrid course. Faculty reported working on their first hybrid course two to three months before teaching it. Most began with placing a few elements of the course online.

Keep your design student-centered and focused on the learning outcomes. One teacher who mentored other teachers to become more student-centered and outcome focused in their course design uses a 2009 YouTube video titled, "Teaching Teaching and Understanding Understanding" (http://www.youtube.com/watch?v = iMZA80XpP6Y); whose subject is constructing knowledge versus transmitting knowledge. Adults learn best when knowledge is constructed, and for knowledge to be constructed, learning activities must be student-centered and not teacher-centered.

Plan and design your course before beginning to teach it. Teachers emphasized the need for careful planning of the in-class and out-of-class components of the hybrid course, especially focusing on the integration of the two, which has been discussed in detail in Chapter 4, Question 3.

Remain organized, and learn from what you are doing. Teachers stressed the importance of remaining organized to avoid confusion among students and to use their time wisely. It was also suggested that teachers learn from failures and successes, should keep a log of what works and what doesn't, and review it prior to designing their next hybrid course.

Avoid trying to do too much. Some teachers said they wanted to keep their courses current; to do so, they frequently added assignments involving a news event or newly reported research findings. They learned rather quickly to replace another assignment with the new material. If they failed to do that, the course work became too much.

Attend a workshop and work with a mentor. Many said attending a workshop on hybrid course design helped them in designing and teaching their first hybrid course. Others mentioned that having an experienced hybrid teacher as a mentor was important because they could run ideas by the mentor before implementing them in their courses.

Let technology serve as a tool versus a prescription for how and what to teach. Several teachers cautioned against using technology that was complicated, difficult to support, and unfamiliar. They also cautioned against letting technology dictate design instead of using technology as a tool to assist learners in achieving learning outcomes.

Set student expectations during the initial F2F class. Teachers advised clearly explaining student expectations during the first F2F class. Interviewees emphasized the importance of making students aware that reduced in-class time did not equate to reduced time spent on achieving learning outcomes.

Be prepared in how you respond to failed technology. Sometimes technology fails. One teacher said she successfully used the same technology in her classes a number of times. When she used the same technology in her large lecture class of 300 students, the technology no longer worked properly. After hearing from several students, she quickly canceled the assignment to avoid wasting students' time, causing them frustration. She then had to make some rather quick adjustments in assignments to compensate for the failed assignment.

Be present in all components of your class. Interviewees stressed the importance of being present for the out-of-class learning activities as well as the in-class ones. As one teacher put it, "Otherwise students get the impression that it is just *their work*, and therefore is not technically part of the class."

Be sure your instructions are specific and clearly written. Teachers emphasized that their getting it wrong in the online portion of the class is very counterproductive in time management for the teacher and the students. This may imply lack of parity in different instructional modes. If unclear directions are given repeatedly in online instruction, students begin to question rather quickly why the teacher is teaching online and why they have enrolled in a hybrid course.

View your course from a student perspective. One of the primary reasons many hybrid faculty workshops are taught in a hybrid format is to help faculty learn to see things from the students' perspective. As one interviewee recommended,

> Walk yourself through your entire course. Ask yourself, "If I were a student, where would I get caught up?" As I walk through each assignment, I invariably find mistakes, or I see something that I thought was clear at the time that I wrote it, but later recognize that it is no longer so. If you don't fix these things, it will definitely be a future problem for you and the students.

Advice to Novice Hybrid Students

The primary purpose of this section is to assist hybrid teachers with knowing what to tell students as they begin their work in a hybrid course. Just as hybrid may be a new experience for teachers, it is also a novel experience for many learners, especially if they are primarily accustomed to teacher-centered designs. At the close of a hybrid class, asking students to develop a bulleted list of recommendations for hybrid students can be helpful in preparing future students for a successful hybrid learning experience.

Don't be afraid to ask for help. Students who are enrolled in a hybrid course for the first time often have questions regarding scheduling of in-class and out-of-class time. Interviewees recommended that students read the syllabus carefully and be sure to ask questions regarding anything that is unclear.

Be prepared to schedule more time for a hybrid class as compared to a F2F class. As with anything else, there is a learning curve associated with a new way to learn. Therefore plan on spending more time doing the work for your initial hybrid class.

Avoid the use of jargon and acronyms when posting. Because a hybrid learning experience generally involves frequent online interaction with peers and the teacher, it is important that others are able to understand what you are communicating. Posting without using jargon or undefined acronyms helps in this regard. One teacher commented, "I actually give my students a little handout of how to be a helpful blended learner."

Post responses in word processing software before posting to the CMS. Most CMSs do not have sophisticated word processing capabilities. Thus, from a time management standpoint, it is helpful to post your work in a word processing software, then copy and paste it in the CMS.

Make sure your hardware and software are up to date, and that you have access to a high-speed connection on a regular basis. Although top-of-the-line computer hardware is not necessary, dependable hardware that is fairly current is necessary to fully participate in course activities. Access to a high-speed connection to view videos or participate in video conferencing is very important.

Be aware of how to get technical support if needed. Many universities have technical support personnel available to students enrolled in online or hybrid classes. If it is not stated in the syllabus, be sure to ask how to access your school's technical support department and when it is available.

Be comfortable using commonplace technology. Although it is not necessary to become a technical wizard, being familiar with commonplace technologies such as e-mail, the web, search engines, library databases, and the university's CMS will better prepare students for success when taking a hybrid course.

Do the work over multiple sessions instead of working on it all day. Rather than attempting to complete all assignments for the week in one sitting, schedule multiple periods during the week to complete work. The literature on adult learning indicates that incremental learning is more effective for adults (Knowles et al., 2005).

To avoid wasting time, organize work. Systematically organize work, as less time will be spent looking for things and getting frustrated when unable to find them. Simple organizing tactics like creating topic folders for the course and faithfully uploading course files and work into appropriately labeled folders may be significant time savers. Placing these entire file folders on a readily transportable flash drive provides access to academic work when traveling.

Take advantage of technical support as needed. Universities usually have tutorials to familiarize students with the CMS and other frequently used technologies. Some universities also have F2F technology workshops. Taking advantage of these services may save an enormous amount of time and frustration.

Expect to assume responsibility for your own learning. Hybrid courses are generally very student-centered. Students are expected to add value to the class by preparing for online and F2F discussion and by sharing relevant sources of information and life experiences with peers and teachers. Be prepared to do this in any hybrid course.

Recognize that the contributions you make to the class affect the quality of the class. As one student interviewed said, "It takes high quality students to have a high quality hybrid experience." Much of the learning activities are dependent upon collaboration with others in the class. Peer review is often a component as is small group work.

In summary, the goal of this chapter is to present what several hybrid teachers have learned through years of practice in designing and teaching hybrid courses. Most of what has been said is aligned with the current literature on hybrid teaching and learning and adult learning theory and principles. The next chapter explores more specific practices these teachers routinely apply in their hybrid course designs.

CHAPTER TWELVE

WHAT THE BEST HYBRID TEACHERS DO

So, when you have everybody in the room, what you should be doing is so transformational that it can only happen to people in that room.

—Stephen Laster (personal communication, September 23, 2009)

T HIS CHAPTER, written in a question-and-answer format, describes how experienced hybrid teachers apply important hybrid design principles to their hybrid courses. For the most part, responses have been summarized for brevity, although in some cases direct quotes are included for emphasis, context, and clarity.

How Do You Develop Social Presence in Your Hybrid Class?

As you may recall from Chapter 4, social presence refers to open communication and group cohesion with the ultimate goal of developing emotional bonding and camaraderie. According to experts in adult education (Knowles et al., 2005; Maslow, 1972), creating social presence is an important factor in effective adult learning environments.

Several respondents mentioned they began their hybrid courses with a F2F class in which students introduced themselves and gave specific information about themselves and their families or significant others. One respondent said she begins by posing a question related to the topic of the day, asking the students to introduce themselves in the context of that topic. For example, she may ask students to identify how their life experiences have influenced their thinking about diversity. She often continues the discussion online. Another said she asked students to reveal something about themselves in the F2F class that will help everyone remember them online. This teacher said she will never forget the student who stated that she had 13 Christmas trees every year.

A number of respondents said their activities were designed to establish social presence specific to the F2F and online portion of the class. Many asked students to introduce themselves in both environments; pictures and favorite websites were often included in their online introductions. Some respondents mentioned creating places (virtual lounges) in the CMS where students could chat on any topic that interested them and others enrolled in the class. Many said they used small groups, no larger than six students, to work together on certain assignments, including discussion assignments. Some respondents said they changed group membership every few weeks, and others left groups in place for the entire term. One individual reported he used discussion forums almost exclusively for developing social presence because of their versatility. Another said he had students work in small groups to solve crossword puzzles relating to exam questions prior to taking exams, and that helped them develop social presence.

One teacher said she made frequent online announcements to let students know she was present and engaged in their learning. Another teacher said he provided feedback on initial assignments within a day or two of submission so students would better understand expectations for assignments. In this way he began developing social presence with them early in the course. Another teacher said she used Audacity (http://audac ity.sourceforge.net), a free and simple-to-use audio recording and editing software, to record podcasts spontaneously to give the class overall feedback on a routine basis. Another respondent said:

> I think it important to create social presence in both environments. I use spontaneous activities that require energy and may be completed quickly, such as brainstorming, in the F2F classroom. Online we do things like icebreakers and scavenger hunts that help students develop social presence virtually while also becoming familiar with the CMS.

One respondent said after she got to the know students, she developed social presence on an individual basis, depending on the need of the student. Some students needed more frequent interaction while others did not. Another teacher said the less-sensitive discussions took place during the F2F class, and once students knew each other better, the more sensitive and more difficult discussions occurred online. Another teacher said, "Use of humor; hobbies; children—we set time aside for that. I tell the students, 'Don't give offense, but don't take offense.' Many students who are quiet in class participate fully online."

In summary, these experienced hybrid teachers develop social presence in F2F and online environments somewhat differently, using what they perceive works best for each environment. Learning activities in both environments include the frequent use of social interaction regarding course topics and how they apply to real-life situations. According to the interview data, it appeared they created a learning environment of intentional informality whereby mutual trust and respect were equally as important as learning.

How Do You Orient Students to the Hybrid Design of Teaching and Learning?

Responses to this question fell into one of three categories: orientation to the hybrid design itself, orientation to a student-centered approach to learning, or orientation to the various technologies used throughout the course. Responses have been categorized applying that taxonomy.

Hybrid course design. Although universities have improved in identifying course designs in their list of course offerings, identifying the mode of course delivery still remains a challenge in some academic environments. In all fairness to students, they should know before the first class that the course is being taught in a hybrid mode, and they also should have at least a rudimentary understanding of what constitutes a hybrid course. Thus, several respondents said they e-mailed enrollees well in advance of the first day of classes to explain how the class would be conducted. However, many times some of the students did not yet have an e-mail address associated with the university, in which case teachers called or e-mailed the admissions office for contact information.

The information provided to students before the first day of classes included general information about a hybrid learning approach, the syllabus and schedule of F2F classes, and the technology that would be used throughout the course. Teachers also emphasized that fewer F2F classes did not lighten the workload for the course. Some teachers said they explained to students the necessity of reading the syllabus carefully and developing a calendar for F2F class times. They encouraged students to remain on target with due dates for online and F2F assignments. Teachers stressed the need for time management skills, including blocking off time on a calendar to complete online work. For additional information, some teachers directed students to the university's website on hybrid learning.

Finally, a few teachers asked students to take an online survey containing several questions about their comfort with technology, their level of technological skills, and their time management skills. They were also asked the degree to which they took initiative for their own learning and how comfortable they were working independently. If students scored low on this survey, they weren't prohibited from enrolling in a hybrid course, but they were cautioned that this type of learning environment may be difficult for them to adjust to. An example of such a survey can be found at https://esurvey.tlt.psu.edu/Survey.aspx?s = 246aa3a5c4b64bb 386543eab834f8e75.

Student-centered approach to learning. Many interviewed mentioned the importance of explaining to students that the class was designed to be very learner centered, meaning students needed to take responsibility for their own learning by actively preparing for and participating in the online discussions as well as the F2F components of the class. Furthermore, students were told that what they contributed to the class influenced their colleagues' learning experience as well as their own. Students were told that the primary role of the teacher in a student-centered course was to make certain the learning activities helped them achieve the learning outcomes. Some interviewees said students often needed to be reminded about these points throughout the duration of the course.

Technology. Several interviewees mentioned the importance of being certain that e-mail exchanges were functional. Some teachers sent an initial welcoming e-mail to students, asking them to confirm receipt, which helped ensure the functioning of e-mail correspondence by identifying and resolving any problems before the class began.

Other technological aspects mentioned included orienting students to the CMS during the first F2F class and through online activities such as scavenger hunts, including links in the syllabus to tutorials or help sheets for the CMS or for other technologies, making certain at least one student in a small group has good technology skills, encouraging students to ask for help rather than wasting time and becoming increasingly frustrated, using readily available and simple technologies that instructors had technical knowledge of and could offer technical support, emphasizing students need to plan for technology failures and go to a library or another public place with accessible technology to complete work if their home technology isn't functioning, and making certain students have contact information for ongoing technological support.

How Does the Size of Your Class Influence Your Course Design?

This section focuses on large class enrollments, greater than 100 students. Two teachers interviewed routinely taught large lecture classes in a hybrid format. Both said the large enrollments significantly influenced how they structured the class.

One of the teachers said 50% of the lecture portion of the class was placed online synchronously with collaborative learning software that allowed for exchanges between students and teacher. Students were able to use icons to indicate when they had a question or were confused about a concept. These synchronous sessions were archived so that students who missed the lecture could view and listen to it at another time, and students who already attended the lecture could listen to it again for review. The remaining 50% of the lecture was F2F with the teacher using clickers during class. This teacher emphasized the importance of ongoing interaction with students—even with a class of 500. As he put it, "I think the value of what happens during live interactions outweighs the decreased flexibility [meeting online at a specific time] when you have synchronous sessions."

This same teacher said that after he had tried to conduct asynchronous discussions in a class that size, it failed miserably even with the help of two teaching assistants. He stressed that automation in all things is key with a large class. All his exams were objective, and answers were electronically scanned to determine scores. Scores were electronically transmitted to the CMS grade book, sometimes within hours after the exam. He said a downside of such a large class was the inability to assess students' competencies when writing about vital concepts. He suggested making the syllabus for the course much more detailed than for a F2F course. As he put it, "If you do this it will save you tons of hours and headaches."

Finally, this teacher said that although students may be familiar with technology to a certain extent, especially for fun, he often found that knowledge of technology for learning purposes was lacking. He commented, "That's sort of my counter argument for the digital generation. . . . when I say this software works better with Firefox than Internet Explorer, some students will ask, 'What's Firefox?' One student asked if it was a library browser."

The other teacher who routinely taught large lectures with 300 students and also taught hybrid classes with enrollments of 10 to 50 students stated:

> It is really different because in small classes my goal is to engage students in thoughtful reflections, have them engage with each other in discussions that may not otherwise happen in the classroom, or to introduce them to new topics that I prepared. So the focus is much more on interaction and collaborative learning that takes place online. In the large lecture, it becomes more of putting material out there [electronically] and hopefully engaging students through online strategies to learn the material, to think reflectively, but I don't see the depth of their reflection, nor do peers see it at the same level as in a smaller class. So I think it's far harder to engage them and have that interaction with them and push them to think at the same level that I could in a small class.

This particular teacher used F2F classes for her lectures. However, during the F2F sessions, she also incorporated time for small groups (4–6 students) to discuss more difficult concepts briefly before moving forward with the lecture. Her goal was to incorporate small group interaction for those who learned best this way; this also encouraged student participation in a large lecture class. She stated:

> The large lecture becomes much more of an active place of learning. What I have found is if I say to a group of 300, "What is the answer?" no one is going to raise a hand because who wants to raise a hand in a group of 300 people? But if I say, "Ok, Team 15, you've spent a few minutes discussing this question. What is your team's answer?" that becomes a whole lot easier.

Her two teaching assistants served as facilitators for permanently assigned groups of about 30 students who met weekly for 50 minutes to discuss course content and logistics. Team skills were emphasized during these discussion sessions. The sessions also included student peer review of other groups' work. Additionally, asynchronous discussion took place in each discussion group, and the teaching assistant facilitated those online discussions. It is important to emphasize with this model that teachers and discussion leaders must have a unified vision for implementing hybrid instructional concepts and procedures.

These two examples illustrate different approaches in designing a hybrid learning experience for large lecture classes. Both these instructors recognized the importance of interaction as a primary learning tool, and with the help of teaching assistants, both found creative ways to incorporate frequent means of interaction into the large lecture course design.

How Do You Schedule the F2F Time and the Out-of-Class Time?

Teachers interested in teaching in a hybrid course design often want to know how much of their class should be online and how much F2F time should be reduced. Many factors should be considered, including course content, level of instruction (graduate vs. undergraduate), university policy, teaching style, and previous hybrid teaching experience. Most expert hybrid teachers recommend novice hybrid teachers begin by placing a small amount of the course online. Because those interviewed were experienced hybrid teachers, all responses presented here may not necessarily work well for novices.

In response to how the course should be scheduled, most interviewed said it depended on the topic and the learning activities. One teacher said she put all the elements of her course on index cards. She then thought about how to teach those elements and designed her course accordingly. Another teacher said he believed it was dependent on teaching style. For him, reducing the F2F time by one third "felt right." One teacher said that a 50% reduction of F2F worked well for the biology class he was teaching. Another teacher said the university predefined the amount of F2F time that could be reduced, which she said wasn't always ideal, but she worked within the guidelines as best as possible. Another teacher scheduled more F2F time at the beginning of a qualitative research class, but as the class progressed, the learning activities were better suited for online work, so the class met less frequently. Overall, she reduced class time by about 50%. One teacher reduced F2F time by 80%, knowing that by doing so, the university would classify the course as totally online, which meant that class enrollment would be capped at 25 students, giving her the advantage of going from 50 to 25 students, making the class more manageable.

One teacher had the following strong views regarding how to schedule F2F time:

> Ten years ago I'd say you really need to get the class together at least every four weeks. It's different today; my view is when you get the class together (F2F), there had better be a really good reason, and if you are going to bring them together to lecture to them, may the gods help you. So, when you have everybody in the room, what you should be doing is so transformational that it can only happen to people in that room. How often should you do that? It depends on what is happening in the flow of the course. And so it's very much dependent on the material you're covering, the goals of the course and your teaching style. And the demographics also influence this; the younger the students, the more there is a babysitting factor. I don't think there is any magic formula.

The variability in these responses supports the idea that no one specific rule appears to work best for all hybrid course designs and for all teachers and students. Instead, many factors are involved in how much F2F time should be reduced and when it should be reduced. Another consideration is that the widely accepted concept of F2F time being directly proportional to learning may not be true. Instead, learning may be more directly related to the amount of time students spend on the subject; in fact, findings from the U.S. Department of Education (2009) support this relationship.

How Do You Integrate F2F and Out-of-Class Components?

It is important to note that in general integration of F2F with online learning activities is critical in creating an effective hybrid design. As one teacher stated:

> When I first started teaching hybrid courses I didn't feel the need to bring online work into the F2F class and students were viewing the online week as a week off, but then when I realized I had to hold them

accountable for that online work by bringing it back into the classroom, it significantly improved the quality of the online work.

One teacher said she often began discussions in the F2F classroom and continued them online. She did this for several reasons, including time management, opportunity for participation, and depth of discussion. More in-depth discussion occurred online, she said, especially with sensitive topics. Another teacher said she assigned readings, giving students questions regarding those readings before the F2F class where they would then discuss the questions. Another teacher said she placed the didactic portion of the course online and left the F2F time for experiential learning activities and student presentations. Yet another teacher said she designed online investigations followed by an online discussion using a discussion rubric. She informs students in advance what they will be discussing during the F2F time.

One teacher approached integration a bit differently: "So I guess it's like I treat the whole class like an online class and then I think about how I can take advantage of a F2F meeting. The class that I teach is a project class, so I try to use the F2F time to encourage creative ideas." Another teacher said he has a series of components for each of the topics he teaches during the semester. He decides which of those components should be online and which should be part of the F2F class, but in all cases all components are very much integrated with one another regardless of where they take place. For example, he said his course often included a section on Islam. He may begin by having students bring some questions to class with them. They could view a video on Islam during class and answer questions about the video. They may continue the discussion online, where he asks them additional questions about features of Islam, and he may also give them an online quiz. Then he might conclude by bringing in a guest lecturer, knowing that the students will be well prepared at that point to ask some great questions. Another teacher said she avoided bringing sensitive topics discussed in depth online back into the F2F classroom. She believed it made some students uncomfortable to further discuss their comments in a F2F situation.

From these examples, it is clear experienced hybrid teachers view their class as one integrated learning experience that involves frequent interaction regardless of where that interaction occurs. Just as in the case of addressing how much F2F time to schedule, there seems to be no magic formula. Rather, how the integration of learning environments occurs is a question of class size, teaching style, content being taught, and an array of other variables.

How Do You Avoid Creating an Excessive Workload for Hybrid Students and for You?

As one teacher put it, "You can't add the online component without getting rid of something." It's somewhat analogous to living situations; if something new arrives, then something old goes, otherwise the living environment becomes unlivable. So it is with a hybrid course. It can't be designed with the online component as an add on. Instead, the entire course is redesigned to create a student-centered learning experience that takes place in multiple environments and at the same time meets the student learning outcomes. As several interviewed pointed out, workload is not only a challenge in a hybrid environment, but one that occurs in F2F and online classes.

Focus on the learning outcomes. Several interviewed mentioned it was important to focus on learning activities that had a direct impact on one or more of the learning outcomes. Another teacher recommended not hesitating to cut a learning activity from the class if the activity was not going as planned.

Chunk major assignments. Several interviewed mentioned the importance of chunking the material with multiple due dates versus giving large assignments with one due date. Chunking the work was viewed as beneficial because it gave the teacher an opportunity to provide feedback on a portion of the assignment so students could improve on their work instead of receiving an unsatisfactory grade on a major assignment. Chunking also reduces the likelihood of students procrastinating.

Don't assign multiple tasks due at the same time. Several teachers said students generally have a certain number of hours per week to complete their work. Thus, when work is not spaced evenly throughout the duration of the course, it causes unnecessary stress and leads to a higher incidence of poor-quality work.

Frequently ask students and yourself about workload. One interviewee said a law professor used open discussion forums for her students. She didn't like to read from the computer screen, so she printed hundreds of pages of discussion postings, which she felt compelled to respond to because students had put so much time into them. To avoid these types of situations, the interviewees recommended evaluating the workload frequently.

What Particular Teaching and Learning Activities Are Well Suited to the Hybrid Design?

This section primarily focuses on ideas that have not yet been covered.

Building and sharing web libraries. A few interviewees mentioned the value of students' being asked to build a web library throughout a course and share those web resources with others in the class. This helps everyone keep current in the topic area by exposing them to multiple perspectives, which also provides opportunities for critical analysis and further discussion.

Reflective practice. Much has already been said about the benefits of reflecting on topics outside the classroom, where time constraints are generally not as much of a challenge. Reflective practice often occurs online in asynchronous discussions.

Peer review, including sharing drafts of written assignments. Several teachers interviewed mentioned that peer review works well in a student-centered course that has an online component. Student reviewers and the students whose work is being reviewed benefit from the process in that reviewers gain new knowledge and different perspectives and those being reviewed get feedback on their work, providing them with an opportunity to improve on it before final submission. The teacher also benefits from submissions of higher-quality work.

Video, simulations, and graphic analysis. The number of graphics, simulations, and videos available on the Internet makes this type of assignment easy to construct. Some interviewees mentioned that when used appropriately, video, simulations, and graphics can be very engaging and effective tools for learning.

More exposure to international guest speakers. The accessibility to podcasts, video conferencing, and asynchronous discussion makes it much easier to invite international guest speakers into a hybrid classroom. One interviewee brought several Chinese students into her hybrid course to discuss views on gender equality in an asynchronous discussion. Neutral gender names were assigned to all participants so those involved in the discussion did not know if they were responding to a male or female, which was reported to have changed the dynamics of the discussion considerably. On another occasion, she brought into an asynchronous discussion guests from Singapore and Vietnam.

Small group work. Several hybrid teachers mentioned they used small groups for many learning activities. Reaching consensus and collaborating within a small group was reported to be more time efficient than working together as an entire class. Feedback could also be given at the group level versus at the individual level, which saved teachers time.

Case analysis. Case analyses were often discussed in small groups online and then with the class during the following F2F meeting. Analyses were compared and contrasted, and students learned from the multiple perspectives. Some teachers had students narrate PowerPoint slides of their case analysis online, and a F2F or asynchronous discussion would follow. One teacher had students review a case study during a F2F class. The teacher provided some insights, then an online role play followed in the form of a talk radio show where students called in to speak with the show's host, in this case the teacher, to argue specific positions. A debriefing in the form of an online discussion followed.

Sharing and evaluating research. Some teachers reported having students work in small groups to develop a critical literature review. Findings were then presented during a F2F class or online, followed by a discussion.

Experiential learning activities occurring in the community. The teacher whose students went into the community and analyzed public art also interviewed community members regarding their thoughts on the art. Analyses and the interview data were discussed in the classroom and online, and formed the basis of students creating a piece of public art to be displayed in the community.

Continuing dialogue. The activity mentioned the most frequently was continuing a discussion beyond the F2F class. Interviewees cited increased participation and many other positives about ongoing interaction and learning.

One interviewee commented, "I'd actually ask, 'What doesn't work in a hybrid design?' I think courses that are built on active learning principles work across disciplines. On the other hand, I think a straight lecture class would be one format that wouldn't work as nothing would occur between F2F classes."

What Technologies Do You Use on a Regular Basis When Teaching a Hybrid Course?

Table 12.1 gives the type of technology, the number of teachers interviewed who were using it, and its purposes. Names of specific software mentioned by those interviewed are included to provide examples in a specific category. Note that these experienced hybrid teachers are using relatively few technologies, which are for the most part simple to use, more readily accessible, and likely to be supported by the university and are compatible with the CMS.

A teacher who teaches technology said:

> As much and as fast as everything changes, nothing's changing. . . . One of my hobbies is wood working. There are two kinds of wood workers. There are the ones that buy the tools, use them well and have them in their toolbox forever and there are the ones that seem to have to buy a new tool every month and never master how to use them. The key is that the tools you put in your toolbox must help you achieve the outcomes you set out to achieve. The same is true with technology. I want

Table 12.1 Technology Used by Experienced Hybrid Teachers

Type of Technology	Number of Teachers Using It	Purpose
CMS (blackboard, D2L, WebCT)	15	Discussion, small group discussion, grade book, e-portfolios, whiteboard, posting narrations, posting course materials, posting links to websites, drop box to store student work, quizzes, surveys, online journaling, synchronous chat
Narrated PowerPoint slides	6	Mini lectures
Video clips	5	Apply concepts
Multimedia editing software (Audacity, Breeze, Camtasia, Nero, Voice Thread)	5	Provides podcasts, gives students spontaneous narrated feedback, and provides narrated video demonstrations
Collaborative learning software (Elluminate, Wimba)	3	Can conduct synchronous class with audio and video capability; teacher and students interact with one another in real time
Clickers	2	Immediate feedback to teacher regarding whether students are learning a concept correctly

the simplest delivery method I can have to elegantly deliver my teaching and learning. The more complicated, the worse it is.

What Do You Do When Technology Fails?

Responses to this question were straightforward and fairly consistent. With students who were experiencing technology problems, teachers said that for the most part they talked about the problems with the students and they solved them together. Most teachers said if a certain technology failed for them they were likely not to use it again. For example, one teacher scheduled a synchronous chat and less than one quarter of the class logged on. Some students logged on as much as 20 minutes late. She never scheduled another chat because she came to the conclusion that it wouldn't work well for her student demographic. One teacher commented it was far easier to solve technology problems in a class of 12 than in a class of 300. Another commented, "It's an awful feeling when the technology fails. That's why I really tend to keep it simple."

In closing, it is no surprise that the experienced hybrid teachers interviewed design their courses continually applying practices the adult learning literature espouses as most effective in achieving student learning outcomes. It was also clearly evident that each of these teachers is passionate about learning and cared deeply about the quality of the learning experience designed for the students. As one hybrid teacher put it, "The most important thing for people to realize is that blended learning isn't a unique method. If you think about it, it's how learning has been happening. There are different degrees of blended, but basically to be effective, you have to know how to blend if you want to reach today's students."

CONCLUSION

CHAPTER THIRTEEN

COMING FULL CIRCLE, FUTURE RESEARCH, AND FINAL REFLECTIONS

Mentors and apprentices are partners in an
ancient human dance, and one of teaching's
greatest rewards is the daily chance it gives us
to get back on the dance floor.

—Parker Palmer (1998, p. 25)

W E BEGAN THIS JOURNEY by describing what hybrid is and is
not. Through that descriptive process, the major elements that
constitute a good hybrid course design were discussed, including creating a student-centered teaching and learning experience where
the student takes primary responsibility for learning and where the
teacher focuses on how to best design learning experiences that target
learning outcomes. The role of the teacher and the role of the student are
blurred through the richness of shared life experiences that are a vital
part of any interactive learning experience.

Next we discussed adult learning theory that supports the importance
of student-centered learning experiences as an effective way of achieving
student learning outcomes. As learning by definition implies a change in
behavior as a result of receiving and acting upon new information, adult
learning theory focuses on the learner versus the teacher. As teachers we
may positively affect student learning by creating engaging and reflective
learning experiences, inviting and encouraging student participation. Yet

we come to understand that whether students choose to engage in those experiences and at what level they choose to do so is ultimately their choice, which is often heavily influenced by their life circumstances. With adult learning theory as a foundation for inquiry, we identified planning questions for teachers to consider as they began designing a hybrid course. Important topics such as workload and the thoughtful integration of online and F2F learning activities were discussed and demonstrated through the use of several examples.

The focus then shifted to primary tools typically used in designing student-centered hybrid learning experiences. Throughout the discussion and application of these tools the discussion included how learning could be measured, making assessment a vital component of any effective hybrid design. The versatility and the value of asynchronous discussion were demonstrated through the use of multiple examples. An important part of any learning process is providing timely and effective feedback, while an important component of any assessment process is the frequent solicitation of student feedback. Both of these topics were thoroughly discussed, using examples to illustrate important points. The benefit of using small groups as an effective learning strategy was explored. The hybrid course design invites the observation and evaluation of online group process as well as group outcomes. Small group learning strategies also give teachers an opportunity to observe small group behaviors, engaging in coaching when ineffective behaviors occur.

Meeting student expectations in a hybrid course is not too different from meeting student expectations in any teaching and learning environment. Students deserve to be treated with respect and to be treated fairly and equitably. Students want the opportunity to safely express their views and to know they are being heard in a nonjudgmental and unbiased environment, without fear of retaliation from the teacher or fellow students. They desire constructive feedback and easy access to learning tools. All of these attributes have been discussed in the context of creating a student-friendly hybrid learning experience.

Technology, including the Internet, provides us with multiple opportunities to creatively design interactive hybrid learning experiences. Emphasis was placed on using simple and stable technologies as tools for hybrid design in lieu of designing a course with the use of specific technologies in mind. In other words, think first about learning outcomes, then think about how the use of technology may enhance students' achievement of those outcomes. When technology is chosen carefully, it has the potential of enhancing learning significantly. When not chosen carefully, technology becomes an impediment to learning and often a major frustration for students and teachers.

The numerous shared revelations of experienced hybrid teachers and students throughout the book serve to validate and enrich the current literature on hybrid teaching and learning, which in many ways is an application of adult learning theory.

I conclude this section with what one of the teachers interviewed said in response to what challenges and opportunities he faced with teaching hybrid. He said that for him teaching hybrid was liberating, and it freed him from the primary obligation of presenting content. He stated, "The students now have that primary obligation, and they undertake it." He went on to say that one of the challenges he faced was coteaching with faculty who didn't want to change from a teacher-centered course to a student-centered course. When asked why he couldn't persuade his colleagues to change their style of teaching, he commented:

> I think it is the same arrogance that I had for a long time. You think, "I'm a good teacher and I'm not going to change." You know we all get these letters from students from time to time, telling us they got into medical school, thank you so much, I enjoyed your course so much, my first biochemistry course, blah, blah, blah. . . . so we think we are doing ok. What we forget is the ones that wrote these letters are the ones that would have done fine with or without you. And there are, for every one of those success stories, a couple of hundred students that are struggling and could use a little more help, and they're not stupid either; so they could *potentially* go to medical school and they could *potentially* get good grades.

He went on to say that his initial semester teaching hybrid was a little rough because he knew there were better ways of doing some things, but he also knew that hybrid was working. He said, "The principal change for the second semester was I abandoned all the attempts to lecture on substance for the first time in class." He added that he had students interacting with the content and with each other about the content before coming to class. He saved class time for students to ask questions on content they had already become familiar with. Students may have worked together to solve content-specific crossword puzzles or they may have taken an online quiz or participated in an online discussion. The point he made was that to be successful in the course, students had to interact with the content before coming to class, which had helped them achieve the learning outcomes.

Questions for Future Research

All the areas of research that could potentially advance the practice of hybrid as a means of teaching and learning would take another book for sure, as little research specific to hybrid has been published thus far. Yet the opportunities for inquiry are abundant. The following few questions may be considered worthy of future research:

1. As related to achieving student learning outcomes, how might we apply Anderson's theory to better determine the most effective mix of content-to-content, teacher-to-student, and student-to-student interaction in our hybrid course designs? And what additional variables are most likely to influence that mix? Is it the content itself? Is it the type of student demographic? Is it teaching style? Is it all of these? What other influencers are likely?

2. What is the role of an instructional designer in creating effective hybrid learning experiences? To be most successful in working with faculty, what qualifications should people in those roles have? What is the role of the teacher in relationship to the instructional designer? How much instructional design support is sustainable for institutions of learning in the long run? How much will actually be necessary in the long run? What models are in practice thus far? How successful are those models? How is that success defined and measured?

3. What hybrid faculty development programs are most likely to encourage and engage faculty in learning how to design, teach, and evaluate hybrid learning experiences? What models are currently in place? How successful have they been? How has success been defined and measured?

4. How much time does it take to develop fluency in using a specific technology for teaching and learning in hybrid courses? How transferable are those skills when using tools that have similar purposes? What is the role of teachers and administrators in evaluating and deciding what technological tools are sustainable and most likely to enhance learning in hybrid environments?

5. How might social networking tools be applied to hybrid teaching environments? How might social networking tools be used to achieve student learning outcomes?

6. What level of technical support should be available to students and teachers for hybrid programs to be successful? What models are in practice? How successful are they? How is that success defined and measured?

7. Is blended online course design comparable to hybrid in regard to learning outcomes and student satisfaction? What models are in practice? How successful are they? How has that success been defined and measured? Does the blended online model decrease the time commitment of faculty who are currently teaching totally online courses?

8. What can we learn about good hybrid design from the students enrolled in hybrid classes? What is the least intimidating and least biased way of collecting this data?

9. What impact if any does a hybrid design, which tends to be student-centered, have on students' willingness and ability to take responsibility for their own learning beyond the hybrid class-room?

10. What is the danger that technology in education, including its use in hybrid courses, will lead to a form of standardized teaching and learning that jeopardizes creative thinking and makes learning environments too rigid for teachers and students?

11. Is there a difference in how teaching should be assessed when using different instructional methods? For example, should the teaching in a F2F class be assessed in the same way as in a hybrid class?

12. Would hybrid learning be effective in K–12 environments?

These questions and a multitude of others may be worthy of further exploration for those interested in the scholarship of teaching and learning and for those passionate about creating significant hybrid learning experiences.

Final Reflections

For a long time I have felt compelled to write this book because I viewed it as an opportunity to thank, in a small way, the many gifted teachers, students, and colleagues who have mentored me over the years, most without knowing they have done so. My life has been rich in learning experiences, and for that I will always be grateful. I have had the fortune of living in a democracy, which values women as well as men. I had the privilege of having parents with a moral compass who loved me and supported my quest for knowing. I enjoyed the benefit of having teachers with integrity who encouraged me to learn, and culturally diverse colleagues and friends who challenged my way of thinking. I have a family that gave me the freedom to pursue my life's work without making me feel guilty about the long hours I often put in as I did so. I once found a sentence (author unknown) that hangs in my office: "If you love what you do, you will never work another day in your life." This thought has served me well throughout my career. Whenever what I do becomes work, I know it is time for me to move on to a new adventure. And I never underestimate having the freedom to do that.

Finally, I've had the privilege of learning, working, and teaching in safe academic environments that view teaching and scholarship as a symbiotic relationship and not a dichotomous one, where teaching and scholarship are viewed in partnership with community, and where diversity is celebrated and not shunned. What I've written is, in essence, a reflection and a culmination of my life experiences as a learner and a teacher. If proven helpful to even a few, it serves as a tribute to all those valued mentors from the past and the present whom I've had the joy of working with. I will forever be humbled by your wisdom and grateful for your mentorship.

REFERENCES

Allen, I. E., & Seaman, J. (2007). *Online nation: Five years of growth in online learning.* Needham, MA: Sloan Consortium. Retrieved from http://www.sloanconsortium.org/sites/default/files/online_nation.pdf

Anderson, J. R., Reder, L. M., & Simon, H. A. (1996). Situated learning and education. *Educational Researcher, 25*(4), 5–11.

Anderson, T. (2003). Getting the mix right again: An updated and theoretical rationale for interaction. *The International Review of Research in Open and Distance Learning, 4*(2). Retrieved from http://www.irrodl.org/index.php/irrodl/article/viewArticle/149/230

Anderson, T., & Garrison, D. R. (1998). Learning in a networked world: New roles and responsibilities. In C. Gibson (Ed.), *Distance learners in higher education* (pp. 97–112). Madison, WI: Atwood.

Angelo, T., & Cross, K. P. (1993). *Classroom assessment techniques: A handbook for college teachers* (2nd ed.). San Francisco, CA: Jossey-Bass.

Aycock, A. (2006, September). *Re: Hybrid faculty development* [Online forum comment]. Retrieved from http://d2l.mu.edu

Bandura, A. (1977). *Social learning theory.* Englewood Cliffs, NJ: Prentice Hall.

Barman, C. R., & Barman, N. (1996). Two teaching methods and students' understanding of sound. *School Science & Mathematics, 96*(2), 63–68.

Bates, A. (1993). Theory and practice in the use of technology in distance education. In D. Keegan (Ed.), *Theoretical principles of distance education* (pp. 213–233). New York, NY: Routledge.

Bates, A. W., & Gallagher, M. (1987). Improving the educational effectiveness of television case-studies and documentaries. In O. Boyd-Barrett & P. Braham (Ed.), *Media, knowledge and power* (pp. 319–338). London, UK: Croom Helm.

Beard, C., & Wilson, J. (2006). *Experiential learning: Best practice handbook for educators and trainers* (2nd ed.). Philadelphia, PA: Kogan-Page.

Bender, T. (2003). *Discussion-based online teaching to enhance student learning: Theory, practice and assessment.* Sterling, VA: Stylus.

Benedict, S. C., & Coffield, K. (1989). The effect of brain hemisphere dominance on learning by computer assisted instruction and the traditional lecture method. *Computers in Nursing, 7*(4), 152–156.

Biner, P., Bink, M., Huffman, M. L., & Dean, R. S. (1995). Personality character-istics differentiating and predicting the achievement of televised-course students and traditional-course students. *American Journal of Distance Learning*, *9*(2), 46–60.

Blanchard, K. (2010). Retrieved from the Thinkexist website: http://thinkexist.com/quotation/feedback-is-the-breakfast-of-champions/348677.html

Bloom, B. S. (1956). *Taxonomy of educational objectives, Handbook I: The cognitive domain.* New York, NY: David McKay.

Boettcher, J. V., & Conrad, R. (2004). *Faculty guide for moving teaching and learning to the web* (2nd ed.). Phoenix, AZ: League for Innovation in the Community College.

Boud, D. M., & Ellison, N. B. (2008). Social network sites: Definition, history and scholarship. *Journal of Computer-Mediated Communication, 13*(1), 210–230. Retrieved from http://onlinelibrary.wiley.com/doi/10.1111/j.1083-6101.2007.00393.x/full

Boud, D., & Walker, D. (1991). *Experience and learning: Reflection at work.* Geelong, Victoria, Australia: Deakin University Press. Retrieved from http://www.eric.ed.gov/PDFS/ED384696.pdf

Bourne, K., & Seamon, J. (2005). *Sloan-C special survey report: A look at blended learning.* Needham, MA: Sloan Consortium.

Boyd, R., & Apps, J. (1980). *Redefining the discipline of adult education.* San Francisco, CA: Jossey-Bass.

Boyle, T., Bradley, C., Chalk, P., Jones, R., & Pickard, P. (2003). Using blended learning to improve student success rates in learning to program. *Journal of Educational Media, 28*(2–3), 165–178.

Bower, G. H., Karlin, M. B., & Dueck, A. (1975). Comprehension and memory for pictures. *Memory & Cognition, 3,* 216–220.

Bracher, M. (1993). *Laca, discourse, and social change: A psychoanalytic cultural criticism.* Ithaca, NY: Cornell University Press.

Brint, S., Cantwell, A., Hannerman, R. (2008). Two cultures: Undergraduate academic engagement. *CSHE* 4.08 (March 2008).

Britzman, D. P. (1998). *Lost subjects, contested objects: Toward a psychoanalytic inquiry of learning.* Albany, NY: SUNY Press.

Brookfield, S. D. (1986). *Understanding and facilitating adult learning.* San Francisco, CA: Jossey-Bass.

Brookfield, S. D. (2006). *The skillful teacher: On technique, trust, and responsiveness in the classroom.* San Francisco, CA: Jossey-Bass.

Brookfield, S. D., & Preskill, S. (2005). *Discussion as a way of teaching: Tools and techniques for democratic classrooms* (2nd ed.). San Francisco, CA: Jossey-Bass.

Brown, D., McCray, G., Runde, C., & Schweizer, H. (2001). *Using technology in learner-centered education: Proven strategies for teaching and learning.* Boston, MA: Allyn & Bacon.

Brunner, J. S. (1961). The act of discovery. *Harvard Educational Review, 31,* 21–32.

Brunner, J. S. (1966). *Toward a theory of instruction.* Cambridge, MA: Harvard University Press.

Bryan, V., Danaher, M., & Duay, D. (2005). Relationship among key variables and students' and students' perceptions toward learning online in postsecondary environments. In C. Crawford et al. (Eds.), *Proceedings of society for information technology and teacher education international conference 2005* (pp. 1128–1134). Chesapeake, VA: Association for Assessment in Counseling and Education. Retrieved November 28, 2008, from http://www.editlib.org/index.cfm?fuseaction = Reader.ViewAbstract&paper_id = 19174

Burns, R. A. (1985, May). *Information impact and factors affecting recall.* Paper presented at Annual National Conference on Teaching Excellence and Conference of Administrators, Austin, TX. (ERIC Document Reproduction Service No. ED 258 639).

Cable, C. (1997). *Welcome to the auscultation assistant.* Retrieved from http://www.wilkes.med.ucla.edu/inex.htm

Carini, R., Kuh, G., & Klein, S. (2006). Student engagement and student learning: Testing the linkages. *Research in Higher Education, 47*(1), 1–32.

Caulfield, J. (2007). Why should I tell you how you teach? An expectancy theory perspective. *International Journal for the Scholarship of Teaching and Learning, 1*(1), 1–19. Retrieved from http://academics.georgiasouthern.edu/ijsotl/v1n1/caulfield/IJ_Caulfield.pdf

Caulfield, J. (2010). Applying graduate student perceptions of task engagement to enhance learning conditions. *International Journal of the Scholarship of Teaching and Learning, 4*(1), 1–18. Retrieved from http://academics.georgiasouthern.edu/ijsotl/v4n1/articles/PDFs/Article_Caulfield.pdf

Caulfield, J., & Waldschmidt, S. (2004, September). *Re: Leading teams and groups* [Online forum comment]. Retrieved from http://d2l.mu.edu

Coggins, C. C. (1989). Preferred learning styles and their impact on the completion of external degree programs. *American Journal of Distance Education, 2*(1), 25–37.

Cottrell, D. M., & Robinson, R. A. (2003). Blended learning in an accounting course. *The Quarterly Review of Distance Education, 4*(3), 261–269.

Cronbach, L., & Snow, R. (1981). *Aptitudes and instructional methods: A handbook for research on interactions.* New York, NY: Irvington.

Csikszentmihalyi, M. (1990). *Flow: The psychology of optimal experience.* New York, NY: Harper & Row.

Daly, B. (1993). The influence of face-to-face to groups working via computer-mediated communication channels on collective induction. *Accounting, Management & Informational Technology, 3*(1), 1–22.

Davis, B., & Sumara, D. J. (1997). Cognition, complexity and teacher education. *Harvard Educational Review, 67*(1), 105–125.

Dean, C. (2005, August 30). Scientific savvy? In U.S., not much. *New York Times* (pp. 1–2). Retrieved from http://www.nytimes.com/2005/08/30/science/30pro file.html

DeBello, T. C. (1989). *Comparison of eleven major learning styles models: Variables; appropriate populations; validity of instrumentation; and the research behind them.* Paper presented at the National Conference of the Association for Supervision and Curriculum Development, Orlando, FL.

DePree, M. (1989). *Leadership is an art.* New York, NY: Doubleday.

De Vita, G. (2000). Inclusive approaches to effective communication and active participation in the multicultural classroom: An international business management context. *Active Learning in Higher Education, 1*(2), 168–180.

Dewey, J. (1938). *Experience and education.* New York, NY: Simon & Schuster.

Dunn, R. (1990). Rita Dunn answers questions on learning styles. *Educational Leadership 48*(2), 15–19.

Dunn, R., & Dunn, K. (1992). *Teaching elementary students through their individual learning styles: Practical approaches for grades 3–6.* Boston, MA: Allyn & Bacon.

Dunn, R., & Dunn, K. (1993). *Teaching elementary students through their individual learning styles: Practical approaches for grades 7–12.* Boston, MA: Allyn & Bacon.

Dunn, R., & Dunn, K. (Eds). (1998). *Practical approaches to individualizing staff development for adults.* Westport, CT: Praeger.

Dunn, R., & Dunn, K. (1999). *The complete guide to the learning-styles inservice system.* Boston, MA: Allyn & Bacon.

Dziuban, C., Hartman, J., & Moskul, P. (2007). Everything I need to know about blended learning I learned from books. In A. G. Picciano & C. D. Dziuban (Eds.), *Blended learning research perspectives* (pp. 265–285). Needham, MA: Sloan Consortium.

Ellsworth, E. (1997). Review of teaching positions: Difference, pedagogy and the power of address. *Educational Studies, 30*(1), 74–79.

Engle, M. (2008). *How to evaluate the information sources you find.* Retrieved from http://www.library.cornell.edu/olinuris/ref/research/evaluate.html

Evaluate web pages (n.d.). Retrieved from the Widener University website: http://www.widener.edu/libraries/wolfgram/evaluate

Ewell, P. T. (2002). *An analysis of relationships between NSSE and selected student learning outcomes measures for seniors attending public institutions in South Dakota.* Boulder, CO: National Center for Higher Education Management Systems.

Fenwick, T. (2001). *Experiential learning: A theoretical critique from five perspectives.* Columbus: Ohio State University. Retrieved from http://www.eric.ed .gov.proxy.lib.wayne.edu/PDFS/ED454418.pdf

Fenwick, T. (2003a). *Learning through experience: Troubling orthodoxies and intersecting questions.* Malabar, FL: Krieger.

Fenwick, T. (2003b). Reclaiming and re-embodying experiential learning through complexity science. *Studies in the Education of Adults, 35*(2), 123–141.

Fink, D. (2003). *Creating significant learning experiences.* San Francisco, CA: Jossey-Bass.

Foley, G. (1999). *Learning in social action: A contribution to understanding informal education.* New York, NY: Zed Books.

Foucault, M. (1988). Technologies of the self. In L. Martin, H. Gutman & P. Hutton (Eds.), *Technologies of the self: A seminar with Michael Foucault* (pp. 16–49). Amherst: University of Massachusetts Press.

Fujishin, R. (2007). *Creating effective groups: The art of small group communication* (2nd ed.). Lanham, MD: Rowman & Littlefield.

Gardner, H. (1993). *Frames of mind: The theory of multiple intelligences.* New York, NY: Basic Books.

Gardner, H., Csikszentmihalyi, M., & Damon, W. (2001). *Good work: When excellence and ethics meet.* New York, NY: Basic Books.

Garrison, D. R., & Kanuka, H. (2004). Blended learning: Uncovering its transformative potential in higher education. *The Internet and Higher Education, 7*(2), 95–105.

Garrison, R., & Vaughan, N. (2008). *Blended learning in higher education: Framework, principles, and guidelines.* San Francisco, CA: Jossey-Bass.

Gesick, C. (1988). Time and transition in work teams: Toward a new model of group development. *Academy of Management Journal, 31*, 9–41.

Gibson, C. (1996). Toward an understanding of academic self-concept in distance education. *The American Journal of Distance Education, 10*(1), 23–36.

Gibson, C. C., & Graff, A. O. (1992). Impact of adults' preferred learning styles and perception of barriers on completions of external baccalaureate degree programs. *Journal of Distance Education, 2*(1), 39–51.

Goleman, D. (1995). *Emotional intelligence.* New York, NY: Bantam Books.

Graham, C. R. (2006). Blended learning systems: Definition, current trends, and future directions. In C. J. Bonk & C. R. Graham (Eds.), *The handbook of blended learning: Global perspectives, local designs,* (pp. 3–26). San Francisco, CA: Pfeiffer.

Gross, C. (2010, March 20). Fewer graduate students plan to enter academia. *Daily Californian.* Retrieved from http://www.dailycal.org/article/104060/fewer_graduate_students_plan_to_enter_academia

Harris, T. E. (1988). Mastering the art of talking back. *Management World, 17*(3), 9–11.

Hart, M. (1992). *Working and educating for life.* London, UK: Routledge.

Harter, S. (1990). Causes, correlates, and the functional role of self-worth: A lifespan perspective. In R. J. Sternberg & J. Kolligan (Eds.), *Competence considered* (pp. 67–97). New Haven, CT: Yale University Press.

Hayes, N. (1997). *Successful team management.* London, UK: International Thomson Press.

Head, A. J., & Eisenberg, M. B. (2010). *Assigning inquiry: How handouts for research assignments guide today's college students.* Retrieved from http://proj ectinfolit.org/pdfs/PIL_Handout_Study_finalvJuly_2010.pdf

Hergenhahn, B. R., & Olson, M. (2000). *An introduction to theories of learning* (6th ed.). Upper Saddle River, NJ: Prentice Hall.

Hershberger, M. (2008, April). *Understanding the national online higher education market.* Paper presented at a meeting of the U.S. Distance Learning Association, St. Louis, MO. Retrieved from http://www.significantfederation.com/ resources/wp-content/uploads/2008/07/eduventures-usdla-presentation-4-23-08.pdf

Hofstede, G. (2007). Cultural constraints in management theories. In J. Osland, M. Turner, D. Kolb, & I. Rubin (Eds.), *The organizational reader* (8th ed.). Upper Saddle River, NJ: Pearson Prentice Hall.

Holmberg, B. (1995). *Theory and practice of distance education.* New York, NY: Routledge.

Honeyman, C., & Yawanarajah, N. (2003). *Beyond intractability: Mediation.* Retrieved from http://www.beyondintractability.org/essay/mediation/

Houle, C. O. (1961). *The inquiring mind.* Madison: University of Wisconsin Press.

How to evaluate research materials after you find them (n.d.). Retrieved from the University of Arkansas website: http://www.uark.edu/libinfo/refdept/instruc tion/evaluation.html

Howard, R. W. (1995). *Learning and memory: Major ideas, principles, issues and applications.* Westport, CT: Praeger.

Janis, I. L. (1972). *Victims of groupthink: A psychological study of foreign policy decisions and fiascoes.* Boston, MA: Houghton Mifflin.

Jarvis, P., Holford, J., & Griffin, C. (1999). *The theory and practice of learning.* Sterling, VA: Stylus.

Jonassen, D. H., & Grabinger, R. S. (1988). *Independent study: Personality, cognitive, and descriptive predictors* (ERIC Document Reproduction Service No. ED 295 641).

Kaleta, R., Aycock, A., & Caulfield, J. (2004, August). *Preparing faculty to teach hybrid courses: A faculty development model.* Paper presented at the 20th Annual Conference on Distance Teaching and Learning, Madison, WI.

Kaleta, R., Garnham, C., & Aycock, A. (2003, August). *Hybrid courses: Obstacles and solutions for faculty and students.* Paper presented at the 19th Annual Conference on Distance Teaching and Learning, Madison, WI. Abstract retrieved from http://www.uwex.edu/disted/conference/Resource_library/pro ceedings/03_72.pdf

Kaleta, R., Skibba, K., & Joosten, T. (2007). Discovering, designing, and delivering hybrid courses. In A. Picciano & C. Dziuban (Eds.), *Blended learning: Research perspectives* (pp. 111–143). Needham, MA: Sloan Consortium.

Kane, S. (2009). *The multigenerational workforce: Managing and motivating multiple generations in the legal workplace.* About.com. Retrieved from http://legal careers.about.com/od/practicetips/a/multigeneration.htm

Katzenbach, J., & Smith, D. (1993). *The wisdom of teams.* Cambridge, MA: Harvard Business School Press.

Keegan, D. (1996). *Foundations of distance education.* London, UK: Croom Helm.

Kern, G. M. & Matta, K. F. (1988). The influence of personality on self-paced instruction. *Journal of Computer-Based Instruction, 15*(3), 104–108.

Kim, H. B., & Fisher, D. L. (1999). Assessment and investigation of constructivist science learning environments in Korea. *Research in Science & Technological Education, 17*(2), 239–250.

Kitchener, K. S., King, P. M., & DeLuca, S. (2006). Development of reflective judgment in adulthood. In C. Hoare (Ed.), *Handbook of adult development and learning* (pp. 73–98). New York, NY: Oxford University Press.

Klahr, D., & Nigam, M. (2004). *The equivalence of learning paths in early science instruction: Effects of direct instruction and discovery learning.* Retrieved from http://www.psy.cmu.edu/faculty/klahr/KlahrNigam.2-col.pdf

Knowles, M. S. (1980). *The modern practice of adult education: Andragogy versus pedagogy.* New York, NY: Association Press.

Knowles, M. (1984). *The adult learner: A neglected species.* Houston, TX: Gulf.

Knowles, M. S. (1990). *The adult learner: A neglected species.* 4th ed. Houston: Gulf.

Knowles, M. S., Holton III, E., & Swanson, R. (2005). *The adult learner: The definitive classic in adult education and human resource development.* Boston, MA: Elsevier.

Kolb, D. (1984). *Experiential learning: Experience as the source of learning and development.* Englewood Cliffs, NJ: Prentice Hall.

Kosslyn, S. M. (1994). *Image and brain: The resolution of the imagery debate.* Cambridge, MA: MIT Press.

Lackey, J. F. (Producer). (2010). *Can we become homeless?* [DVD]. Milwaukee, WI: Urban Anthropology.

Larkin, J., & Simon, H. (1987). Why a diagram is (sometimes) worth ten thousand words. *Cognitive Science, 11,* 65–99.

Lave, J. (1988). *Cognition in practice: Mind, mathematics and culture in everyday life.* Cambridge, UK: Cambridge University Press.

Lave, J., & Wenger, E. (1991). *Situated learning: Legitimate peripheral participation.* New York, NY: Cambridge University Press.

Lawson, C. (n.d.) *The connections between emotions and learning.* Retrieved from http://www.cdl.org/resource-library/articles/connect_emotions.php

Lea, S., Stephenson, D., & Troy, J. (2003). Higher education students' attitudes to student-centred learning: Beyond "educational bulimia?" *Studies in Higher Education, 28*(3), 321–334.

Levi, D. (2007). *Group dynamics for teams* (2nd ed.). Los Angeles, CA: Sage.

Lewin, K. (2010). Retrieved from Thinkexist website: http://thinkexist.com/quotation/there_is_nothing_so_practical_as_a_good/176589.html

Lipscomb, L., Swanson, J., & West, A. (2004). Scaffolding. In M. Orey (Ed.), *Emerging perspectives on learning, teaching, and technology.* Retrieved from the University of Georgia website: http://projects.coe.uga.edu/epltt/

Lowney, C. (2003). *Heroic leadership.* Chicago, IL: Loyola Press.

Mangrich, A. (2006, September). *Re: Hybrid faculty development* [Online forum comment]. Retrieved from http://d2l.mu.edu

Marks, M., Mathieu, J., & Zaccaro, S. (2001). A temporally based framework and taxonomy of team processes. *Academy of Management Review, 26*(3), 356–376.

Maslow, A. H. (1972). Defense and growth. In M. Silberman, J. S. Allender, & J. M. Yanoff (Eds.), *The psychology of open teaching and learning* (pp. 43–51). Boston, MA: Little, Brown.

Matisse, H. (2010). Retrieved from Thinkexist website: http://thinkexist.com/quotation/creativity_takes_courage/144595.html

Mazza, R. (2004). Monitoring students activities in course management systems with CourseVis. In L. Cantoni & C. McLoughlin (Eds.), *Proceedings of World Conference on Educational Multimedia, Hypermedia and Telecommunications 2004* (pp. 686–687). Chesapeake, VA: Association of Community and Continuing Education (ACCE). Retrieved from http://www.editlib.org/p/12562

McAuliffe, G. (2006). The evolution of professional competence. In C. Hoare (Ed.), *Handbook of adult development and learning* (pp. 476–496). New York, NY: Oxford University Press.

McGrath, J. E. (1990). Time matters in groups. In J. Galegher, R. Kraut, & C. Egido (Eds.), *Intellectual teamwork: Social and technological foundations of cooperative work* (pp. 23–62). Hillsdale, NJ: Erlbaum.

McGrath, J. E., & Hollingshead, A. B. (1994). *Groups interacting with technology.* Thousand Oaks, CA: Sage.

McLaren, P. (1995). *Critical pedagogy and predatory culture: Oppositional politics in a postmodern era.* New York, NY: Routledge.

McTighe, J., & Wiggins, G. (2004). *Understanding by design.* Alexandria, VA: ASCD.

Merriam, S., Caffarella, R., & Baumgartner, L. (2007). *Learning in adulthood: A comprehensive guide* (3rd ed.). San Francisco, CA: Jossey-Bass.

Merriam, S., & Clark, M. C. (2006). Learning and development: The connection in adulthood. In C. Hoare (Ed.), *Handbook of adult development and learning* (pp. 27–51). New York, NY: Oxford University Press.

Mezirow, J. (1991). *Transformative dimensions of adult learning.* San Francisco, CA: Jossey-Bass.

Mezirow, J. (1996). Contemporary paradigms of learning. *Adult Education Quarterly, 46*(3), 158–173.

Michaelsen, L. K., & Knight, A. B. (2004). Getting started with team-based learning. In L. K. Michaelsen, A. B. Knight, & L. D. Fink (Eds.), *Team-based learning: A transformative use of small groups in college teaching* (pp. 27–50). Sterling, VA: Stylus.

Michelson, E. (1996). Usual suspects: Experience, reflection and the (en)gendering of knowledge. *International Journal of Lifelong Education, 15*(6), 438–454.

Middendorf, J., & Kalish, A. (1996). The change-up in lectures. *National Teaching and Learning Forum, 5*(2), 1–5.

Miller, C. (1992). *What students can tell us about the multicultural classroom.* Minneapolis, MN: Center for Interdisciplinary Studies of Writing. Retrieved from http://writing.umn.edu/docs/publications/Miller.pdf

Miller, N., & Boud, D. (1996). Animating learning from experience. In D. Boud & N. Miller (Eds.), *Working with experience* (pp. 3–13). London, UK: Routledge.

Mischel, W. (1973). Toward a cognitive social learning reconceptualization of personality. *Psychological Review, 80,* 252–283.

Moore, M. G. (1990). *Contemporary issues in American distance education.* New York, NY: Pergamon.

Moore, M. G. (1993). Theory of transactional distance. In D. Keegan (Ed.), *Theoretical principles of distance education.* New York, NY: Routledge.

Moore, M. G., & Kearsley, G. (1996). *Research on effectiveness, distance education: A systems view.* Belmont, CA: Wadsworth.

Myers, S. A., & Anderson, C. M. (2008). *The fundamentals of small group communication.* Los Angeles, CA: Sage.

National Center for Education Statistics. (1997). *1993 national study of postsecondary faculty: Retirement and other departure plans of instructional faculty and staff in higher education institutions.* Retrieved from http://nces.ed.gov/pubs98/web/98254.asp

Oblinger, D. (2003, July–August). Boomers, Gen-Xers, Millennials: Understanding the new students. *Educause,* 37–47. Retrieved from http://net.educause.edu/ir/library/pdf/erm0342.pdf

Oliver, R., Herrington, J., & Reeves, T. C. (2006). Creating authentic learning environments through blended learning approaches. In C. J. Bonk & C. R. Graham (Eds.), *Handbook of blended learning: Global perspectives, local designs* (pp. 502–514). San Francisco, CA: Pfeiffer.

Ormondroyd, J., Engle, M., & Cosgrave, T. (2009). *Critically analyzing information sources.* Retrieved from http://www.library.cornell.edu/olinuris/ref/research/skill26.htm

Parker, P. (1998). *The courage to teach*. San Francisco, CA: Jossey-Bass.

Parks, C., & Sanna, L. (1999). *Group performance and interaction*. Boulder, CO: Westview.

Pegrum, M. (2006). Socrates and Plato meet neoliberalism in the virtual agora: Online dialog and the development of oppositional pedagogies. In J. Lockard & M. Pegrum (Eds.), *Brave new classrooms: Democratic education and the Internet* (pp. 13–34). New York, NY: Peter Lang.

Peters, O. (1993). Distance education in a postindustrial society. In D. Keegan (Ed.), *Theoretical principles of distance education* (pp. 36–54). New York, NY: Routledge.

Phipps, R., & Merisotis, J. (1999). *What's the difference? A review of contemporary research on the effectiveness of distance learning in higher education*. Washington, DC: Institute for Higher Education Policy.

Pintrich, P., & Schunk, D. (1996). *Motivation in education: Theory, research and applications*. Englewood Cliffs, NJ: Prentice Hall.

Postman, N. P. (1985). *Amusing ourselves to death*. New York, NY: Viking Penguin.

Power, M. (2008). The emergence of an online blended learning environment. *MERLOT Journal of Online Learning and Teaching, 4*(4), 503–514.

Pritchard, A. (2009). *Ways of learning: Learning theories and learning styles in the classroom*. New York, NY: Routledge.

Pyrczak, F. (2008). *Evaluating research in academic journals: A practical guide to realistic evaluation* (4th ed.). Glendale, CA: Pyrczak.

Quaglieri, P. (1980). Feedback on feedback. *Supervisory Management, 25*(1), 34–39.

Quinn, R. (2006). Mastering competing values: An integrated approach to management. In J. S. Osland, M. E. Turner, D. A. Kolb, & I. M. Rubin (Eds.), *The organizational behavior reader* (8th ed., pp. 77–87). Upper Saddle River, NJ: Pearson Prentice Hall.

Remen, R. N. (2006). *In the service of life*. Retrieved from http://www.rachelremen.com/service.html

Rhodes, R., & Whitten, J. (1997). Early intervention with at-risk Hispanic students: Effectiveness of the Piacceleration program in developing Piagetian intellectual processes. *Journal of Experimental Education, 65*(4), 318–329.

Roberts, G. (2003). *An interpretation of Dewey's experiential learning theory*. Gainesville: University of Florida. Retrieved from http://www.eric.ed.gov/PDFS/ED481922.pdf

Robinson, J. P. (2001, August). *Workplace skills needed by today's workers*. Retrieved from http://www.aces.edu/crd/workforce/publications/8-30-01-Workplace-Skills-Needed-by-Today's-Workers.pdf

Rogers, E. M. (1995). *Diffusion of innovations* (4th ed.). New York, NY: Free Press.

Rooney, J. E. (2003). Blending learning opportunities to enhance educational programming and meetings. *Association Management, 55*(5), 26–32.

Ross, B., & Gage, K. (2006). Global perspectives on blended learning: Insight from WebCT and our customers in higher education. In C. G. Bonk (Ed.), *The handbook of blended learning* (pp. 155–168). San Francisco, CA: Pfeiffer.

Salomon, G. (1983). *Using television as a unique teaching resource for Open University courses.* Milton Keynes, Buckinghamshire, UK: Open University Institute of Educational Technology.

Salomon, G., & Perkins, D. N. (1998). Individual and social aspects of learning. *Research in Education, 23*(1), 1–24.

Sawada, D. (1991). Deconstructing reflection. *Alberta Journal of Educational Research, 37*(4), 349–366.

Schmidt, M., Arndt, M. J., Gaston, S., & Miller, B. J. (1991). The effectiveness of computer-managed instruction versus traditional classroom lecture on achievement outcomes. *Computers in Nursing, 9*(4), 159–163.

Schön, D. A. (1987). *Educating the reflective practitioner.* San Francisco, CA: Jossey-Bass.

Schwartz, D., & Heiser, J. (2006). Spatial representations and imagery in learning. In R. K. Sawyer (Ed.), *The Cambridge handbook of the learning sciences* (pp. 283–298). New York, NY: Cambridge University Press.

Schwartz, P., Mennin, S., & Webb, G. (2001). *Problem-based learning: Case studies, experience and practice.* London, UK: Kogan Page.

Semple, A. (2000). Learning theories and their influence on the development and use of educational technologies. *Australian Science Teachers Journal, 46*(3), 21–28.

Sexton, T. (2008, April 9). *What is social loafing and how can it be avoided?* AC Associated Content. Retrieved from http://www.associatedcontent.com/article/699855/what_is_social_loafing_and_how_can.html

Short, J. A., Williams, E., & Christie, B. (1976). *The social psychology of telecommunications.* New York, NY: Wiley.

Shulman, L. (1998). Theory, practice, and the education of professionals. *Elementary School Journal* [Special issue], *98*(5), 511–526.

Shulman, L. (2005). Signature pedagogies in the professions. *Daedalus, 134*(3), 52–59.

Shunk, D. H. (1991). Self-efficacy and academic motivation. *Educational Psychologist, 26*, 207–231.

Siegler, R. S. (1998). *Children's thinking.* Upper Saddle River, NJ: Prentice Hall.

Skinner, B. F. (1965). *Science and human behavior.* New York, NY: Free Press.

Skinner, E., & Belmont, M. (1993). Motivation in the classroom: Reciprocal effects of teacher behaviour and student engagement across the school year. *Journal of Educational Psychology, 85*(4), 571–581.

Stanley, C. (2010, May 20). Hybrid courses will return. *Vanguard.* Retrieved from http://www.dailyvanguard.com/hybrid-courses-will-return-1.2267710#4

Starenko, M., Vignare, K., & Humbert, J. (2007). Enhancing student interaction and sustaining instructional innovations through blended learning. In A. G. Picciano & C. D. Dziuban (Eds.), *Blended learning research perspectives* (pp. 161–178). Needham, MA: Sloan Consortium.

Stefanakis, E. (2002). *Multiple intelligences and portfolios: A window into the learner's mind.* Portsmouth, NH: Heinemann.

Sternberg, R. (2002). Successful intelligence: A new approach to leadership. In R. Riggio, S. Murphy, & F. Pirozzolo (Eds.), *Multiple intelligences and leadership* (pp. 9–28). Mahwah, NJ: Erlbaum.

Stevens, D., & Levi, A. (2005). *Introduction to rubrics: An assessment tool to save grading time, convey effective feedback and promote student learning.* Sterling, VA: Stylus.

Sullivan, W. (2005). *Work and integrity: The crisis and promise of professionalism in America* (2nd ed.). San Francisco, CA: Jossey-Bass.

Sumara, D., and Davis, B. (1997). Enlarging the space of the possible: Complexity, complicity, and action research practices. In T. R. Carson and D. J. Sumara (Eds.), *Action research as a living practice* (pp. 299–312). New York, NY: Peter Lang.

Thalheimer, W. (2008a). *Providing learners with feedback, part 1: Research based recommendations for training, education and e-learning.* Retrieved from http://www.work-learning.com/documents/Providing_Learners_with_Feedback_Part1_May2008.pdf

Thalheimer, W. (2008b). *Providing learners with feedback, part 2: Peer-reviewed research compiled for training, education and e-learning.* Retrieved from http://www.work-learning.com/documents/Providing_Learners_with_Feedback_Part2_May2008.pdf

Thielfoldt, D., & Scheef, D. (2004, August). Generation X and the Millennials: What you need to know about mentoring the new generations. *Law Practice Today.* Retrieved from http://www.abanet.org/lpm/lpt/articles/mgt08044.html

Thompson, M. (1998). Introduction. In C. C. Gibson (Ed.), *Distance learning in higher education: Institutional responses for quality outcomes* (p. 8). Madison, WI: Atwood.

Tuckman, B., & Jensen, M. (1977). Stages of small group development revisited. *Group and Organizational Studies, 2,* 419–427.

Turner, J. H. (1988). *A theory of social interaction.* Stanford, CA: Stanford University Press.

Tynjala, P. (1998). Traditional studying for examination versus constructivist learning tasks: Do learning outcomes differ? *Studies in Higher Education, 23*(2), 173–190.

University of California, Berkeley (2011). *Encouraging participation.* Retrieved from http://gsi.berkeley.edu/teachingguide/sections/participation.html

Updike, J. (2009). Retrieved from Quotesummit website: http://www.quotesummit.com/john-updike-you-cannot-help-but-learn-more-quote/141841

U.S. Census Bureau. (n.d.) *2005–2007 American community survey.* Retrieved from http://factfinder.census.gov/servlet/STTable?bm = y&-geo_id = 01000US &-qr_name = ACS_2007_3YR_G00_S1401&-ds_name = ACS_2007_3YR_G00

U.S. Department of Education, Office of Planning, Evaluation, and Policy Development. (2009). *Evaluation of evidence-based practices in online learning: A meta-analysis and review of online learning studies.* Washington, DC: Author. Retrieved from http://www.ed.gov/about/offices/list/opepd/ppss/reports.html

von Prummer, C. (1990). Study motivation of distance students. *Research in Distance Education, 2*(2), 2–6.

Vygotsky, L. (1978). *The mind in society: The development of higher psychological processes.* Cambridge, MA: Harvard University Press.

Walvoord, B. (2004). *Assessment clear and simple.* San Francisco, CA: Jossey-Bass.

Weiner, B. (1994). Integrating social and personal theories of achievement motivation. *Journal of Personality and Social Psychology, 15,* 1–20.

Wenger, E. (1998). *Communities of practice: Learning meaning and identity.* Cambridge, UK: Cambridge University Press.

Wiesenmayer, R., Kupczynski, L., & Ice, P. (2008). The role of technical support and pedagogical guidance provided to faculty in online programs: Considerations for higher education administrators. *Online Journal of Distance Learning Administration, 11*(4). Retrieved from http://www.westga.edu/~distance/ ojdla/winter114/wiesenmayer114.html

Wilson, B. G., & Myers, K. M. (2000). Situated cognition in theoretical and practical contexts. In D. Jonassen & S. M. Land (Eds.), *Theoretical foundations of learning environments* (pp. 57–88)/Mahway, NJ: Erlbaum.

Winn, W., & Snyder, D. (1996). Cognitive perspectives in psychology. In D. H. Jonassen (Ed.), *Handbook of research for educational communications and technology* (pp. 112–142). New York, NY: Simon & Schuster.

Wirt, J., Choy, S., Gerald, D., Provasnik, S., Rooney, P., Watanabe, S. & Tobin, R. (2002). *The condition of education 2002.* Washington, DC: National Center for Education Statistics, U.S. Department of Education, and Institute of Education Sciences. Retrieved from http://nces.ed.gov/Pubsearch/pubsinfo.asp? pubid = 2002025

Wong, S. (1992). Approaches to study of distance education students. *Research in Distance Education, 4*(3), 11–17.

Wood, D., & Wood, H. (1996). Vygotsky, tutoring and learning. *Oxford Review of Education, 22*(1), 5–17.

Wood, M. R., & Zurcher, L. A. (1988). *The development of postmodern self: A computer-assisted comparative analysis of personal documents (contributions in sociology).* New York, NY: Greenwood Press.

World Bank. (2007). *Building the skills for a new economy.* Retrieved from http:// siteresources.worldbank.org/INTMONGOLIA/Resources/building_the_skills_ for_new_economy_ENG.pdf

Yannie, M. (2000). Technology is us: Do we have time to learn: A librarian's perspective. *TechTrends, 44*(4), 42–43.

York-Barr, J., Sommers, W. A., Ghere, G. S., & Montie, J. (2001). *Reflective practice to improve schools: An action guide for educators.* Thousand Oaks, CA: Corwin Press.

Young, J. R. (2010, July 22). How social networking helps teaching (and worries some professors). *Chronicle of Higher Education.* Retrieved from http://chronicle.com/article/How-Social-Networking-Helps/123654/

Zorn, T., Jr., & Tompson, G. (2002). Communication in top management teams. In L. Frey (Ed.), *New directions in group communication* (pp. 253–272). Thousand Oaks, CA: Sage.

INDEX

REFERENCE INDEX

Also available from Stylus

The New Digital Shoreline
How Web 2.0 and Millennials Are Revolutionizing
Higher Education
Roger McHaney

Two seismic forces beyond our control—the advent of
Web 2.0 and the inexorable influx of tech-savvy Millennials
on campus—are shaping what Roger McHaney calls "The
New Digital Shoreline" of higher education. Failure to chart
its contours, and adapt, poses a major threat to higher education as we know it.

These forces demand that we as educators reconsider the learning theories, pedagogies, and practices on which we have
depended, and modify our interactions with students and
peers—all without sacrificing good teaching, or lowering standards, to improve student outcomes.

Achieving these goals requires understanding how the indigenous population of this new shoreline is different. These students aren't necessarily smarter or technologically superior, but they
do have different expectations. Their approaches to learning are shaped by social networking
and other forms of convenient, computer-enabled and mobile communication devices; by in-
stant access to an over-abundance of information; by technologies that have conferred the ability to personalize and customize their world to a degree never seen before; and by time-shifting
and time-slicing.

Roger McHaney not only deftly analyzes how Web 2.0 is shaping the attitudes and motiva-
tions of today's students, but guides us through the topography of existing and emerging digital media, environments, applications, platforms and devices—not least the impact of
e-readers and tablets on the future of the textbook—and the potential they have for disrupting teacher-student relationships; and, if appropriately used, for engaging students in their
learning.

This book argues for nothing less than a reinvention of higher education to meet these new
realities. Just adding technology to our teaching practices will not suffice. McHaney calls for
a complete rethinking of our practice of teaching to meet the needs of this emerging world
and envisioning ourselves as connected, co-learners with our students.

22883 Quicksilver Drive
Sterling, VA 20166-2102

Subscribe to our e-mail alerts: www.Styluspub.com